Ron White and Michael White

Que Corporation
201 West 103rd Street, Indianapolis, IN 46290

MP3 Underground

International Standard Book Number: 0-7897-2301-8

Library of Congress Catalog Card Number: 99-067326

Printed in the United States of America

First Printing: November, 2000

03 02 01 00   4 3 2 1

Trademarks

Warning and Disclaimer

Associate Publisher
Greg Wiegand

Acquisitions Editor
Angelina Ward

Development Editor
Gregory Harris

Managing Editor
Thomas F. Hayes

Project Editor
Karen S. Shields

Copy Editor
Megan Wade

Indexer
Sharon Shock

Proofreader
Benjamin Berg

Technical Editor
Robert Patrick

Illustrator
Steve Adams

Team Coordinator
Sharry Gregory

Interior Designer
Kevin Spear

Cover Designer
Anne Jones

Production
Darin Crone

Table of Contents

About the Authors

Ron White is a senior editor of *Ziff-Davis Smart Business for the New Economy*, and a former executive editor of *PC Computing*, where he has written the CD-Ron, Web Kahuna, and Freeloader columns. His work for the magazine has been nominated for a Maggie award. He is the author of the award-winning bestseller, *How Computers Work*, also published by Que. He acquired his musical tastes during the '70s, which helps explain some of the more obscure references in *MP3 Underground* and his frequent lapses of memory. People regularly make fun of him when he sings. He can be contacted at ron@MP3Under.com.

Michael White, Ron's son, has been a guitarist for 17 years, five of them as bass player, backup singer, and co-songwriter for the Boston-based rock bands White, Woods and Matthews, Chronic Jones, and We Are Not the Tupperware Ninnies. This is his first book. He can be contacted at michael@MP3Under.com.

Dedication:

This is dedicated to the one I love. Doo-wop.

Acknowledgments

The authors are deeply indebted to researcher Margaret Ficklen, to several people at RealNetworks, including Gary Cowan, Kari Day, Pat Boyle; Wes Robinson at Golin Harris for his assistance with MusicMatch; Greg Williams and Jim Carey at PC Data; CDDB's Ann Greenberg; David E. Weekly; John Van Scoter at Texas Instruments; Kimberly Strop at Liquid Audio; and Douglas Cogen. At Que, the authors thank Angelina Ward, Gregory Harris, Aaron Price, Craig Atkins, and tech editor Robert Patrick. There are surely many others whom we've neglected unintentionally; we thank them as well.

Tell Us What You Think!

As the reader of this book, you are our most important critic and commentator. We value your opinion and want to know what we're doing right, what we could do better, what areas you'd like to see us publish in, and any other words of wisdom you're willing to pass our way.

As an associate publisher for Que, I welcome your comments. You can fax, email, or write me directly to let me know what you did or didn't like about this book—as well as what we can do to make our books stronger.

Please note that I cannot help you with technical problems related to the topic of this book, and that due to the high volume of mail I receive, I might not be able to reply to every message.

When you write, please be sure to include this book's title and author as well as your name and phone or fax number. I will carefully review your comments and share them with the author and editors who worked on the book.

Fax: 317-581-4666

Email: consumer@mcp.com

Mail: Greg Wiegand
          Associate Publisher
          Que
          201 West 103rd Street
          Indianapolis, IN 46290 USA

1

What Is MP3 Internet Audio and Why Should I Care?

♪ *What Are MP3 and Internet Audio?* ♪ *How Do MP3s Work?* ♪ *How Do Sound Waves Become Digital Data?* ♪ *How Does the MP3 Audio Codec Work?* ♪ *What Is the MP3 Revolution?* ♪ *What Do I Need to Get Started?*

Okay, rock 'n' rollers, here's the short version. MP3 and other forms of Internet audio use a technology that allows people to record incredibly good music as a very small computer file. But there's more. It gives you unimagined, complete control over where, when, and how you listen to music and other audio. It makes music your love slave! If you think a day without music is like a day without... well, music, then pay attention.

MP3 is not just a technology. It's a revolution that's going to affect television, movies, and the whole range of entertainment—perhaps even how we teach, exchange ideas, and learn. So, I'll make this deal with you. I'll tell you about everything you need to know to download, create, and play e-music, including the secret stuff the recording industry would rather you didn't know, and I won't bore you with a little lecture about how if you respect a performer, you'll want him to get paid, yadda yadda yadda. The truth is, I don't care what you do with the information. I've thought long and hard, and I don't see any way you can actually kill somebody with a song. And if nothing you do with MP3 is fatal, I say have a ball. I won't try to be your mother. In turn, you don't try to pass the blame on to me when the thought police bust down your door and confiscate your hard drive.

There. If all that sounds okay to you, then keep on readin'. If, on the other hand, you don't give spit about music, you have bought the wrong book. Return it before you bang up the cover and the clerk gives you a dirty look. A lot of people don't care what MP3 is. They just want music the way God intended, on CDs and a home entertainment center from Target. Hey, that's fine.

The rest of us are going to have some fun. I'm figuring you and I are of like mind. Back in the days of vinyl, how many times did you buy the same LP because the record invariably got scratched? I've bought *Abbey Road* five times on vinyl, twice on CD, and I can find only one of them today. How many of you have paid over and over again for the same CD because you want it at home, in the car, and in the office? I've done this only with *Dark Side of the Moon*, but that's a special case involving various superstitions. Still, I'd like to have the economy of buying a CD only once but still have the convenience to play it anywhere I am. After all, what am I buying? The plastic compact disc or the right to hear the music on it?

How many of you have paid 20 bucks for a CD that has only one song on it you really like? The record companies plaster the radio stations and MTV with one terrific cut from a CD when they know the rest of the tracks suck. I used to fall for one-hit wonders all the time, until I just said, "I'm mad as hell, and I'm not going to take it anymore."

When an MP3 Isn't an MP3

When I write *MP3*, most of the time it's a lazy way of referring to all computer audio formats associated with online music.

continues

continued

What I really mean is "e-music"—audio in any of several file formats, including MP3, Wave, RealAudio, Liquid Audio, Windows Media Audio, and others we'll encounter throughout the book.

How many times have you thought how you'd like to have a music CD that contains nothing but your very favorite songs? And wouldn't it be wicked if it had 100 songs instead of 15? Sound good? It gets better. We're going to do all this without stuffing anymore of our hard-earned lucre into the filthy coffers of the record magnates—at least no more than we have to do to live with our personal ghosts.

You don't need to be a computer geek to use a personal computer to transform your musical life. In the following chapters, we'll go hand-in-hand amidst the software and hardware you'll use.

What Are MP3 and Internet Audio?

A personal computer makes sounds in three different ways. One is the simple beep you hear only while your PC is booting or when something goes wrong, such as a stuck key on your keyboard. The second way is with the *musical instrument digital interface* (MIDI). MIDI works by applying a digital description of what an instrument is supposed to sound like to an actual melody. No real instruments need to be involved at any time, and MIDI often sounds unlike any real musical instrument.

The third way for a computer to make sounds is to decipher music that has been encoded as a series of 1 and 0 bits. This is the way music compact discs work; they use a digital audio format called *CD-DA*. It's also the way Windows records and plays wave files—audio files with the extension .wav. A *wave* file has the same characteristics as the CD-DA tracks on a music CD, which is why your PC can play music CDs on its CD-ROM drive. The quality of a wave file is the same as that on a music CD—and so is the size, which is where the problem comes in. A wave file uses about 10 megabytes of hard drive space for each minute of music. At that rate, a music album that plays for an hour would consume 600MB of disk storage. And if you want to send that same album over the Internet, using an ordinary 56K modem, it would take about 22 hours.

That's where MP3 comes in. MP3 is one of several ways to encode audio so the resulting file is squeezed to a tenth the size of a wave file while still packing the same quality sound. Using software called *rippers*, anyone with a PC can painlessly convert tracks on a music CD into computer files. Now that 600MB album becomes 60MB, a size that takes only two and a half hours to send over a modem connection. And on Internet connections, such as cable, DSL (digital service line), and T1 connections found at businesses and on campus, the download time becomes virtually a nonissue. Our hour's music now takes only a few minutes to download.

MP3 is not the only type of audio compression being used to store music. We'll discuss the others in more detail later in this chapter. Nor is downloading compressed music files the only way to enjoy audio from the Internet. *Streaming* audio, which you can think of as being radio stations on the Internet, is a source of both canned and live audio. We'll look at streaming audio in more depth in Chapter 7, "How Do I Play MP3 Files? And How Do I Keep Track of 1,000 Songs?"

...And Why Should I Care?

If music is important to you, you should care about MP3 and Internet audio. Even if you have a humongous collection of every CD-ROM, cassette, and vinyl record in the known, civilized world, you should still care about MP3. Why? Because it changes the entire experience of listening to music.

How do most of us listen to music—pre-MP3? We turn on the radio when we're in the car; maybe we play it while in the office or puttering around the house. Or we listen to music on anything from a Walkman to a boombox to a state-of-the-art home sound system. In all these instances, we're entirely passive. We can change stations on a radio, but that's not really like being in command of the radio's broadcasts. On whatever channel we choose, we listen to what some program director at a local Top 40 station decided we'd want to listen to. Even the most capable sound system still leaves little choice beyond choosing which tape or CD to play. Oh, sure, CD players have a button to shuffle the order in which they play tracks. Whoopee.

A PC has the power to give you control. Here's how. Usually when we think of *multimedia*, the hype is always about the pizzazz that sound and video bring to boring, old computer programs. Really, it's the other way around. Computers bring to media a way to organize all music and video, to manipulate it, store it compactly, and send it over the Internet. It relieves you of the purely passive role. You decide what you want to listen to, when you'll listen to it, and even how it sounds.

The following is a fast rundown of the reasons anyone who loves music and likes to tinker must know about MP3 and all the other forms of Internet audio.

Free Illegal Music

Let's not kid ourselves. One of the reasons you bought this book was because you want to snag free music from Bands You've Actually Heard Of (BYAHO). MP3 and software to find MP3 songs make the Internet a smorgasbord of songs from the latest riser with a bullet to golden oldies you'd have a hard time finding in a music store. We'll get into the legalities in more detail in Chapter 2, "Is This Going to Get Me Thrown in Jail?"

Free Legal Music

You can, of course, find illegal copies of songs on the Internet. But even ignoring the thousands of bootleg brand-name songs, the Internet is a reservoir of free music. Sometimes, you'll find a free song from someone such as Alanis Morissette or Jimmy Page, put online to promote a new album. But more often, the music comes from unknown performers and groups, called indies because they are independent from the major labels, trying to bust through to the big time by way of the Internet.

New Music

Don't turn your nose up at bands just because you've never heard of them. In the days before MP3, the popular musicians were a combination of performers and composers with undeniable talent and acts who were the creation of clever marketing. But basically, the five major record labels—Sony, BMG, EMI, Universal, and Warner Bros.—decided who had a shot at fame and fortune. If you think that's a good idea, I have a few Menudo and New Kids on the Block CDs you're welcome to. But now, *après* MP3, any band with a demo tape can be heard on the Internet. Many Web sites with engines to search out MP3s can match your preferences for BYAHO to indie groups that are similar to your favorites. And if your tastes lean toward the obscure or the offensive, the Internet may be your best source for niche music.

The Hunt

For some, listening to music is not as much fun as finding it. If all you can remember of a favorite song from years past are some snatches of lyrics, the Net provides sites that let you track down that almost-forgotten song, even if you never knew the name of the song or its performers. This is the thrill of collecting for collecting's sake, not unlike the intrepid butterfly collector.

Getting Only the Music You Want

How many music albums have you bought because you liked one song on it? Then when you listen to the entire recording, you find that's the *only* song you like. You're paying $17–$20 for a single song. Although they're hard to find, single tracks by brand-name bands may be bought from the Internet for as little as a buck. And it'll get better.

Digitally Perfect Copies

MP3s, and to a lesser extent, other forms of digitized music, let you make copies of songs that are as good as the original. When you copy CDs to tape, a loss in quality is inevitable. The more stages of reproduction that analog copying goes through, the worse the copy will sound. But MP3s use the same computer bits that store your letters, stock portfolio, and Quake levels. Bits don't change from copy to copy as analog copies do. This is also part of the reason the big record labels don't like MP3. They were perfectly happy with your making a copy of a CD to cassette tape because they knew the tape wouldn't be a faithful reproduction of the disc. But with digital formats, bootleggers can create thousands of rip-off CDs that are all indistinguishable from the original.

Creating Custom CDs

Remember that CD we were talking about a few paragraphs ago—the one you bought only to discover you didn't like any of its songs except for the one song that tricked you into buying it in the first place? How often are you going to put the CD in a player to listen to that one track? Not often. It's not worth the effort. With the software on this book's CD and a recordable CD drive, you can take that one song and dozens like it from other CDs and create your own custom CD of one-hit wonders—an entire CD filled with only the best of your music collection. And you can make more than one copy of it so you have the same music available at home, work, and in the car.

Rescuing Your Antique Recordings

In the back of countless closets and garages throughout the nation are cardboard boxes filled with 12-inch discs of black vinyl. For those of you in the X generation, these discs are called "records." They used to be the only form of recorded music you could buy over the counter. And some music/sound afi-cionados insist that vinyl sounds better and conveys more nuances of a per-formance than digitized music can capture. I don't know about that. But I do know that many of these LPs (which stands for "long-play") are becoming obso-lete simply because few people still produce the turntables and needles needed to play them. Plus, the vinyl itself is fragile, subject to skips, scratches, and crackles. With MP3, you can save your old media in a form that will never dete-riorate, and the software on the book's CD-ROM even lets you clean up the noise that pops out of damaged vinyl.

Being Your Own DJ

Computerized music gives you a chance to organize your music collection with a versatility and convenience that are simply not possible in any other medium. Accompanying computerized music files can be tags that contain information about the name of the performers, the song title, the album it's from, the track number, and more. Then, you create playlists of songs designed to match one mood or another. A playlist with the best of James Taylor, Joni Mitchell, and Carole King works for those laid-back retro moods while another playlist of Korn, Nine Inch Nails, and Marilyn Manson is good for those days when you don't really like anybody very much. Or, you create a playlist of Yanni, John Tesh, and Kenny G for those days when you have no musical taste at all.

The same songs can be part of more than one playlist without your having to create a copy of the song for each list. And the really neat part of creating playlists is that you don't have to manually enter all the information about title, artist, and so on. In fact, you don't even have to know the names of the songs. With the RealJukebox and MusicMatch Jukebox software on this book's CD-ROM, you can effortlessly add tags to the tracks from your music CDs by automatically pulling the information down from an online database.

World Wide Radio

Internet audio frees you from the law of physics that says you must live within 30 or so miles of a radio station's transmitter. Streaming audio lets you to listen to radio stations from anyplace in the world. In addition, this radio provides the name of the artist and song, and tells you what song's coming up next. You'll be able to attend concerts virtually and capture that music to your own files for later listening.

Better Portable Music

Say bye-bye to the Walkman and hello to the portable MP3 player. MP3 has made possible a new breed of portable music stored on memory chips on players that are smaller than so-called portable CD players, which, face it, aren't really that handy because they're too bulky to slip into a pocket or clip to a belt. Portable MP3 players are even smaller than portable cassette tape players, sound much better than other portables, and give you instant access to any song—something tape just can't manage at all.

Becoming a Media Mogul

Internet audio is the chance for you to get your band out of the garage. Make your demos in MP3, and dozens of Web sites will make them available for free download. Other sites let you sell your music directly to your audience. Or, you use a program such as Shoutcast, to create your own radio station that is based, legally, on your personal music collection. (For licensing reasons, we can't include all the files needed to set up your own Webcasts, but they are available on the Net at http://www.shoutcast.com/download/broadcast.phtml.)

There. If not a single one of these scenarios appeals to you, I'm amazed you've read this far. If, however, this all sounds like a splendid idea—why, maybe even something you'd like to do yourself—then read on. If you're anxious to get your hands on the MP3 Toolkit supplied on the book's CD-ROM, you can skip the rest of this chapter, which tells you how MP3 files work—helpful for a deeper, more Zen-like understanding of computer audio, but not essential.

How Do MP3s Work?

MP3s are not the only kind of audio files you can play on your computer. Before MP3, wave and MIDI files (identified by the extensions .wav and .mid) were commonly used. Wave files are the sounds you hear as you use different functions of Windows. These are the sounds your PC makes when you start or shut down Windows and when Windows pops up an error box or a dialog box with an exclamation point or question mark. They are most often digitized recordings of actual sounds, music, or special effects. (We'll get to what a digitized recording is in a minute.)

MIDI (musical instrument digital interface) imitates different musical instruments based on a mathematical description of the sounds each instrument produces. It's like a musical impersonator. MIDI is popular with musicians because they can use it, for example, to make the music coming from a keyboard sound as if it were coming from a violin. MIDI also has the advantage of using less disk space for a file describing the sound than a wave recording of the same sound. But MIDI music sounds artificial, and it can't capture the full range and complexity of recorded audio.

So, that leaves us with wave files, which reproduce sounds roughly of the same quality as music tracks that come from factory-made music CDs. In fact, wave files, as we'll see in Chapter 8, "How Can I Create My Own Music CDs?" can be copied to writable compact discs and played in any music CD player, such as those in a home entertainment center or car.

Wave files are created by converting analog values to decimal values. Sound, like much of the information we receive through our senses is *analog*—continuous and constantly changing. A watch with hands is an analog clock because the hands are constantly moving, constantly changing the value of the time they represent. A digital clock, on the other hand, changes in one-second or one-minute increments, which it expresses with decimal numbers. One moment, it's 10:39 p.m., and the next moment it's suddenly 10:40 p.m. For computers to do anything with analog sound waves, the sounds must be converted into a series of discrete values represented by the 0 and 1 bits of computing. Figure 1.1 shows how analog becomes digital.

How Do Sound Waves Become Digital Data?

If a tree falls in a forest, and there's no one there to hear it, does it make a sound? I don't know, but if there is someone there to hear it, and they have a recording device, Figure 1.1 shows how that noise can become a computer sound file:

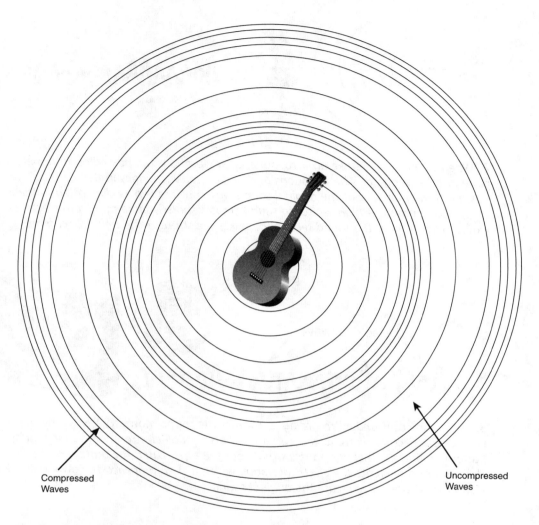

Compressed
Waves

Uncompressed
Waves

Figure 1.1   *1. When we hear sounds, we're actually sensing, with an amazing degree of discrimination, the vibration of particles that make up air. All sounds are created when something—a bell, a larynx, shattering glass, an oboe—vibrates. The vibration first pushes one way against the surrounding air, creating a wave of denser air; then it pulls back from the air, making the wave less dense. Our ears detect changes in the frequency of the wave as pitch; the higher the rate of vibration, the higher the pitch. We register the amount of energy in the wave as volume. We also detect a pattern of variations in the wave caused by the materials making the sound. A C-sharp produced by a bell and a xylophone are both sounds waves vibrating at the same frequency, but we recognize their origins by the distinctive distortion each instrument overlays on the waveform of pure C-sharp.*

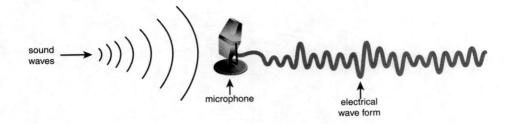

sound waves → microphone electrical wave form

2. *When sound waves strike a microphone, their vibrations are passed on to a metal plate or other material. The vibrations of the plate cause changes in the electrical current passing through it so that the original sound wave pattern is now duplicated in the flow of electrical current. A higher-pitched sound creates shorter, more numerous electrical waves. The stronger the sound hitting the mike, the stronger the electrical current.*

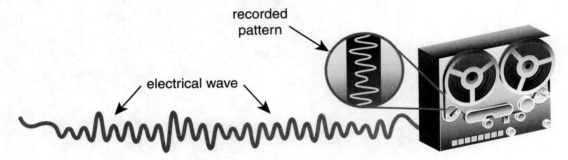

recorded pattern

electrical wave

3. *Audio tape uses analog recording to capture the sound, now represented by the variations in the electrical current. The current powers a small electromagnet that creates a pattern among the metallic particles that coat the tape. Later, the pattern of the particles is used to re-create the electrical signal, which is then amplified to power a speaker so that it vibrates to re-create the original sound.*

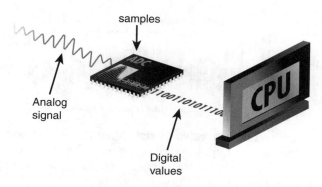

4. *Digital recording begins with the same sound being turned into an electrical wave-form. That current runs through a microchip called an analog-to-digital converter (ADC). The ADC constantly samples the signal to determine its exact pitch and volume and generates a number that represents the analog value of the current at that moment. Audio on musical CDs and wave files is sampled 44,000 times a second.*

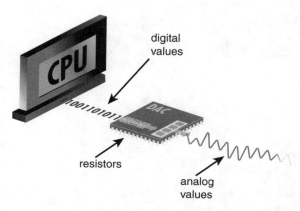

5. *On the output end, analog currents are needed by most stereo speakers. A digital-to-analog converter (DAC) changes a string of digital values into rapidly changing voltages. The DAC manages this by routing current through a matrix of resistors, which are components that resist the flow of electricity. The resistors are weighted to present different degrees of resistance. By sending current along different patterns through the resistors, the resulting analog stream of current is varied to correspond to the digital data.*

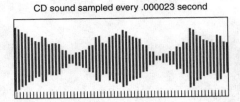

CD sound sampled every .000023 second

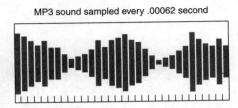

MP3 sound sampled every .00062 second

6. *The precision of an ADC/DAC conversion is affected by how often the analog signal is sampled, a measurement called the sample rate. Samples made more frequently create more realistic sound. Not all types of audio require the same sample rate. For ordinary speech, a rate of 60 samples a second creates acceptable recordings.*

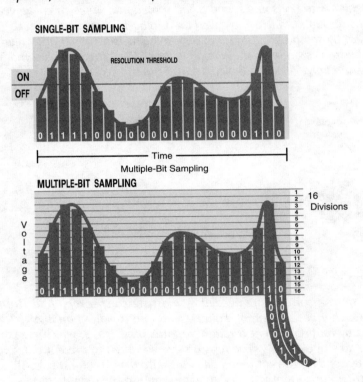

7. *Resolution, the precision with which a converter detects changes in the analog signal, also affects the accuracy of the digital recording. Resolution depends on the number of bits a converter can devote to the digital translation of the analog values, a measurement called the bit-rate. If the converter has only one bit to represent any one sample of the analog signal, it can only show if the analog signal is on or off. While a resolution of*

two bits is sufficient for, say, scanning printed black-and-white text, it doesn't hold enough information for audio. Most sound cards use 16 bits of data—65,535 different values—to describe audio each time it's sampled.

Adapted from How Computers Work, Millennium Edition by Ron White, Que, ISBN: 0-7897-2112-0.

Ordinary music CDs are recorded digitally. The analog audio signal is converted to digital values that are written as a series of 0s and 1s on one continuous, spiral track. The 1s are recorded as tiny *pits* in the metallic surface of a CD; smooth sections of the spiral, called *lands*, represent 0s. When you insert the CD into your computer or any CD player, a laser beam shines against the surface. If the beam strikes a land, it is reflected to a type of microchip called a *diode* that translates the laser's energy into a pulse of electricity. When the beam hits a pit, the light is scattered and the player interprets the lack of an electrical pulse as a 1.

The tracks on store-bought CDs and their computer cousins, wave files, have one major obstacle. They're big—about 10–11 megabytes of disk space for each minute of sound, or 1,400 megabits for each second of stereo sound. The solution to this problem is *compression*, reducing the number of bits of data required to hold effectively the same amount of data. Some files you may already be familiar with use compression. Zipped files are compressed using a system that lets every bit of data be restored when the files are unzipped. This is called *lossless compression* because none of the information is lost during the compression/decompression process. Lossless compression is vital for information in which the change of even one bit of the data could be disastrous, such as financial information, serial numbers, and software code. But music and the human voice aren't nearly so demanding. Audio can be compressed using *lossy compression*. Some of the information in the original file is discarded entirely to reduce the file's size. The trick is in figuring out what information is expendable.

The most common algorithm, or formula, for lossy compression of audio files is MP3. The MP part of the name and the file extension, .mp3, come from *MPEG*. Pronounced "EM-peg", it's a set of standards developed by the Motion Picture Experts Group for compressing and storing digital audio and video, and it's used to compress DVD versions of movies. The 3 in the name refers to MPEG Audio Layer 3, the part of MPEG that stores the audio. It reduces audio files to about one-tenth their original size, or about 1MB for each minute of sound—a size that lets MP3 songs be downloaded even on a 28.8Kbps modem in a reasonable time and doesn't hog your whole hard drive. Yet when the MP3 files are decoded back to the analog signals that create sound, virtually no loss in sound quality occurs between them and the original CD tracks.

The secret word here is *virtually*. Some sound information is actually lost, but not anything we would notice; this is called *psychoacoustics*. The most common example of psychoacoustics has happened to most people who listen to a car radio. As you're driving along, you hear a song on the radio you particularly like and you turn up the volume a bit. While stopped at a railroad crossing, you turn up the music again so you can hear it over the rumble of the train. Later, when you hit the highway, you crank up the music another notch to overcome the noise from tires and wind that accompanies high-speed driving. Then you turn it up again just for the hell of it.

This is fine until you stop and turn off the car. A while later, when you get back in the car and start it up again, your radio blares at you like a bullhorn, and you think to yourself, "Was I really listening to the radio that loud?" Yes, you were. You just didn't notice because of one of the peculiarities about how humans perceive sound: When a sound doubles in volume, our brains register only a 25-percent increase. Psychoacoustics works by only recording the JND— the *just noticeable difference*—between a sound in one sample and the sound in the next sample. The JND between any two sound samples is not a constant. It varies with the frequency, volume, and rate of change. An MP3 file, or other compressed music file, works by stripping out the parts of the music you won't miss hearing. (See the following section, "How Does the MP3 Audio Codec Work?")

MP3 files are based on psychoacoustics—the study of how the human brain perceives sound. This science has determined that not all the sound we hear is perceived by the brain. To create an MP3 file, an MP3 encoder reads a wave file and then strips out the parts you won't miss hearing. For example, most people can't hear sounds above 16kHz, so the encoder strips out any sounds above a preset threshold level. Loud sounds will mask quieter sounds at or near the same frequency; the encoder removes these, too. By whittling away the parts you don't hear, the encoder creates a file that sounds almost the same but is dramatically smaller.

If this strikes you as a cavalier attitude to have toward music, consider this: Your brain is constantly ignoring and discarding sensory information. Step outside and look just to the side of a bush or tree. You can see the plant in your peripheral vision, but only in general terms as a splash of green that your brain interprets as some bush-thing. If you look directly at the bush, you can see individual leaves, with individual shapes and shades of color. Look away again, and the leaves blend into a green blotch again. If your senses and brain couldn't play such tricks, the brain would immediately suffer a sensory overload as it tried to process every bit of information reaching it through not just your eyes, but all your senses. After you've sat on a chair for a bit, your brain filters out the sensation of your rear against the seat. If you think about it, you can feel the pressure. But the point is you don't think about it. The clock that seemed to tick so loudly when you first got it soon becomes silent as far your brain is concerned because it discards the ticking sound unless you suddenly wonder whether you wound the clock last night. MP3 compression, although it might be scorned by audiophiles—the type who spend more on their sound equipment than their kids' education—is simply duplicating what your brain does naturally.

How Does the MP3 Audio Codec Work?

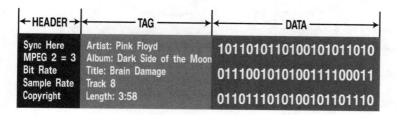

Figure 1.2 *1. Frame Structure*

Every MP3 file is made up of millions of equally sized frames—packets of audio data similar to the packets used to send data over the Internet. Each frame is broken into three parts.

Header: *At the beginning of each frame is a header that identifies the packet. The headers act as synchronizers, setting up points throughout the MP3 file at which playback can begin in the middle of a song. The headers permit fast forwarding and reverse.*

Tag: *Following the header is the tag. This contains information about the song, including name, artist, album, length, and track number. The MP3 player uses this information for its display while the song is playing. The tag also can point to lyrics and album cover graphics embedded in the file.*

Data: *The rest of the file is audio data, in the form of bits, that has been compressed during the creation of the file.*

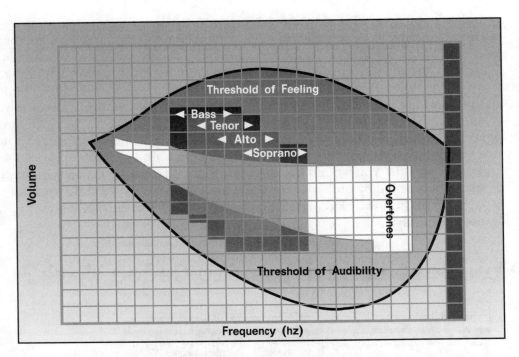

Adapted from Audio Cyclopedia, *by Howard Tremaine.*

2. Hearing Thresholds

The MP3 codec (compression/decompression) process reduces file size by discarding sounds that would never be heard anyway. These are sounds the human ear cannot detect—generally those below 2Hz (20 vibrations a second) and those above 20KHz. As sounds approach the upper and lower limits, they must also be louder to be heard. By not recording frequencies recorded at volumes the ear can't detect, MP3 eliminates unnecessary data.

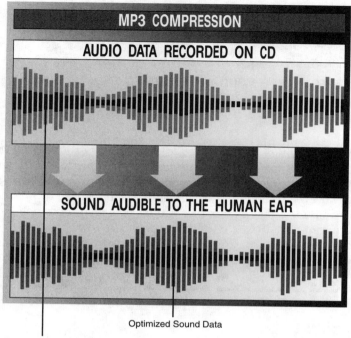

Original Sound Data

Optimized Sound Data

3. Masking

The MP3 codec eliminates some of the audio data based on a psychoacoustic model of human hearing. The codec compares two simultaneous sounds and determines that one sound is so loud that the other sound is drowned out, like a whisper at an AC/DC concert. The data for the softer sound is discarded. It is not replaced during decompression.

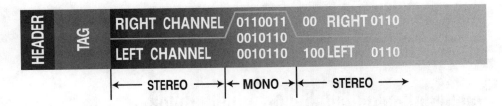

4. Joint Stereo

Ordinarily, two separate streams of data are used to record music in stereo. But the ear can't detect the location of some sounds, such as bass drum beats. During such passages, MP3 records only one channel of the sound combined with clues, where necessary, to indicate how the second track would differ. The bits saved by not duplicating bass sounds is used for higher pitches that can be located in space and that require more data to record.

5. Byte Reservoir

For less complex sounds, some frames may not use all the data bits allotted to them. These bits are used by other frames that need more space. When the MP3 file is replayed, the scattered bits are reassembled in the correct order.

6. Hoffman Compression

The last step in compression is called Hoffman coding, the same compression scheme used by Zip files. It identifies repeated patterns of bits and replaces them with shorter symbols that are decoded at playback. Hoffman compression reduces file size by about 20 percent.

7. Decompression

During playback, the MP3 file is again processed by the codec. It is expanded by reverse Hoffman compression. Some sounds are permanently discarded. Others are re-created from audio clues and bits scattered through different frames. From the codec, the file goes to a DAC, which changes the digital data into an analog stream of electrical current.

What Is the MP3 Revolution?

Consider the possibilities: You can make faithful copies of any music CD, copies so small you can pack 10 albums onto a single writable CD, so small you can zip them across the Internet in seconds. Sounds like a good excuse for a party, doesn't it?

It did to college students. Linked in their dorms to colleges' high-powered connections to the Internet, students swap music like grade-school kids trading Pokémon cards. Hey, dude, students are *supposed* to be rebels. And they're usually rebels low on cash. The record industry couldn't have asked for anything scarier. For them, the spookiest thing about MP3 is that the file format is in the public domain. Any freshman can figure out how they work and how to create them. Better yet, he doesn't have to. Dozens of free programs to create MP3s already exist. It's too late to do anything for the past or present.

Not that the bloated, capitalist pigs don't try. The recording industry has responded to MP3 with a demand for a *Secure Digital Music Initiative (SDMI)*, a form of something called *intellectual rights management* that preserves the music publishers' traditionally tight control of how music is made, distributed, and sold. The threat of MP3 has inspired other ways to create compressed music files—most of them with the capability to prevent illegal copies. Windows Media Player uses Microsoft's own compression scheme—.wma for Windows media audio—which Microsoft, of course, hopes will become the industry standard. Real Networks, creators of the RealPlayer and RealJukebox included on this book's CD-ROM, has its own compression methods. Another format you're likely to run across on the Internet is Liquid Audio. Most of the rivals to MP3 claim to produce either smaller or better sounding music files. And all of them have one or more different ways for the big record companies to control the spread of music. Some systems limit how many copies can be made or what devices music can be copied to. Other systems may put a time bomb in a music file so that it can't be played after a certain date. And sooner or later, some kid with a skin condition is going to figure out how to crack those formats, too.

How we get our music—and in the future our video, movies, books, and news—is changing. All forms of intellectual content will have to be distributed electronically and for free. Why? It's a reverse of Murphy's Law: People will do whatever they can do. If they have a way to receive music and information for free, they'll receive it free. Part of the new economy is going to be figuring out how musicians, writers, artists, teachers, and companies all get paid for producing new music, new books, new art.

What Do I Need to Get Started?

You've probably already got it. The CD-ROM that comes with this book provides all the software you'll need to create, play, and play with MP3 files. And you're likely to have all the hardware you need, at least to get started.

Software

Frankly, a lot of CDs that come with books are shovelware, any old shareware and public domain programs grabbed at the last moment just so the book can say, "Includes CD!" We didn't want to throw 20 MP3 encoders and 30 MP3 players at you just to fill up the disk. We spent long hours looking at all the MP3 players, recorders, rippers, and assorted other programs to get more out of computerized music, and the contents of this book are planned around the capabilities of the programs we chose for the CD. We hope the final product will be one-stop shopping for all your MP3 need, giving you the best products for each different MP3 job—think of an MP3 Suite—along with a straight-shooting printed manual that tells how to best use the software together.

At the heart of the suite are two programs, RealJukebox—part of the Real Entertainment Center—and MusicMatch Jukebox, which have different ways of copying songs off CD, organizing and playing the songs, and creating your own CDs. RealJukebox is included because it has the best combination of ease and versatility. MusicMatch offers features you won't find in RealJukebox, including—at press time, anyway—making higher-quality MP3 files from your music CDs. But it is so awkwardly designed that only a programmer's mother could love it. Use MusicMatch Jukebox to *rip* CDs—create MP3s from them—but listen to them with RealJukebox.

RealPlayer, another part of the Real Entertainment Center, is software for listening to Real's version of streaming audio, which is music being piped in real-time over the Internet. MusicMatch has the same capability to play streaming MP3 files, but RealPlayer plays many more audio and video formats and is far easier to use.

For legal and licensing reasons, we were unable to include all the programs discussed in the book. In these cases, we'll give you the internet address you'll need to download them. You can also find links to the most current versions of all the programs covered in this book by going to the book's own Web site, MP3Under.com.

One of the programs you should download is called MP3 Fiend. It helps you find downloadable music from FTP sites—the members-only places where a lot of underground music lurks. Another program, Napster, gives you access to the huge community of MP3 users who are willing to offer their files for download to other MP3 collectors.

At the risk of spamming you with duplicate software, we're including two programs to help you download music. Go!Zilla tracks and organizes downloads from Web sites; it's handy for all your downloading, not just MP3s. CuteFTP simplifies greatly the task of pulling down files from those tricky FTP sites you'll find with MP3 Fiend. In addition to the files on the CD, there are instructions on how to use your Internet browser to download MP3s hidden in newsgroups.

You'll also find a collection of helpful tools for the perfectionist who wants to edit and organize audio files to within a inch of their little, digital lives. The CD is rounded out with similar programs for Mac users and programs that aren't essential to using MP3s, but which make music on a computer more fun. I know. You can't imagine that it actually gets better. It does.

Hardware

The obvious piece of hardware you'll need is a computer. If you have a PC purchased in the last three or four years, it should be powerful enough to handle all your MP3 operations. Our testing was done on two Pentium IIs and a first-generation Pentium, both running at modest processor speeds, although they are all souped up with additional memory. For all your computing—not just MP3s—the more memory, the better. You should have at least 64 megabytes of RAM, and even if you have to sell the family dog, get still more.

A sound card is a necessity, and any recent computer has one. Our test PCs are running the ultimate in sound boards for playing with music: the Creative Labs Live!Drive. The board provides digital as well as analog outputs. It comes with all the software you could want for mixing, surround sound, and environmental audio (which is more for games, but what the heck; who says you can't play Quake as you listen to Sarah McLachlan?). What really makes the Live!Drive useful is the jack plate that installs into an empty half-height drive slot. It goes on the front of your computer, where you can actually reach the jacks without crawling on the floor. It has jacks for S/PDIF in and out, MIDI in and out, headphones, and a microphone (the last two of which also have their own volume controls). (S/PDIF—Sony/Philips digital interface allows the transfer of audio from one digital device to another without the conversion to and from an analog format, which degrades the signal quality.) The sound card is very cool, but just about any sound card that costs $100 or more gives you everything you need for the basics in MP3.

If you have a hard drive with a capacity smaller than 10GB, think about getting a bigger one. Sure, one of the advantages of MP3 files is that they take up less storage space. But it's a law of MP3: Once you start your song collection, it will grow to fill all available drive space. And consider this. To edit songs, the audio files must be in the Windows wave format (.wav). Waves take up as much space as the same tracks on a CD—that is, roughly 10 times the size of their MP3 translations. That means a music CD in wave format takes up 650MB of space. If you want to do a lot of editing or your appetite for digital songs is ravenous, consider an additional hard drive. Most PCs have room for another drive, and the prices lately have been real bargains—20 gigabytes for a little over $200. At $10 a gig, that's awfully cheap storage.

The most important upgrade may be speakers. If you're using the cheap, tiny speakers that until recently were standard equipment with new PCs, you can do better. Several good speaker systems that include a pair of good midrange/high-range stereo speakers and one big subwoofer you can put anywhere may be found at your local computer or electronics store. Get the best your budget allows because in the end, your MP3s will only sound as good as your speakers. There's a lot of argument about MP3, Liquid Audio, and Windows media audio formats when it comes to bit rates and compression schemes and which is the best for music. But the differences among them are less important than the speakers the sound finally comes from.

Got good speakers with your stereo system? If they're in the same room with your computer—or can be without anyone complaining about their disappearance—they could be a fine, free solution. Note, however, that computer speakers have amplifiers built into them. If you use speakers designed for the typical home sound system, you have to use the system's amplifier, too.

Also, look at the newer digital speakers. These are interesting because they don't require a traditional amplifier. Some of them come in amazing designs that allow them to be less than an inch thick. Just make sure you have a digital output jack on your sound card.

A CD-ROM drive is a necessity if you want to convert your traditional music CDs to computer files. You probably already have a CD drive in your computer. What you want, if you don't have it, is a drive capable of *digital extraction*. Without that feature, the only way you can convert music tracks into MP3 files is to let your computer record the music *as* it plays. That means a music CD that plays for 60 minutes will take 60 minutes to convert. With digital extraction, the computer pulls the musical data off the CD as fast as the CD drive can spin. That lets you convert an entire CD to MP3s in 10–15 minutes.

If you don't know whether your current CD-ROM drive has digital extraction, install MusicMatch Jukebox from the book's CD, plop a music disc in the drive, and try to convert it. (Details are in Chapter 6, "How Do I Convert My Music CDs to MP3 Files?") If you don't have digital extraction, Jukebox will tell you. If you don't, you can buy a drive that has the feature for as little as $50.

The final piece of hardware you'll want is a writable CD drive. This lets you make extra copies of your music CDs or put together your own compilation of songs that you can play in traditional sound systems, your car, or a Walkman. The songs must be in CDA format, which is similar to .WAV format, to work outside a computer although several products are on the horizon that bring the MP3 format to the car and component sound system.

If you must buy a writable CD drive (CD-R), consider getting a *re*writable CD drive (CD-RW). The CD-R can record files to a disc only once. They're unerasable. A CD-RW drive, which can also be used with CD-R discs, can record to a CD-RW disc, erase what's on it, and record to it again. They are useful for creating backups of files that change frequently.

Okay. Got everything you need? Good. This'll be fun.

Is This Going to Get Me Thrown in Jail?

In this corner, the perp—19 years old, weighing 143, glasses held together with Band-Aids, and with all the financial resources of someone who still has to write home for money—the college student. In the opposite corner, the victim—weighing umpteen tons, money belt held together with lawsuits, and with enough money to buy whatever it wants, from talent to companies to U.S. reps. It's the Big Five, the five largest record labels. In this chapter, you'll see how these two slug it out.

Considering that all the Big Five's money comes from the perp and his friends, you'd think they'd cut him some slack if he were to share the latest Smashing

Pumpkins ditty with a friend. But the Big Five labels—Warner, Sony, Universal, EMI, and BMG—are the descendants of the steel and railroad barons who ruled their industries with a power unknown to some Roman emperors. These are the same companies that paid black doo-wop groups $500 flat for all rights to a song in perpetuity. The labels made millions from these deals while the real talent wound up playing nostalgia gigs at colleges and bars for gas money.

Here's how a typical record deal works today. One of the five biggies approaches an up-and-coming band and offers to put $100,000 into cutting a record and promoting it. The company will own the masters and all copyrights associated with them. The lucky band will get 10 percent of the sales. Not a great deal, but most unknown bands would give their collective left nuts for a chance at the big time. Oh, but there are "recoupables." These are expenses such as recording, manufacturing, promotion, and touring. They are recouped by the record company from the band's 10 percent—which means that the label puts the money up front, but the band still winds up paying for everything. A record must sell half a million copies *before* the band members see any money. Then, their profit is only about a dollar a record, on something you and I pay $17–$20 for.

If the band doesn't like that deal, it's free to go to any one of the remaining four big record labels, who'll offer more of the same. What a band—even a hit band—is left with are the concessions. The band's real money comes from T-shirts, posters, and associated paraphernalia sold at concerts.

Remember, the record companies are supposed to be the *victims* in the MP3 revolution. If MP3s really represent stealing from musicians, the record companies' real beef is that outsiders are horning in on their action.

What's Legal? What's Not?

MP3 does have legal uses. These include copying the CDs you own to MP3 format on your computer and making recordable CD copies of those same recordings. (Although the record companies won't officially concede those uses are legal.) The best the Big Five will allow is that it's legal to download music files recording companies have put on the Internet to promote an album. But most MP3 stuff—the *good* stuff—is illegal. An estimated 90 percent of the MP3 downloads that take place on the Net are pirate booty. It doesn't matter that you do it only for your own amusement or that you're not making a dime off the songs. While most of this is yet to be tested in the courts, as far as the Big Five are concerned, anything you do besides giving them money is illegal.

But are common, everyday use, downloading, and swapping of songs in any format going to land you in jail? No. "But you said it's illegal!" Yes, in the same way booze was illegal under Prohibition, only without the organized crime. In fact, the average mugging is a more organized and heinous crime than swapping MP3s. The sheer disorganization of the MP3 community is your best assurance against jail time. With the exception of some Internet download sites that are essentially commercial sites trading MP3s of copyrighted songs for your clicks on sex-site banners, none of this is organized or permanent enough for the cops to track, assuming they've run out of murders, robberies, and rapes to investigate.

But First a Message from Our Lawyers

I want to make my publisher's lawyers happy. Nowhere in this book am I advising you to make illegal copies of music, download illegal songs, or give them to others. And I'm not even telling you it's okay morally, that because the record companies are such rich pigs, you've got a little coming back to you. And I'm not telling you the laws are wrong and that you should be able to dabble in music copying with impunity. No way. None of that. Nada. And when I write MP3s aren't going to land you in jail, hey, don't take me seriously. It's a joke! I don't mean it.

Don't get too cocky. Some things can send you to jail. Making thousands of copies of a hot new compact disc, printing labels, and jewel case covers that look like the originals, and selling these on the black market—that *will* get you thrown in jail. Not that it takes anything as obvious as that. In 1999, Jeffrey Levy, a student at the University of Oregon, drew the attention of the university's guardians of computing when he sent out seven gigabytes of files in just a few hours. Pretty soon the FBI was involved, and Levy was charged, under the No Electronic Theft (NET) Act, with making available for download some $70,000 worth of copyrighted materials, including 1,000 MP3 songs. He pleaded guilty and got two years' probation and a limit on his Internet access. He could have gone to the big house for three years and have been fined a quarter of a million dollars.

Of course, Jeffrey was a bit of an overachiever. But you have been warned. Don't waste your one phone call on me.

The Digital Difference

Now I hear you saying, "I've been making cassette tapes off CDs and the radio for years. I give them as Christmas presents. Does that make me a criminal?"

Maybe, maybe not. But even if you are technically guilty because you gave away a copy, the reason the recording companies don't care is that tape copies are imperfect. And copies made from those imperfect copies are still more imperfect. Serial copying with cassettes doesn't threaten the record companies.

MP3 is a different animal. It's digital. Each copy of an MP3 song is as good as the one that came before it—or the hundredth one that came before. And then there's the Internet. The physical nature of a cassette means you have to mail it, ship it, hand-carry it, or somehow get it to each person on your receiving list. The combination of the Internet and the small size of an MP3-compressed song means you don't even have to get off your lazy ass to give a perfect copy of a song to thousands of people.

The RIAA (Recording Industry Association of America) started worrying about digital copies a decade ago when the electronics industry was trying to bring the digital audio tape (DAT) recorder to market. Instead of recording music as complex, wavering analog signals—a technology that dates to Edison's first gramophone in 1877—digital recorders use the 0s and 1s of computer data to make tape copies that are as faithful to the original song as a store-bought CD. The record companies didn't like that. And they acted.

There Is No Such Thing As Free Music

As much as music may want to be free, *somebody's* paying for it. Even music from radios, restaurants, bars, and elevators is paid for in some way. Radio stations and the like pay fees to the American Society of Composers, Authors, and Publishers (ASCAP), Broadcast Music, Inc. (BMI), the Harry Fox Agency, and SESAC (Society of European Stage Authors and Composers). A portion of that money, in turn, goes to composers and artists although how they figure out to apportion it is anyone's guess. It's not like they have someone sitting in every bar with a notepad checking off every time someone plays "Heartbreak Hotel" on the jukebox.

The Laws

The result of the record companies' action was the 1992 Audio Home Recording Act (AHRC). It requires certain digital music devices to have a chip that functions as a *serial copy management system* (SCMS). Basically, the system prevents people from making a copy of a copy of a song. The idea is if you copy a song and give it to friend, that's okay. But if the friend wants to make a copy of the copy, he can't. The problem with this solution is that personal computers aren't considered to be music devices. PCs have no built-in copy management system, and there's no incentive for them to have one. After all, how much of a selling point is it that your computer *can't* do things others can? This doesn't mean that making copies of songs becomes legit just because you use a PC. The same rules apply. It's just easier.

If you record music to writable CDs, even under legal circumstances, one feature of the AHRC has you *already* paying for real or imagined piracy. In an attempt to make you angry and bitter—which, of course, describes the ideal customer—the law charges you a 3-percent tax on the sales of blank digital tapes, cartridges, and writable CDs. This is just in case you're a song bandit who owes money to the labels. One-third of this tax goes into a "musical works fund," which is administered by a couple of federal agencies that distribute it to songwriters and music publishers. Two-thirds of the money goes to record companies, who pass along 40 percent of their share to big-name artists. A small part of it goes to unknown performers, studio musicians, and others who probably need it the most. This has inspired the I'm-going-to-pay-for-it-anyhow-so-I-might-as-well-steal-the-music school of moral rationalization.

The other law you should know about is the Digital Millennium Copyright Act of 1990. It was written to protect Internet providers from any illegal activities they might unknowingly host. It's the same thing as not holding the phone company liable because someone uses its phone system to plot a crime. But if a provider is aware of someone letting others download copyrighted songs, it must kick the scurrilous scoundrel off the service, which is why MP3 pirate sites disappear all the time, only to reappear somewhere else.

In the Crosshairs

As for individuals, even the RIAA says it's not after MP3 violators on the consumer level.

"Technically speaking, ripping a song from a CD and putting it on your hard drive may violate the law. However, those are not situations that the RIAA will enforce," Frank Creighton, senior vice president director of antipiracy at the RIAA told *Wired* magazine. "We never target the individuals downloading the files, even though they may be causing the reproduction and distribution and violating the law. It doesn't mean we're not concerned about it. But we're focusing on people that are posting the material."

Part of the reason for the RIAA's seemingly magnanimous stand may be the fact that personal use has never been tested in the courts. Under the sleeping-dogs theory of law, you're sometimes better off not forcing an issue. By declining to press personal use cases, the RIAA leaves open the door to declare that personal use is also forbidden should it be forced to take a last-ditch stand.

Also, personal users are small potatoes—potatoes without names or faces or big checking accounts. Prosecuting folks like you would cost more in legal fees than the songs are worth. Instead, the RIAA has unleashed on some of the more inventive Internet companies more lawyers than you'd find at a 50-car pileup on Interstate 101. Some of the legal issues go to the heart of what possession means and what it is we're buying when we pay for an intellectual creation.

In the Courts

Most of the computer software and hardware that pertains to digital music is not covered by the AHRA because it is not used exclusively for copying music, and some of the technology didn't even exist when the law was passed. So, CD burners, MP3 encoders, and computer hard drives do not have to include an SCMS chip. The courts have ruled that portable MP3 players—in the specific case, it was the Diamond Rio—are legal because they aren't recording devices, which would have been covered by the AHRA. The Rio merely stores and plays MP3 recordings that had been created on a PC.

Score one for the consumers. But don't count the labels out. They have the resources to out-litigate the Justice Department, much less dot-com startups that don't even show a profit. And they will apply those resources because in dispute are not simply copyright violations. Those are just an excuse for battle. The record companies see the MP3 revolution as a threat, not just to sales of their CDs, but to their control over the bands that produce music, the distribution system, and the devices we use to record and listen to music. MP3 and the Internet lead to a world in which there is no need for record labels at all.

In 1999, MP3.com, the premier MP3 site, began its My.MP3.com service. It was designed to let someone listen to his own, legally bought collection of music regardless of where he is. It works like this: You connect to MP3.com using the site's Beam-it program. You then put one of your store-bought CDs into your disc drive and it's copied to MP3's servers. From there, you can listen to it as *streamed* audio, a sort of personalized Internet radio that we'll look into in Chapter 7, "How Do I Play MP3s? And How Do I Keep Track of 1,000 Songs?"

Or rather, that's the way I thought it worked when I first heard about it. I assumed it was similar to Web sites, such as Idrive.com and Freespace.com, that let you have 50MB–300MB of free storage. But with My.MP3.com, what actually happens is that an MP3 duplicate of your disc already resides on the site's servers. It's one of some 45,000 CDs bought by MP3.com just for this project and encoded to the hard drives on its servers. So, if MP3.com already has the same disc you have, what's the point in copying yours? The end result is the same: a perfect digital image on MP3.com's hard drive of a CD sitting in your CD-ROM drive. Beam-it merely checks to identify that the original CD is really in your drive. If it is, Beam-it adds the contents of that CD to the list of songs you can stream no matter where you are.

And while we're at it, if I happen to beam up a CD identical to yours, isn't it just silly to have two copies of the same songs on MP3.com's drives? They're the same! You can use just one of them for everyone who wants to stream the song. Except for providing backups and more bandwidth, duplicates are a waste.

MP3.com got it. It got how computers were going to change the marketplace, especially the storage and delivery of digital data. But as sensible a notion as that might be from the standpoint of computer users, the record companies were buying none of it. The RIAA filed suit against MP3.com, and a judge ruled for the record companies. The potential fines could have run to $6.75 billion, although four of the record labels settled for $20 million judgments and a deal for MP3's future use of their songs.

In early 2000, the RIAA and Metallica sued Napster, Inc. (The company is named after its only product, which is software that lets people directly swap MP3 files over the Internet.) Unlike MP3.com, Napster's Web site contains not a single song to be downloaded or streamed. All Napster's own servers have are lists of songs other people are willing to let you copy off their hard drives. (For a fuller explanation, see Chapter 5, "What's This Napster? How Can I Use It to Swap Music with Others?")

Handy Rationales

The untested nature of copyright laws in the age of computers lends itself to some arguments that downloading even copyrighted songs is legal under certain circumstances. It depends on what it is we're actually buying when we fork over $17 for a CD (which, by the way, costs about 50 cents to manufacture). We're surely not buying this little plastic disc inside a plastic case that will break as soon as we get it home. The disc itself is worthless. And we're not buying the songs the discs contain. Possession of the songs remains with the record companies that bought the copyrights from the composers, musicians, and singers. So, that leaves us with this: We have paid for the right to listen to the music. Nothing limits when or where we can listen to the music. It's pretty much a 24/7 license. And nothing limits what we use to reproduce the music. You're not legally bound to use only a CD player. You can use a computer's CD-ROM drive.

So, let's take this back a couple of decades to all those vinyl albums and 8-tracks I bought in the '70s. For sentimental reasons, I keep them in the back of a closet. But I don't listen to them because my once state-of-the-art turntable bit the big one in the '80s. Here's the point: I don't remember there being a time limit on the music that I'd bought the rights to listen to. So, if I still have that right, by downloading MP3S of the songs that sit silently in the closet, I'm merely exercising the right I paid for years ago.

Works for me.

Lars Ulrich, the drummer for Metallica, and a lawyer showed up at Napster's Silicon Valley headquarters with 13 boxes of computer printouts purported to contain the names of 335,435 Napster users who had swapped Metallica MP3 files. The documentation also identified 1.5 million MP3 files of 95 different Metallica songs that were supposed to have been available for anyone to download over a two-day span.

Now if you recall, the Digital Millennium Copyright Act does not put responsibility on Internet providers if it's found that some of their users are violating copyright law. Internet providers are just expected to deny service to those identified as breaking this law.

Napster said that if the claims were submitted properly, it would disable the users Metallica had identified. Of course, the names used on Napster are *handles*, pseudonyms such as CyberBoy and PhatPhillie. Tracing most of the names is impossible. They belong to people on dial-up connections for which the Internet address changes with each phone call. And if someone is denied access to Napster's databases, all she has to do to get back on is register again with a different handle.

The Napster case is in the courts at the time of this writing. But it's a lose-lose situation for the RIAA. Even if it puts Napster out of business, there are already slicker and trickier Sons of Napster creating online communities that can't be policed effectively without an invasion of privacy the public would not tolerate. The most effective solution may be the one being worked out between MP3.com and some of the record giants. It enables MP3.com to stay in business and apply its expertise to putting music catalogs online in some way that profits MP3.com and the record companies.

The Secure Digital Media Initiative

Lawsuits have been just the record industry's knee-jerk first reaction to a threat they don't understand. Currently, aside from frequent cease-and-desist letters and the occasional lawsuit, the record industry, still as ignorant of computing as ever, is putting its faith in SDMI (the Secure Digital Media Initiative).

Consisting of 150 members from the record labels and electronics manufacturers, SDMI has as a goal some sort of system to prevent music piracy—if they can agree on a method. The general plan works in two phases. The first is the Phase I device, which failed to materialize as scheduled in time for the Christmas 1999 electronics buying frenzy, that can play music encoded in either a protected or unprotected format. But to play much of the commercial digital music of the future, a user will have to upgrade a device to Phase II, which uses a digital watermark. SDMI is responsible only for coming up with the specifications for the phases. Other companies will supply the actual technology.

How Digital Watermarks Work

A song's *digital watermark* is made of a continuous stream of digital messages that can be detected by computer components but not by the human ear. The messages run throughout the song so that less than a second of the audio contains all the information in the watermark. The mark can contain a copyright holder's name as well as a serial number that uniquely identifies the disc. The watermark is encrypted and can't easily be read unless you know what it's supposed to say. Removing the watermark is impossible without destroying the sound quality. *Bots*—software agents that work without direct supervision—could scour the Net looking for runaway songs.

One form of copy protection uses two watermarks, one strong, and the other weak, as shown in Figure 2.1. The *strong* watermark survives a song being converted into MP3 format. The *weak* watermark, on the other hand, is destroyed by the compression process. An SDMI-compliant device detecting the strong watermark would then know to look for the weak one. When it couldn't be found, the device would know it was a copy and follow appropriate instructions, such as not allowing the copy to be copied.

SDMI decided in 1999 to use watermark technology from Verance Corp. Since then, several companies have been competing for a Phase II technology that will be compatible with the Verance watermark. But the SDMI is not a happy family. Many of its members have been jousting to get a copy-protection technology adopted that favors their products and a few lawsuits have even been thrown about. SDMI members are too busy trying to make other members blink to pay attention to interoperability—how well products made by one company work with devices made by other companies. In a year and a half, an SDMI product has yet to reach the market.

If a Phase II player ever does make it to market, who's going to buy it? Certainly not people with large—and conceivably perfectly legal—MP3 collections. Sensible shoppers will wait until the inevitable incompatibilities that accompany all new technologies have surfaced and been fixed.

Then, when SDMI compatibility is working as designed, the following will happen: After a certain date, all new songs will have embedded in them Phase II technology that stops them from working with current CD players for the house and the car, not to mention Walkman-style players and, presumably, even computer CD drives. You will have to be content with music from only the 20th century, or else you'll have to shell out a thousand bucks or more to replace the perfectly good electronics you already have.

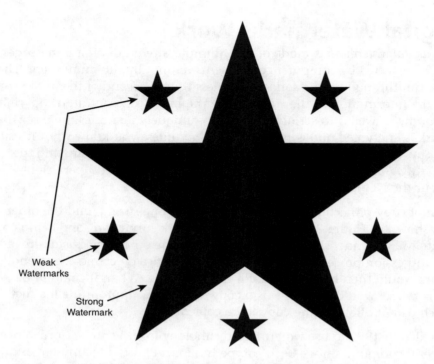

Uncompressed Watermark

Compressed Watermark

Figure 2.1 *How a digital watermark works.*

One form of copy protection embeds two codes called watermarks. One watermark is intentionally designed to be destroyed if the song is compressed.

Does this seem like a good idea? It does to all the record labels that see this as a way to end piracy. It does to the electronics manufacturers that will be selling you new sound equipment. The only one not invited to the party is the customer. The consumer doesn't get anything extra out of all this. The record labels need to research the history of software. They'd find that, at first, the software makers used copy protection, too. But, understandably, it was never popular with customers, who always found ways to defeat the protection. There's no reason—no reason at all—to assume that SDMI copy protection will get a different reception. As some in the industry have observed, the best feature for any player to boast of will be "*Not* SDMI-compliant."

Record labels, musicians, and music retailers—everyone busy stoking the star-maker machinery behind the popular song—will have to learn something. All music is now free. It's not a matter of whether it's legal or moral. It's simply a fact. And there's no returning to the days when possession was the divine right of bully companies. If the labels are to survive, they will need to start by giving away the music because if they don't, the music will be taken from them. The labels will have to find ways to add value to something that's already free. TV has done it in the form of HBO, ESPN, and Showtime. Software has done it with shareware that is routinely given away free so happy customers will pay to register and get extra features or fewer nag screens. Even computer writers realize they must do it, too. It's called evolution. Adapt or sleep in the tar pits.

3

Where Can I Find MP3 Music?

♪ *Web Sites* ♪ *What's FTP?* ♪ *Searching for HTTP and FTP Music Files* ♪ *Newsgroups—MP3s the Hard Way*

Someday MP3s—or some improvement on current MP3 technology—will completely replace the CD recordings we buy over the counter these days. Getting a small, high-quality audio file will be as simple as turning on the water tap. Too bad. We'll have lost the thrill of the hunt. Collecting music is like any collection—each item added individually, only after it's pulled from the morass of pop culture, and each item has a history, a story, a separate *raison d'etre*.

So here's the skinny on this chapter: Two types of Internet sites let you download MP3s and other forms of music: HTTP, which in practical terms often translates to "legal," and FTP, which means "jail bait." We'll look at how to find music on both types of sites, using online search sites and the software included on the book's CD-ROM. At the end of this book, musician Michael White has written detailed reviews of the top 101 MP3 sites. We'll also see how to find songs hiding as text messages.

Web Sites

If you look at a Web address your browser displays, you'll see it prefixed with "http," which means simply that the site uses *hypertext transfer protocol*. This isn't as foreboding as it sounds. If you already surf the World Wide Web, you're already familiar with HTTP sites, because that's the only kind the Web has. It really has to do with the fact that HTTP lets site creators use programming code called *hypertext markup language (HTML)* to design sites with graphics and fancy fonts and all the other bells and whistles that so enchant us.

With a dedicated, full-time connection to the Internet, you can set up an HTTP Web site on your own personal computer. But it's not a good idea. If the site's successful, you can forget about using the computer for anything else. It will have its circuits full just responding to requests for pages and downloads from surfers, especially if you post your MP3 collection. Usually Web sites are not located physically in the same building as the person or company that created it. Instead, you rent space from Internet *hosts*, who have scads of storage, fast file servers, and multiple links to a high-speed T1 or T3 Internet connection.

Although HTTPs can generally be interpreted as "legal sites," this isn't always true. There are perfectly respectable-looking Web pages that contain enough outlaw MP3s to fill a clandestine Tower Records. The record industry's enforcers regularly patrol MP3 Web sites, and when they find unauthorized songs, they lean heavily on the company that is physically hosting the site to close it. But usually no trail leads to the individual who set up the site, and it may appear again on a different rented server.

Generally, though, you can download anything you find on an HTTP site without getting the law hot on your trail. These legal downloads include two species of artists. The first is bands you've actually heard of, or as they're known as in the wilds, *BYAHO*. At the same time, you have a chance for another adventure—discovering new artists who are happy to give away their music for free just for the chance to break into the big time, where they actually get paid by a record company.

What's BYAHO?

While writing this book, I quickly tired of writing "bands you've actually heard of." But everything else I thought of—"star bands," "brand bands" didn't sound right. And so I gave birth to an acronym. And I know. I should be ashamed.

Only a few of the songs at legal Web sites are by BYAHO, at least with the blessing of the bands or their record labels. But with persistence and frequent trolling of the major MP3 sites, such as MP3.com, you can find big-time band downloads that are perfectly legal. The songs are placed there by the record companies to get you hooked so you'll buy the albums they come from. Often you listen to the song in a streaming format rather than downloading it to your hard drive. Occasionally, there are no strings attached to the download. But more often, they'll have some sort of digital rights protection built into them, particularly if they're offered as .WMA or Liquid Audio files.

The requirements of the secure digital music initiative (SDMI—see Chapter 2, "Is This Going to Get Me Thrown in Jail?") are flexible enough to enable record companies to attach different strings. Sometimes a time bomb is built into the file so that it won't play after 30 days. Or, the file might play only on the computer to which it was downloaded. Other schemes won't allow the song to be copied to a writable CD or converted to a wave (.WAV) file. The record industry still hasn't figured out exactly how it wants to use free downloads, and you can expect different strategies from song to song. And way too often, the BYAHO songs are actually simply previews. You get about 30 seconds of Nine Inch Nails, and then nothing (a small file size is usually the tipoff here). Often you'll only be able to download after giving something to the record company—such as your email address. In Chapter 7, "How Do I Play MP3s? And How Do I Keep Track of 1,000 Songs?" you'll see how you can record streaming audio so that you can listen to it offline and how to skirt some of the copy protections so your song doesn't go belly up in a month.

Table 3.1 *The Most Popular Internet Audio Sites*

Rank	Web Site
1	real.com
2	mtv.com
3	shockwave.com
4	mp3.com
5	bmgmusicservice.com
6	columbiahouse.com
7	tunes.com
8	www.com
9	windowsmedia.com
10	listen.com
11	peeps.com
12	launch.com

Table 3.1   *Continued*

Rank	Web Site
13	vh1.com
14	ubl.com
15	nsync.com
16	riffage.com
17	audiohighway.com
18	lyrics.com
19	harmonycentral.com
20	sonymusic.com
21	netradio.com
22	korn.com
23	emusic.com
24	musicmatch.com
25	discjockey.com

Source: PC Data, June 2000

Most of the songs offered for downloads unfettered by copy protection or legalities are from *indie bands*. Indies are independent groups that don't have a contract—at least not with any of the major labels. The Web has given rise to indie labels—online companies trying to figure out how to crash the big time by publicizing their bands through MP3 files. Most of the indie bands, however, are associated with no label at all. These are garage bands who are leveraging PCs to put them on the same playing field as bands backed with more money for recording and promotion. PC sound editing and mixing software let the musicians produce an MP3 without the expense of studios and tape mixers. The Internet gives them a way to distribute their songs, build up a mass following, and get signed by the record companies, who will then use, exploit, and abandon them to a life of playing nostalgia gigs at beer halls.

How Do I Find Which Garage Bands Are Hot?

Surf on over to this book's own Web page, www.mp3under.com. There we've posted links to the top song lists at the top Web music sites, including mp3.com, Rolling Stone, the Big Five music labels, Amazon, and a slew of others.

A lot of the indie bands will never get anywhere near MTV. In addition, some songs are remixes, while others sound like musical parodies. When you open up the music world to anyone with a band and a PC, you're going to get a lot of crap. But you're also going to uncover some treasures you never would have had a chance to hear under the old, oppressive record regime. You might be one of five people in the United States who like Narcoleptic Lovers, and it's only through the Web that you could know about them at all.

The are several different types of MP3 sites. Most specialize in music downloads. But others are better for software, news about music and digital downloads, fan chat rooms, buying CDs, Webcasts, and Internet radio stations.

Some offer it all. These are rich sites with one-stop shopping for all your music needs from free downloads to CD sales. Among the biggest megasites are mp3.com, rollingstone.com, listen.com, and tunes.com. mp3.com is the seminal MP3 Web site. What you can't find at mp3.com, you'll at least find a link to. MP3.com, the company, has set the standard for music sites on its pages and in the courts, where it battles the record companies (not always winning). Any of the sites associated with record labels have lots of pizzazz and some promotional downloads of performers as wide-ranging as Alanis Morrisette and Shania Twain. Others to check out are askmp3.com, which is great for technical background on MP3, and rollingstone.com, which is good for a smorgasbord of downloads from brand-name bands.

At the end of the book, musician Michael White reviews the top 101 MP3 sites. And check out this book's official site, www.mp3under.com. We are a modest link site where you can click through to the latest versions of the software on the book's CD-ROM, as well as programs we didn't have room to include on the CD-ROM. We also have links to the top 100 MP3 sites and many of the also-rans.

MP3—It's Everywhere!

Just for laughs, try going to the address field of your Internet browser and typing *anything*mp3.com. Any combination of *mp3* preceded by any word in the English language has been registered as a domain name by someone. Not all are working sites, but you can make a game out of trying to come up with a cool-sounding name for an MP3 site that hasn't been spoken for already.

Most downloads on Web sites are simple to snag. You're probably already familiar with how to do it. (Clue for the clueless: You *click* something.) But even if Web downloading is old hat to you, check out Chapter 4, "How Do I Download

MP3s Once I Find Them?" where I'll show you a better way of downloading using the free software Go!Zilla, included on the book's CD-ROM.

Buying Music Online

Among the megasites, many allow you to buy music online. Currently, online shopping for music is in a Neanderthal stage of development. Most sites, such as Amazon.com, only allow you to buy a pre-pressed CD, which shows up at your house a few days later via UPS or mail. Sites slightly higher on the evolutionary scale, such as towerrecords.com, riffage.com, and musicmaker.com, let you pick songs from different artists and burn you a custom CD with your personally chosen mix of tracks. Okay, that's nice, but it shows how the record companies are still mired in The Way Things Used to Be.

It's as if they can't imagine selling music any way except on real, hard CDs that must be sent from one end of the country to another on planes, trains, and delivery trucks. It's like settling down to watch a pay-per-view movie on cable, paying for it, and then being told you can watch it in three days when it arrives on a videotape.

Right now only a handful of music sites offer CDs and tracks for sale *and* immediate download over the Internet. One of the best sites for immediate gratification from sucking down BYAHO track by track is emusic.com. Finding a particular artist or album is chancy, but if you page through the alphabetical listings, you'll find performers you recognize. Just in the A's are Ian Anderson, Average White Band, and April Wine. Okay. Not the hottest acts this century, but you can download Liquid Audio or .WMA tracks recorded at an excellent 120 bits a second for 99 cents each.

Earlier in 2000, two of the big name labels, Sony and BMG, announced plans to offer their catalogs for sale as downloadable files. But the companies are experimenting with different types of copy protection and different music formats. By the time you read this, there should be more BYAHO songs sold for immediate download, but don't expect it to be straightforward until the labels figure out exactly how to do it.

Search Wizards

If you can't find the band you love, love the band you find. When some search engines don't come up with a match to what you're looking for—or even when it does—the engines suggest

continues

continued

songs and artists who are supposed to be similar to what you asked for. Sometimes the results are tenuous. A failed search for Barry White at one engine drew suggestions that I might like, instead, to listen to Orson Welles. Yes, sir. Nothing's better for that romantic evening than a fat man reciting Shakespeare. Usually the suggestions aren't that silly, and the search wizards are particularly helpful when you're trying to find the hidden gems among indie sites.

Part of the reason more sites don't offer pay-per-track downloads is the cost of processing a credit card charge. The 99 cent charge costs as much to process as $20 for an entire CD. One site, Mjuice.com, handles the problem by letting you charge Mjuice Dollars—as little as $2 at a time. Then you can download songs, some as cheap as a quarter, until you run out of Mjuice bucks. A record of your purchases are kept with your account so that if, for example, your hard drive dies, you can redownload the song without paying for it again. Another marketing plan you'll see sites experiment with is subscriptions. Ministryofsound.com has two plans, one $10 a month, the other $24.95 for three months. With the subscription, you can download anything from a certain collection, to which about 10 songs a week are added. Don't expect these to be the current top ten from *Rolling Stone*'s best-seller list.

This situation is changing. Several record labels have announced partnerships with online music sites to sell their music as downloads. A lot of the credit for this breakthrough in common sense goes to Liquid Audio, whose versatile copy protection/compression format gives the record executives control over how music is protected. More importantly, it and Microsoft's secure .WMA format are security blankets so the execs don't feel they're giving away the store. But until the record industry finally makes its peace with the Internet, searching for pay-per-track downloads is for people who have very little left to do in life. Using a PC to page through pay sites manually is really contrary to what computers are all about. They're supposed to do dull, monotonous, detailed tasks that would take humans hours, all in a matter of seconds. Why, you ask, can't software do my searching? And as long as you asked, the answer is in the next paragraph.

Search Sites

Some Web sites don't always have a lot of songs to download, but they'll tell you where they can be found. These are *search sites* with online programs that search all the other sites for MP3 and other audio and video files. Now practically every MP3 site you can find has some sort of search function. But the searches are usually of only that site or just a link to a more powerful search engine maintained by someone else, such as look4mp3.com or Lycos. Sites with these limited, simple searches aren't what I mean. We're talking *metacrawler*—an engine that feeds search requests to half a dozen other search engines. Then it compiles the results into a single list for your reading pleasure. A good search site covers as much of the Internet as their indexing computers can handle. Some search the entire Internet, including the notorious FTP sites. Others limit themselves to music on only the Web.

Most don't perform live, as-you-wait searches. Instead, they regularly scan the Net for files with the extensions .mp3 and .wma, and other tell-tale signs that they contain songs, and store the locations of successful hits in their own databases. The advantage is that you get quick results, but the database is not always up-to-date and can't tell you whether any of the sites it suggests are online.

Before you ask, there is not one, perfect, all-encompassing search site. You'll get different results from one search site to another. But all search sites are pretty simple to use. Many of the search engines find both legal Web sites and those suspicious FTP sites.

We'll look at a couple of the better online search engines later in this chapter. But first, we have to confront the *bête noire* of Internet audio: FTP.

What's FTP? 'Cause If I have to Learn One More Three-Letter Acronym, I'm Going to Hurl

If you're like most PC users these days, you're running Windows. Or maybe you're a Macintosh devotee. Either way, your forays into the Internet take place almost entirely within the safe, comfy World Wide Web. The Web is designed to be easy to navigate, even if it sometimes is frustrating and slow. But the Web is only a part of the Internet. Much of the Net remains the way it was before the Web appeared—running UNIX or Linux operating systems with a text-only interface devoid of graphics and frills that's more akin to working at an antique DOS prompt than the Web. In a word, it's geeky.

Now ask yourself, where do you find a lot of brainy geeks, with no responsibilities, lots of time on their hands, little money in their pockets, a passionate belief that the world owes them something, access to high-powered computers, high-speed Internet connections they don't have to pay for, and who like to rock? Look no farther than the nearest college dorm. The FTP phenomenon has flourished among college students for exactly the reasons described. Using computers hooked to their colleges' powerful servers, they have virtually unlimited storage space and bandwidth. They pull songs off CDs and other FTP sites and onto their computers. Then they open their hard drives to others who spread the songs even further across the Internet.

Not all FTP sites are instruments of the devil. Some are operated by companies as a convenient place to download updates and patches to their software. But generally, any time you see an MP3 for download from an FTP site, it's illegal. Often you see disclaimers such as this one, complete with misspellings and questionable grammar:

The mp3's on this site can only be used as backup, that means you have to have the original single/album of the song you're downloading, if not, you have to buy it within 24 hours.

There is NO Illegal or Copyrighted material on this Website. There are links to mp3's which may or may not be copyrighted. I am not doing the distribution here so I hold myself irresponsible if you download any copyrighted material from the links I provide. Linking is not illegal, Hosting and Distributing is!! I'am just provideing the links, so the creator of this page or the ISP hosting any content on this site take NO responsibility for the way you use the information/files provided on this site. These files and anything else on this site are here for private purposes only and should NOT be downloaded or viewed whatsoever! If you are affiliated with any government, or any other related group or were formally a worker of one you can NOT enter this Web site, cannot access any of its files and you cannot view any of the HTML files. All the objects on this site are PRIVATE property and are not meant for viewing or any other purposes other then bandwidth space. DO NOT ENTER whatsoever! If you enter this site you are not agreeing to these terms and you are violating code 431.322.12 of the Internet Privacy Act signed by Bill Clinton in 1995 and that means that you can NOT threaten our ISP or any person(s) or company storing these files, cannot prosecute any person(s) affiliated with this page which includes family, friends or individuals who run or enter this Web site.

IF YOU DO NOT ACCEPT THESE TERMS THEN LEAVE.

Of course, that's a crock. But then lawyers make a good living off that. Whether the crime is the act of offering the download, or performing the download, or copying the disk hasn't really been decided. But there's got to be at least one law broken in there somewhere.

That said, let's get back to the devil's handiwork.

Although FTP sites are part of the Internet, you don't download pages as you do on the Web. FTP sites have no links to click, only something that looks a lot like an old DOS directory listing. To access anything on these sites, you have to work with the *file transfer protocol* that gives FTP its name. A *protocol* is simply a collection of code and signals that let different types of computers communicate with each other; it's a sort of common language. In the case of FTP, the protocol was developed specifically to make files publicly available for transfer over the Internet. No messaging. No browsing. Just transfer. Because you can work with more than one file at a time—whole directories, in fact—FTP is simpler than Web links for mass transfers.

When you first connect to an FTP site, you're likely to be given just look-only access to the files. You can check out a site's collection of MP3s, but you can't download them. Such sites usually have a readme file that explains how you can gain download access to the site's files. Some FTP sites require that you first do something, such as send an email to the site's owner, click some sponsor's banner at a Web site, or visit a porn page. But before you can get even look-only access, you must log on to the site with a recognized username and password. More helpful search engines return not only a site's location but public usernames and passwords so you can make the initial connection.

Ratio Sites

At some MP3 FTP sites, you're required to upload files before you get to download any. These are *ratio sites*. Usually, your uploads are measured in megabytes. That's so no joker can create a bunch of five-second MP3s to satisfy his upload requirements. A site with a 1:5 ratio lets you download 5MB for every 1MB you upload. Ratios range from a stingy 1:2 to as loose as 1:10. In most instances, the credits you get for uploading last only for that session. If you disconnect, you'll have to start over from scratch.

Some sites don't have ratios. Instead, you must go through umpteen porn sites to find the password. Even if the music is free, server space isn't, and so a lot of sites make sponsorship deals with other sites. And stockbrokers aren't likely to sponsor an FTP site; those sponsors are porn. The password deal is to ensure you click the banner ad to make the host site some money. Many FTP sites let you log on with a public password that only allows you to read a text file that tells you what hoops to jump through to get *leech access*, the ability to download all the songs at the site. Other sites give you the password only by email. A few, called *anonymous FTP servers*, let you in with no strings. These are as rare as hen's teeth.

Reading FTP

The Internet address, which is called a *universal resource locator (URL)*, for typical Web pages looks like this: `http://www.mp3under.com`. FTP servers look different from the URL you use for a typical Web page. For example, Microsoft has an anonymous FTP server at `ftp://ftp.microsoft.com` where you can download updated files. But most FTP sites are weirder than that. Most times you'll be dealing with such unlovely names as `ftp://224.12.343.748` and `ftp://382.409.131.24`. The computers that make up the Internet see site names as four sets of numbers separated by dots. (Actually, URL addresses are also numbers, but the World Wide Web is kind enough to translate the numbers to words, which humans have an easier time remembering.)

In theory, you can go to an FTP address using Microsoft Internet Explorer or Netscape Navigator. But don't. Neither browser was designed for FTP, and so the results are awkward and uncertain FTP connections. They're not worth the effort. Instead, we've included on the book's CD a program that lives to connect to FTP sites: CuteFTP. It's an easy way to connect and transfer files. We'll get to CuteFTP in the next chapter, where we cover downloading files. Right now, we need to get back to the current task—*finding* MP3 files.

Searching for HTTP and FTP Music Files: The Quest for Billy Idol

One day, for no apparent good reason, I had an urge to hear Billy Idol singing, "Dancing with Myself." I didn't know why, and I couldn't find my CD, last seen in the vicinity of the black maw under the driver's seat. Still, some urges are not to be denied. Surely on the Internet I can find one song by one has-been glam-punk rocker. Because any two searches for the same song or artist can produce different, overlapping results, the consummate MP3 hunter must master more than one way to search for MP3s. Follow me as I look at using online search engines, a metasearch program—MP3 Fiend—and Outlook Express to search newsgroups.

Using a Web Site Search Engine—Audiogalaxy.com

The search engine at Audiogalaxy.com is good for quick-and-dirty sweeps for FTP MP3s. The engine regularly prowls FTP sites, creating a database of the files each site has and sorting them by artist and song. More importantly, it gives you all the information you need in the form of user ID, password, and port number to log on to a site. Although the information is basic, most other sites don't do as good a job as Audiogalaxy in laying it out so you know what's what.

Take Your Choice

Dozens of music search engines besides Audiogalaxy are on the Web. One that deserves special attention is look4mp3.com, shown in Figure 3.1, because it lets you choose whether to search for HTTP sites or FTP sites. If you find downloading from FTP too daunting—even with the terrific CuteFTP program included on the book's CD-ROM—or if you simply want to stay away from pirate-inhabited FTP sites, or want to hunt for the good stuff that's only on FTP—look4mp3's dual search is the best place to go.

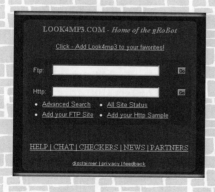

Figure 3.1   *Pick your path at look4mp3—HTTP or FTP.*

Choose HTTP for (mostly) legal songs; FTP takes you into the rich but uncharted outlaw territory.

Using your browser, surf to `audiogalaxy.com`. Right under the banner is a space to enter search terms, such as "Billy Idol." You also can search by title, album, genre—such as techno rock reggae—or anything, really, that someone might have included in the information tags imbedded in an MP3 file. There's a no–ratios box if you don't want the results to list ratio sites, which require uploads before you can make downloads.

Worse than Ratios

The no–ratios check box at Audiogalaxy sounds like a good idea. You'll only download from sites where you don't first have to embark on a life of crime by uploading the latest Mariah Carey warble. But it also means that you're going to run into a lot of banner sites. These sites let you in only far enough to read a message that tells you to go to a Web page and click some of the ads on that page. Doing so eventually reveals the secret password, and you can return to the FTP with full access. At the least, this is a dreary annoyance. At worst, it takes you into one of those pop-up madhouses determined to lure you to a pay porn site. Every time you try to close a site or go back, another banner pops up. I haven't yet figured out the marketing correlation between being irritated and being horny.

If we enter "billy idol" as search terms, the first thing the Audiogalaxy engine does is suggest you narrow the search by choosing one of Billy's song titles, as shown in Figure 3.2. It also suggests other artists that fans of Billy might like, such as Motley Crue and Backstreet Boys. (If you figure out the connection, let me know.)

If you just go barging on down the screen, however, you see a list of FTP sites that carry at least one song by Billy Idol. (Worshippers of other, more obscure butchy rockers may come up empty. And mind you, I'm not suggesting that people rip off sneering, has-been rock stars. It's just that Billy Idol gives me a good excuse to make smart-aleck remarks.) Anyway, if you scroll on down the suggestions, you get to a part of the listing that looks like the screen in Figure 3.3. The callouts in the screen identify the types of information the search engine returns. Some of the information is critical to negotiating FTP sites successfully.

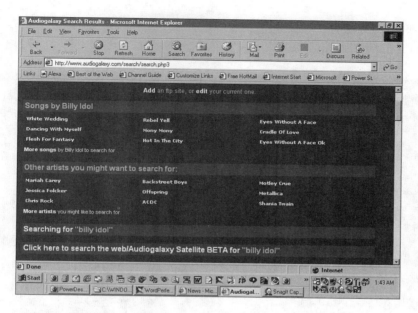

Figure 3.2 *Billy Alikes.*

In addition to finding you a Billy Idol song, Audiogalaxy's search engine suggests other performers it thinks you'll also like.

Pick one of the sites based on its chance of being open and how long it has been since the search engine checked that site to see whether it's online. Also consider whether it's a ratio site and how good a selection of songs it has. When you have one in your crosshairs, copy down the site ID, user ID, and password. All the other information Audiogalaxy supplies is helpful, but the site ID, username, and password are absolutely essential if you're ever going to connect to an FTP site. You'll need them when you get to the next chapter on downloading FTP files.

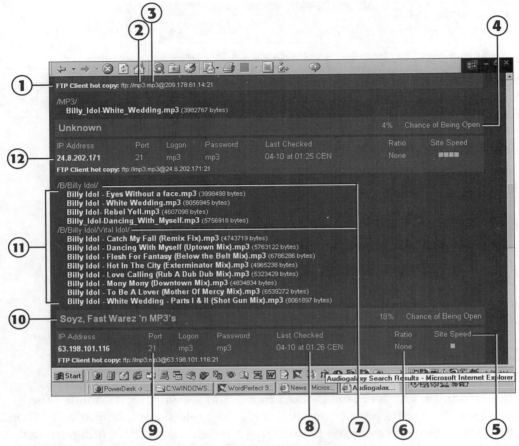

Figure 3.3 *Getting the lowdown on FTP sites.*

Audiogalaxy lists the particulars of FTP sites that carry at least one matching song.

① **FTP Hot Copy:** An easy way to use some Windows FTP programs such as CuteFTP, included on the book's CD-ROM. CuteFTP watches the Windows clipboard and connects automatically to any FTP URL you copy.

② **Logon:** The word the new user must enter as an identity.

③ **Password:** A supposedly secret word needed to connect to the FTP site. If the site does not require ratio uploads, there may be still

another, second password you can find only by following the directions you find at the site, which typically take you to a Web page loaded with advertising.

④ **Chance of Being Open:** This is the chance, expressed as a percentage, that a user will be able to connect to this site. Many sites will allow only a set number of users to access the site at one time. If a site is very popular or the number of users allowed is very low, this percentage will also be low.

5 **Site Speed:** A rough measurement of the average speed of a site, rated from one (slowest) to five blocks (fastest).

6 **Ratio:** If there is a Y or a ratio here, this is a ratio site. You will be required to upload songs before you can download any. A 1:10 ratio requires you to upload 1MB of files before you can download 10MB.

7 **Directory path:** The location of the following song file on the MP3 server.

8 **Last Checked:** The last time the search engine checked the site's status—whether it's online or offline.

9 **Port:** A location on the server that listens for access requests. The conventional port number for FTP is 21, but other numbers are acceptable, depending on the server's configuration. If either the port or the IP address is wrong, you won't be able to connect to the site.

10 **Site Name:** This is a text name for the benefit of humans. It's not necessary to connect to a site. Some sites have no text names.

11 **Song Lists:** Titles and artists of songs found at this site.

12 **IP Address:** This is the Internet protocol address—the way computers on the Net see it, as a group of four three-digit numbers separated by decimals (for example, 123.456.789.012).

Finding Music with MP3 Fiend

As good as Audiogalaxy, or any search engine, may be, it's necessarily limited by the fact that no single, mortal database can exhaustively search the ever-growing, amorphous Internet. To get the best results, you may have to search in several different MP3 databases because the same search terms on different engines will produce different results. (Another popular search engine is Scour.com. Check the reviews of the top search sites in "Top 101 Internet Audio Sites" at the back of the book.) You can find all those sites and other good search engines at this book's Web page, mp3under.com. But first, you should know there's a way to expand the scope of your MP3 searches without trotting from site to site.

MP3 Fiend (see Figure 3.4), a program you run from your own PC, searches 11 of the Web's best MP3 engines simultaneously and then combines the results to display on a single page. What's better, it verifies the results so you don't spend a lot of time trying to connect to an FTP site only to find out it's dead for some reason. The creator of MP3Fiend did not respond to several emails asking permission to include the program on the book's CD. Our killjoy lawyers say we can't distribute it without permission. Instead, surf on over to MP3Fiend.com and download the software. It's worth the effort and connection time. Then install MP3Fiend, and then we'll embark on a *metasearch*, which spans the array of search engines.

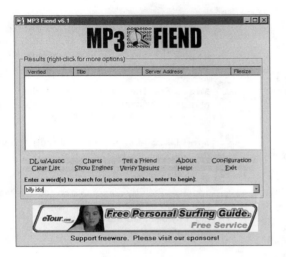

Figure 3.4 *MP3 Fiend's main screen.*

Most functions of MP3 Fiend are launched from this screen. The only menu selections are the words under the large, empty window. They produce a whippoorwill-like sound when you pass the arrow over them. You can turn off the sound.

The first thing you notice when you launch MP3 Fiend (refer to Figure 3.4) is that it has a non-standard look for a Windows program. In fact, in the MP3 world, non-standard, even bizarre, looks are the norm. Some of them are really quite lovely, although incomprehensible. Anyway, don't make any assumptions that something you're used to in other Windows programs still applies. Luckily, MP3 Fiend is so easy to master that you'll get it under your belt in about five minutes. Most of its interface is taken up by a large, blank window where the results of the search will be displayed.

WinMP3Locator Can Locate MP3s, Too

As this book went to press, ReGet Software had just released its WinMP3Locator software. Similar in operation to MP3 Fiend, but seemingly a little slower, WinMP3Locator integrates with your Web browser and download software (such as Go!Zilla and CuteFTP, as well as ReGet's own creation) to search numerous Internet sites for songs. I don't think it's as good as MP3 Fiend, but you can download a free copy at
http://www.winmp3locator.com/.

Pay for Play

The free version of MP3 Fiend is fully functional but advertising-supported. To get rid of the ads, you have to pay. Registration is $25, and for your money you also get your name in the title bar, no ads, and tech support. Fiend's creators will also accept contributions of less than $25.

MP3 Fiend itself does not search the Internet. Instead, it conducts a metasearch among the databases that have been created by other sites' MP3 search engines. It's a search of searches.

To launch a search, type some keywords—artist, title, album name, and so on—in the only space where you can type: the data entry box right above the ad. Fiend keeps track of previous searches, which you can get to by clicking the arrow at the right end of the data entry box. You'll get more results from vague searches. "Billy idol" gets more hits than "dancing with myself."

When we enter "billy idol" and press the Enter key—the only way to launch the search—Fiend sends the search terms to Gnutella, Pathfinder, FTPFind, MP3Board, Kermit's MP3 Search, Gnute, Audiofind, Astraweb, 2Look4, MusicSeek, and Lycos MP3 Search. They're all good search engines on their own, and among all of them it's awfully hard not to find anything you look for. Gnutella and Gnute, in particular, are helpful for finding HTTP downloads, which are much easier to use than FTP sites.

As Fiend conducts its metasearch, the Results Form keeps you posted on the progress of the search. (See Figure 3.5.) On a 56K modem or faster, searching all 11 databases will take less than 3–5 minutes, and even less time if you set up Fiend to look for fewer than 50 matches. You can eliminate any of the searches by clicking the X-buttons in the left column, and you stop the search by clicking the Close button. You'll know when the metasearch is over because you'll hear Austin Powers say, "Yeah, baby!"

Good Gnews

The recent addition of Gnutella to MP3 Fiend's mix is interesting because it's one of the first indications that open-source music is the wave of the future. Gnutella and a program called Napster enable anyone with a PC and an Internet connection to become an ad hoc MP3 download server. This is no small cheese. We'll get into it in depth in Chapter 5, "What's This Napster? How Can I Use It to Swap Music with Others?"

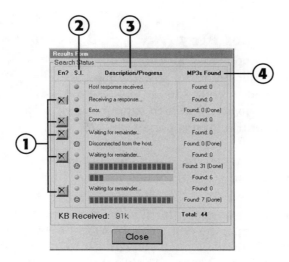

Figure 3.5   *MP3 Fiend Results Form.*

Fiend keeps you posted on the search process, even though the whole deal only takes a few minutes.

① **X-Buttons** disable any or all the search engines even while a search is in progress. Helpful if you've already got enough hits to satisfy you. Disable an engine permanently by clicking the words Show Engines and then uncheck the boxes to the left of the names of search engines you don't want to use. No, I don't know what En? stands for. Does it matter?

② **S.I.** also reports on the metasearch's progress, starting out with all circles green. They turn tangerine—yes, tangerine—as the search progresses, and finally either become a red circle if Fiend encounters an error or transform into happy faces as an inquiry completes. They serve no helpful purpose, but they're nice to look at. And no, I don't know what "S.I." stands for either.

③ **The Description/Progress** column tells you whether Fiend is connecting to a site, is waiting for results, has encountered an error, or is disconnected.

④ **MP3s Found** shows the number of songs that match the search terms for each search engine. A running total is at the bottom of the list.

Each song listed in the results identifies an MP3 file somewhere on the Internet that matches your search. Our quest for Billy Idol homed in on 133 files, four of them HTTP downloads. Each of those files is going to require verification, which is time-consuming. You can make the search more efficient if you narrow the search to a particular song. Right-click anywhere in the results list and choose Subsearch Results. You're given a choice of keeping the results you get with a subsearch or discarding the results. We'll choose to keep them. Enter "Dancing

with Myself" in the entry box and click OK. Immediately, the list is trimmed by 117, leaving us with only 16 sites. Now, mind you, this is not the same thing as finding 16 copies of "Dancing with Myself" that you can actually download. That would be too easy. Because FTP sites dominate the results, you must do more research by verifying them.

Verifying Fiend Search Results

The 11 databases Fiend searches are filled with bad information. It's inevitable on the Internet, especially when you're looking for sites the record companies are closing as fast as they can. Depending on how infrequently each search engine refreshes its search, the results could be woefully outdated. So, the first thing to do is to see which of these results are any good.

You can verify one site at a time, which is the faster way to go if you see only one or two results that intrigue you. Select any result by left-clicking it. You can choose more than one result to test at a time by holding down the Ctrl key as you click results. Then right-click and select Verify Results/Verify Selected Results. Conversely, you can verify all the results at once by clicking the words Verify Results on Fiend's main screen. The verification process takes longer than the search itself because MP3 Fiend sends several commands to each site and has to wait for results. It took just short of four minutes to check out our original 133 Billy Idol songs over a cable Internet connection. During that time, MP3 Fiend tried to log as a user named Anonymous with an email address of anon@anon. Fiend tests each of the sites to see, essentially, how much it can get away with.

The results of the testing are shown in Figure 3.6. If you click the heading of the Server Address column, the results are sorted by site address, and you'll see that the same sites are duplicated several times for different songs. Our original 133 Billy Idol hits come from only 34 individual sites. The verification process rarely comes up with results that say, "Come on in! Download all you want!" Instead you get responses that at first seem to suggest you're shooting all blanks. With a guide to the responses, though, you'll find things aren't as hopeless as they seem. With Figure 3.6 are some of the verification returns MP3 Fiend produces and what they mean:

VERIFIED!

You won't see this often, and when you do, it doesn't necessarily mean someone left the back door unlocked. It sometimes hides a banner or ratio site, but it's still a keeper.

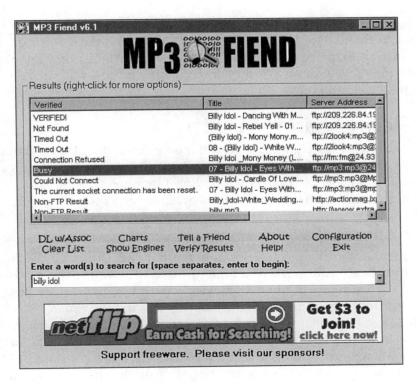

Figure 3.6 *MP3 Fiend verification screen.*

After MP3 Fiend tests all the potential connections uncovered by a search, the results of the test are displayed in a list that needs interpretation to become helpful.

Banner Site

MP3 Fiend believes this is a banner site. This means that the site requires you to travel to a Web site to get a password, and may require you to click on banner advertisements to find it. First, of course, you must have a password to get a password. These sites are so annoying that you may want to skip them altogether. But, if you're determined, you'll see in a few moments how to fish out the information you need to assault the site. Also, MP3 Fiend doesn't claim to be perfectly accurate in detecting banner sites. Some sites it labels as banner sites are not, and many without the label are, in fact, banner sites.

Busy

The site is busy. To keep the site speed running smoothly, FTP owners often put a limit on the number of users allowed on at the same time. FTPs sites with slow connections, such at 56K and ISDN lines—yes, those are slow connections in these

days of DSL and cable—usually allow five or fewer simultaneous connections. Sites with DSL, cable, T1, or T3 hookups allow more people on at one time. To get into them, you must use an FTP client such as CuteFTP, which you'll meet in Chapter 4.

Connection Refused

The site is down or, for some unknown reason, simply refused your connection. Remember, the search results MP3 Fiend comes up with are based on information in the databases of various search engines. Fiend merely reports what the databases say. It doesn't try to actually connect until you run the verification process. For this run, delete any `Connection Refused` results by highlighting the line on which the site is listed and pressing the Delete key, or by right-clicking and choosing Delete.

Could Not Connect

The site is down; delete it from the list.

Not Found

This result could mean one of two things. The first is that the song is missing. The site's owner might have moved that file to another directory. It doesn't mean you can't download it, but that you'll have to connect to the site and do some manual searching first. Or, `Not Found` could mean you have a ratio site that Fiend misinterpreted.

Permission Denied

It's not as bad as it sounds. This almost always indicates a ratio site where you have to upload an MP3 before you can download any. You have to do some manual probing of the site, but you will get the song eventually.

Syntax Error

This error will occur on FTP servers that don't follow the usual rules for communicating with remote clients. All you can do is connect to them manually to see what's going on.

Timed Out

The site did not respond in a reasonable time. Either the site is down or so slow that you might as well delete it.

Non-FTP Result

You've struck an HTTP site, which makes for easier downloading.

Nothing in Verified Column

This result is an MP3 Fiend anomaly. Often, though, sites that are blank in this column are ratio sites.

All files that show file sizes are valid downloads, although they might be banner or ratio sites that require further effort on your part.

That further effort, with any of these results, involves looking at the details of the results MP3 Fiend obtained during the verification. There you'll find the clues to making a successful connection using CuteFTP.

Interpreting MP3 Fiend Verification Logs

To find out exactly what happened when MP3 Fiend probed any of the sites, look at the Verification Log screen for any verified site that suggests it's open to making a connection somehow (see Figure 3.7). The logs help you figure out exactly how.

```
221
220- Rogwilli's New and Improved FTP WAR-FTPD 1.65 Ready
220- Welcome to Rogwilli's FTP Server
220-
220- There is a Byte Ratio on this site!
220- 1:3 here on this site -
220- Please upload 70's crap to me
220- and any ACOUSTIC MUSIC you have!!
220-
220- Good deal huh?
220- Email: ro6willi@hotmail.com
220- or ICQ me at 56813472 for leech access
220-
220- Remember all MP3's must be deleted after 24 hours.
220- OH yeah - This site is Y2K compliant!
220-
220 Please enter your user name.
USER anonymous
331 User name okay. Give your full Email address as password.
PASS anon@anon.com
230 Change DirectoryUser logged in, proceed.
CWD /80s
250 Change Directory"\80s" is current directory.
TYPE A
200 Type is ASCII [No subclass parameter defined, Non-Print used as default.
PASV
227 Entering Passive Mode (24,163,103,169,17,63)
LIST Billy_Idol_-_Dancing_With_Myself.mp3
Send150 Opening ASCII NO-PRINT mode data connection for ls Billy_Idol_-_Dancing_With_Myself.m 3.
-rw-rw-rw- 1 root  sysadmin 5764883 Jan 26 1999 Billy_Idol - Dancing With Myself.m 3
226 Transfer finished successfully. Data connection closed.
QUIT
```

Figure 3.7 *MP3 Fiend verification log.*

A verification log shows you the exact commands MP3 Fiend hurled at a site and the responses it elicited. Enough information is usually in the log to tell you how to complete a successful connection.

Many FTP sites, particularly ratio and banner sites, are deliberately designed to limit your first attempt to connect with them, but in the process, they provide instructions you can incorporate for a second, usually successful, hookup. You find these instructions in the site's Verification Log. To look at the log for any particular site, first left-click the result in the Verification Screen and then right-click and select View Verification Log. If you want to check another site, be sure to left-click it before right-clicking; otherwise, you'll still get the previous log results. The most likely verification results to have useful information in their logs are Verified, Banner Site, Not Found, and Permission Denied.

Mass Deletions

After testing connections with Verify, you don't have to delete unreachable sites individually. Click anywhere in the list and choose Remove Results/Remove Invalid Files. This quickly cuts the list to fewer than a dozen sites. The only problem with this is that it can delete a few sites it shouldn't. If you want to ensure that you look at the verification logs of every site uncovered in the search, do the following: Left-click any site to select it and then right-click and choose View Verification Log. If the log for that one song doesn't have anything useful, none of the results from that same site will be useful either. With the site still selected, right-click and choose Remove Results/Remove All From This Server. Fiend instantly deletes all the results from that same site. Because the results tend to be from only a few sites, you'll quickly check out all the sites this way. Other filters are available for removing sites, but these two are the most helpful.

When you select View Verification Log, a new window pops up with the results of the FTP exchange between MP3 Fiend and the FTP site. Let's take a look at one of the logs to dredge up some useful information. All the lines preceded with numbers are the site's responses to the Fiend. I'll butt in every so often, in the boldfaced type, to point out what we've learned.

220 WEBWORX Microsoft FTP Service (Version 5.0).

USER anonymous

331 Anonymous access allowed, send identity (e-mail name) as password.

Fiend logs on as "anonymous" and the site asks anonymous to enter an email address for a password.

PASS anon@anon.com

230 Anonymous user logged in.

Fiend gives "anon@anon.com" as a password. The site accepts that password and logs in the anonymous user. You now have the two most vital bits of information you can have: a working user ID and password.

CWD /Music

250 CWD command successful.

The site obeyed MP3 Fiend's command to change the working directory (CWD). A good sign. Some sites lock you into one directory until you've uploaded or gone to a banner site to get the "real" user ID and password.

TYPE A

Fiend tells the computer to display only ASCII (text) characters.

200 Type set to A.

PASV

227 Entering Passive Mode (209,226,84,194,5,232).

Fiend sets up the site to receive more commands.

LIST Billy Idol - Dancing With Myself.mp3

Send125 Data connection already open; transfer starting.

550 Billy: The system cannot find the file specified.

Bad news. The site could not find the song that was spotted during the search. The song might be at the site but has moved to a different directory.

RETR Billy Idol - Dancing With Myself.mp3

Send125 Data connection already open; transfer starting.

MP3 Fiend tries a different location on the site and hits pay dirt.

ABOR

426 Connection closed; transfer aborted.

226 ABOR command successful.

QUIT

Fiend aborts the transfer and quits the site.

This is not bad. We've found Billy Idol's "Dancing with Myself," and it's at a site without banners or ratios. At this point we would use MP3 Fiend's automation features to send all the log information to CuteFTP so you can finally suck down the song.

Some of you might have noticed that MP3 Fiend has a main selection, Download w/Assoc, and there's some mention in the configuration screen of feeding Fiend's results directly to either of two programs that specialize in downloads. These two programs are GetRight and Go!Zilla, the latter of which is on the book's CD-ROM. Doesn't that mean we can do our downloading directly from MP3 Fiend? Would that it were so easy. Although Go!Zilla is a terrific program for downloading from HTTP sites, it sucks when it comes to FTP. The same feature that lets Fiend—and Audiogalaxy—trigger Go!Zilla also lets both work with CuteFTP, which is a much better program for reeling in FTP downloads.

But that's in the next chapter. First, just so you'll understand better the twists and turns that accompany FTP sites, let's look quickly at parts of a few other logs:

220- There is a Byte Ratio on this site!

220- 1:3 here on this site _

220- Please upload 70's crap to me

220- and any ACOUSTIC MUSIC you have!!

You'll have to upload 1MB of music, preferably from the '70s, for every 3MB you want to download.

220- Email: ro6wil55@hotmail.com

220- or ICQ me at 56813472 for leech access

Many sites require a person to contact the site's operator through email or the real-time chat program ICQ to receive *leech access*, which allows visitors to download anything and everything the site has.

220- Remember all MP3's must be deleted after 24 hours.

This is a lame attempt to pretend laws aren't being broken.

And another

230-this is a lookie account only... so take a look

230-and if you like what you see, get in touch with me

230-and we can talk trades/leeches.

230-this is NOT a ratio site... so don't waste your time...

A *look account* gives visitors unfettered access to see what songs are at the site, but visitors must contact the site's owner to get download access.

Just about any FTP site that's running and doesn't block you out entirely will at least give you *look access* to see what it has to offer. And as these examples show, the sites usually display some text message to explain what type of site it is and how to get download access. This most often involves either going to a related HTTP site and clicking on advertising banners so the FTP owner makes a few cents or contacting the site's owner by email or ICQ to get the real passwords.

Finding Songs with MP3 Fiend's Music Charts

If you're looking for a song that's on any of today's music charts and you're either too lazy or too dim to figure out some search terms for it, MP3 Fiend provides live updates of seven of *Billboard*'s top 20 music charts. Use them to see what's hot or to fashion a quick-and-dirty search for any of the songs on the chart.

Begin by clicking Charts on Fiend's main screen. A few seconds of delay occur as MP3 Fiend checks for the latest versions of *Billboard*'s charts. You'll get another screen, similar to the one in Figure 3.8. Click the arrow on the drop-down list that reads The Billboard Hot 20. The list that drops down lets you change the selection to one of six other *Billboard* lists. Choose one, and the screen displays that chart's list.

If you want to do a search for any of the songs on any of the charts, double-click any of the titles to generate an effective set of search terms to zero in on MP3s of that song. Press Enter to launch the search and then use the verification process and logs to track down the chart buster.

Newsgroups—MP3s the Hard Way

There is another way in which the wily hunter might track down the elusive MP3 song. This is using the newsreader built into your Internet browser. In a nutshell, this is a primitive way to get MP3s or any other type of file. *Newsgroups*, which communicate over a worldwide network called *Usenet*, are a leftover from the earlier days of the Internet when it was entirely text-based and its primary use was the exchange of notes, messages, and other information that could be expressed by the alphabet, numerals, and ordinary punctuation.

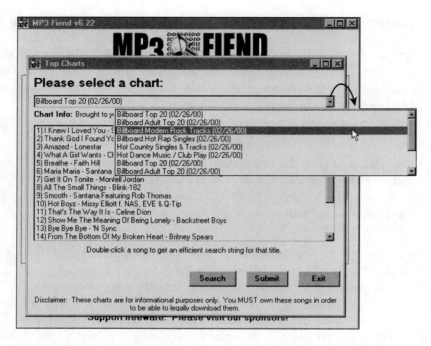

Figure 3.8   *Billboard Charts on DemandBillboardz.*

MP3 Fiend provides Billboard magazine's latest charts for rock, rhythm and blues, rap, country, dance, and adult contemporary songs.

The "news" part of the name is a misnomer. They are really message groups—electronic bulletin boards where everyone reads and replies to everyone else's messages. Each new message can start a *thread*, which is a linked string of answers and replies. Each newsgroup has a specialized area of common interest. For example, alt.binaries.sounds.mp3 is a newsgroup devoted to MP3s. The topics can get endlessly specific, such as alt.sounds.mp3.80s.billyidol.albumsonly. The "alt" means alternative, but not alternative music. Instead, it describes a type of newsgroup that doesn't have all the rules and moderation that other newsgroups have. Binaries tells you to expect to find *binary files*—non-text files that include computer-readable-only data, such as MP3 files, graphics, or software. You can find newsgroups on practically any subject. It's not unusual for a *news server*, where the messages physically reside, to have 50,000 topics going at the same time.

Although news servers are designed to handle text only, someone figured out how to use newsgroups to distribute binary files, which use codes other than those that represent the alphabet. The trick to distributing MP3s via newsgroups is to translate binary codes into combinations of alphanumeric characters. The result, when you open such a message, looks like nonsense to us, but a computer on the receiving end easily converts the gibberish into usable code or data.

Versatility

I don't want to give the impression that newsgroups are used only for distributing bootleg Britney Spears songs. They're also used to distribute nude Britney Spears photos—or at least pix that make that claim—along with other, more genuinely raunchy stuff.

If this seems a roundabout way of doing things, you're right. The advantage of newsgroups is that you can leave a message asking for some obscure song, and someone else with your weird tastes in music, just to be nice, might post the song there. This would probably all be very touching if fundamentally we weren't talking about violating federal law. With the exception of some MP3s from bands, such as the Grateful Dead, which encourage taping of their concerts and so fall into a legal limbo, you can be certain that any popular song you find posted on a newsgroup is illegal.

Not that I care. I'm just going to show you how to find MP3s in newsgroups. In the next chapter, you'll see how to download and decode them. Then you're on your own.

Finding News Servers

If you haven't set up any newsgroups before, that's your first job. When you signed up for Internet service, whoever's providing that service should have told you the name of its *network news transfer protocol (NNTP)* server and whether you need to log on and use a password to get to it. There are three types of news servers:

Free News Servers aren't necessarily free by intention. These are often servers that have been configured incorrectly so that they don't require usernames and passwords. Other servers are free intentionally, but might allow you to only read messages, not post them.

Commercial News Servers charge a subscription fee monthly, quarterly, or yearly. In return, they provide faster service, more reliability, and a wider range of newsgroups than do public servers.

Web-Based News Servers have integrated the drab text of traditional news servers with the graphic look of a Web page. Messages are easier to navigate using the ol' point-and-click. Deja, at `deja.com`, has done the best job of civilizing newsgroups.

Even if you already have a news server, you can tap into others. Not all news servers have the same contents. This means that if you can't find the song you want in one server's newsgroups, maybe you can find it in another's. To find some news servers that will let you hitch a ride, go to `http://www.newsservers.net/` and click on the Servers tab. Then scroll on down past the text and click on Complete List of Free News Servers. Or, just go directly to `http://www.newsservers.net/news_servers/complete.html`. (Another good site is `http://usenet.startshere.net/`.) You'll see a list similar to the one shown in Figure 3.9. The list of free connections at Free Usenet Servers includes the numerical name of the site in the *xxx.xxx.xxx.xxx.* format, followed by the site's text name. For example, the first listing in this screen—128.230.129.221 (dp-news.maxwell.syr.edu)—identifies an open server at Syracuse University. The list also gives you information about the site so you can determine if the site is fast enough, big enough, and stable enough for you to link to.

Whether you use a news server associated with your Internet provider or one of the publicly, if unintentionally, free servers, you must add the server to your newsreader. Many newsreaders are available as shareware. We're going to stick with one that comes with Windows in the form of Outlook Express, which also handles email.

Outlook Express—not Outlook, which is a more powerful program that comes with Microsoft Office—provides a Wizard that steps you through the process. Launch Outlook, click the Tools menu, and choose Accounts. In the Internet Accounts dialog box that pops up, click the News tab. You'll be presented with a list of any news servers to which you've already created links. To add a new news server, click the Add button and then News.

This starts up the Internet Connection Wizard. Most likely, the wizard will already have the first two items it presents for you to fill in: your display name and email address. Change them if you want to be more mysterious. The third

wizard screen asks you to type the name of your Internet News (NNTP) server. Fill in the name you received from your Internet provider or one that you've found in a list of free news servers. The name you type will look something like that in Figure 3.10. Don't check the box about requiring a password unless you've been told to by your Internet service provider.

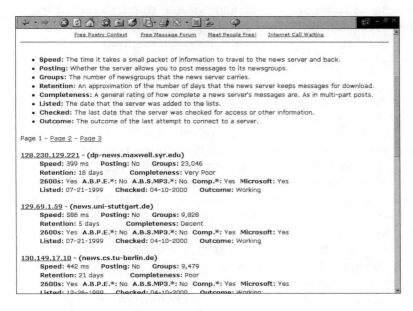

Figure 3.9   *News servers.*

You're not limited to only your Internet provider's news servers. There are others, and they're free for the picking.

Click Next and then Finish. The wizard sends you back to the Internet Accounts dialog, where the news server will have freshly appeared on the list of accounts. The name of the newly added server also appears in the menu on the left side of Outlook Explorer's main screen.

Close the Internet Accounts dialog box. Because you haven't used that news server before, you're asked if you'd like to download newsgroups. Yes, you would. In a few moments, Outlook Express displays a Newsgroup Subscription list that starts off much like the list in Figure 3.11, where newsgroups named with numbers have been sorted to the top of the list. Page down through the list a couple of screens just to get an idea of what it's like. Each one of the items in the list is a separate newsgroup, filled with messages and replies on whatever topic is suggested by the newsgroup's name. Newsgroups are organized into

subject hierarchies, with the first few letters of the newsgroup name indicating the major subject category. Major subject categories are news, rec (recreation), soc (society), sci (science), and comp (computers). The names of sub-categories are separated by dots.

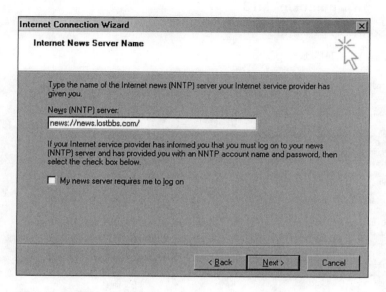

Figure 3.10   *News wizard.*

When Outlook Express's Internet Connection Wizard prompts you, enter the name of a news server to which you want access.

With tens of thousands of newsgroups, you need to narrow down the list by typing "mp3" in the box beneath the instruction "Display newsgroups which contain:". Checking the box to the right, "Also search descriptions" will be more thorough in dredging up groups associated with MP3, but it greatly increases the time the search takes. Most of the time, you can safely leave it unchecked. That way, it takes Outlook no time at all to display a shorter list in which every entry has "mp3" somewhere in its name, like these examples:

> alt.binaries.mp3
>
> alt.binaries.mp3.bootlegs
>
> alt.binaries.mp3.macast.skins_plugins
>
> alt.binaries.mp3.throttle.news.and.piss.off.sabrina
>
> alt.binaries.mp3.zappa

alt.binaries.mpeg.mp3

alt.binaries.music.mp3

alt.binaries.remixes.mp3

alt.binaries.smash_pumpkins.MP3

alt.binaries.sounds.1940s.mp3

alt.binaries.sounds.1950s.mp3

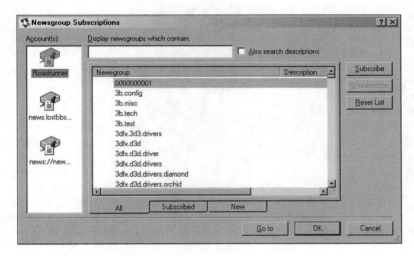

Figure 3.11 *Newsgroup subscriptions.*

If a newsgroup sounds interesting, double-click it to subscribe.

On my computer, as I'm writing this, the complete MP3 list contains 286 newsgroups, with a variety that runs from Beatles to bluegrass, jazz to ninja, acid rock to gospel.

Using a Newsgroup

Scroll through your own list. When you find a newsgroup you like, you can *subscribe* to it so that it is displayed in your Outlook Express Folders list. Subscribing provides easy access to your favorite newsgroups, eliminating the need to scroll through the long list on the server each time you want to visit a favorite newsgroup.

Select the newsgroups to which you want to subscribe by double-clicking them. When you do, an icon of a couple of folders appears to the left of the group's name. When you've selected all you want, click the OK button. Notice that the

names of the newsgroups you selected are added to the Folders window of Outlook Express. The Newsgroup Subscription dialog box is replaced by the Subscription window shown in Figure 3.12.

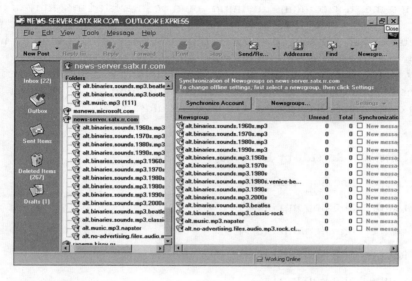

Figure 3.12 *In Sync.*

By subscribing to and syncing with different newsgroups, you can get Outlook to update them with new messages automatically.

The window lists the newsgroups to which you are now subscribed along with columns that show the number of messages you've read and the total messages in each group. The layout is similar to the Windows folder, or directory, structure when seen with Windows Explorer.

Finding Hidden Messages

Outlook Express doesn't always show all the messages that belong to a newsgroup when you double-click the group's name. Your Outlook Express might be set to show only 300 messages at a time. To change this, click Tools, Options, Read and uncheck the box labeled "Get (some number) headers at a time." Also, click View on the program's main menu followed by Current View, Show All Messages.

To see the messages contained in a newsgroup, either left-click the group's name in your Folders column or right-click it and choose Open. Outlook Express displays a list of the messages for that newsgroup. The messages' titles give you a good idea if a message contains anything you'd be interested in. Many of the messages are requests ("REQ:") for specific songs, enticements to MP3 Web and FTP sites, pleas for help, or simply everyday gripes. What you're looking for in particular are messages that contain encoded songs. You'll recognize these because they invariably include the name of the song and usually the artist who performs it, such as the following messages containing a Cyndi Lauper song among other assorted messages. (There were, alas, no Billy Idol songs.)

> The Fixx
>
> REQ.: "Time Will Reveal" by DeBarge - - - -PLEASE?
>
> (Cyndi Lauper) She Bop.mp3 (0/9)
>
> (Cyndi Lauper) She Bop.mp3 (2/9)
>
> (Cyndi Lauper) She Bop.mp3 (3/9)
>
> (Cyndi Lauper) She Bop.mp3 (4/9)
>
> (Cyndi Lauper) She Bop.mp3 (5/9)
>
> (Cyndi Lauper) She Bop.mp3 (6/9)
>
> (Cyndi Lauper) She Bop.mp3 (7/9)
>
> (Cyndi Lauper) She Bop.mp3 (8/9)
>
> (Cyndi Lauper) She Bop.mp3 (9/9)
>
> FREE GAS SAVING TIPS!!! not topic, but important none the less!
>
> Problems with napster
>
> Attn: Folderol - Please Repost Roxanne - Track 3 - TIA :)
>
> GnUtElLa, 10,000 CrAcKs and 10,000 SeRiAlLs, MP3's, NaKeD WoMeN, and MoRe!!!!!
>
> REQ: "Coming Up Close" by Til Tuesday

In addition to the artist's name and song title, another sure clue that messages contain songs is the (0/9)–(9/9) following the message titles. These tell you that "She Bop" has been spread across nine messages. The first number is the order in which the separate parts must be rejoined to re-create the song. You can

open up any single one of the song messages. But it takes several seconds even on a hot Internet connection, and all you'll see is gibberish:

```
M$CY2+O[_B(K>^9%ZL?Z"\A$XLB$"-:5"N6CX>0>E_D[,$Z&````"B*863##*
```

To get Cyndi's song on your hard drive, you must download and decode all the messages that it comprises. It's not difficult, although there is one tricky element. But that's for the next chapter.

How Do I Download MP3s Once I Find Them?

Downloading from Sites on the Web ♪ *Organizing Downloads with Go!Zilla* ♪
Downloading from FTP Sites with CuteFTP ♪ *Downloading from Newsgroups*

Ah, now it gets interesting. After so many pages just jawing about MP3 files, toying with legalities, and cruising some look-but-don't-touch download sites, this is the money shot. At last we're about to reel in some MP3s. And because we're talking about a completely unregulated system that pretty much just grew into what it is today, there's naturally no one, simple way to go about downloading.

MP3 songs exist in three separate Internet environments: the World Wide Web, file transfer protocol (FTP) sites, and the messages swapped in newsgroups. (See Chapter 3, "Where Can I Find MP3 Music?") Plus, other audio formats— Windows WMA and Liquid Audio's LQT— are redefining what a download is. You can, in theory, use the programs that come with Windows to download from any environment. But you really, really don't want to, except for newsgroup downloads. For the Web and FTP, two programs on the book's CD-ROM

will do a much better job than an unaided browser. We'll see how to make Go!Zilla and CuteFTP two of the biggest guns in your MP3 software arsenal, no matter what the audio format.

Downloading from Sites on the Web

You surely have downloaded stuff off the Web, haven't you? I guess it *is* possible that someone today hasn't downloaded a file at least once in their lifetime. Kids do it. Grandparents do it. No big deal, right? Double-click some icon or the word Download, Windows pops up a window, and you get to say where you want the file to go to and what name you want to give it.

I admit, that's really pretty simple. Only two problems with it. One is that it doesn't always work when it comes to downloading audio files. Music sites on the Web have come up with all these twists to the simple act of downloading, particularly when the song is in Windows media audio (WMA) or Liquid Audio (LQT) format. Some sites download their own downloading programs, which take over all downloads without so much as a "Thank you, ma'am." Some take you to another site and tell you to just sit there and wait for the download to start on its own. Some don't seem to give you a choice of where to save a file. Others do nothing.

Here's where we'll look at the best ways to download music files using only your browser, either Windows Internet Explorer or Netscape Navigator. I don't know why music sites, in particular, are off on so many different tangents. But we'll look at the one simple way that always—nearly—works. And for those who are a bit more compulsive and like to have all their downloads in specific folders, named just so, and their origins documented, we'll show you how to incorporate into your everyday downloading a free program included on the book's CD-ROM, Go!Zilla.

The Right Way

You know the old saying: "There are three ways to do something. The right way. The wrong way. And the computer's way." Okay, so it's not an old saying. But it's true. Both Internet Explorer and Netscape Communicator have more than one way to launch a download, and you should know them all.

All downloads on Web pages are identified as some sort of button or other link, such as the name of the file or simply the word Download. We're going to call these *download links*. It doesn't matter whether they're icons or underlined words or animations. The information here applies equally to any link that launches a download.

One way to activate a download link that you surely already know is left-clicking the link. It usually works, especially with MP3 files, and when it works properly, there's no problem. But a better tactic is to *right*-click the download link. Doing so pops up a menu. Select Save Target As (in Internet Explorer) and you're presented with an ordinary Windows Save File As dialog box. (See Figure 4.1.) There you can change the folder for the song and its name. If you're using Netscape Navigator, right-clicking produces a menu with the selection Save Link As. It does the same thing.

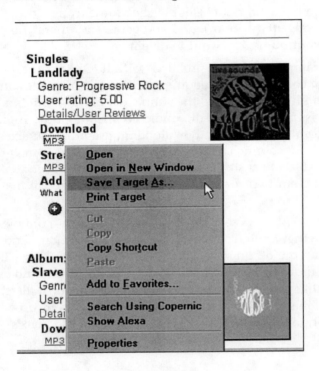

Figure 4.1: *Right-Click Menu.*

Use Save File As in the menu that appears when you right-click a download link.

Right-clicking doesn't always work—particularly with WMA and LQT audio files. That's because many links that look as if they should belong to a download are really links to another Web page, usually stuffed with promos for the band and a real download link hidden someplace so you have to scour the entire page to find it. Or, the bogus download link really launches a Java script or CGI (common gateway interface) script that controls the download process after you've entered your email address, age, Zip code, blood type, and zodiac sign, and agreed to let your mailbox be stuffed regularly with fan news about the performers' songs, T-shirts, posters, and paraphernalia.

If you do right-click on such a link, you'll know it right away because the Save As box, instead of showing you a filename that ends with .MP3, WMA, or LQT, will have the characters "Java," "cgi", or "html" in the name. When that happens, click Cancel, proceed with a left-click, answer all the questions, and then click a file that takes you to still another page, where you might finally find the real link to launch the download.

You may be able to tell in advance whether a link leads to an actual download. Position the pointer over the link and look at the bottom left of the browser's window. In most cases, you see the URL behind the link, such as the one shown in Figure 4.2. If the URL doesn't end in an extension that indicates it's a music file, go ahead and left-click it to take you to the next stage, where a right-click might just work. However, be aware that it's no big trick for Web page designers to override this display with text of their choosing, and sometimes this text can be deceptive. Just because you see a message saying "click here to download" doesn't mean you won't instead be taken to a page full of banner ads first.

Figure 4.2:   *Look Before You Click.*

You can see what a link leads to before you click it.

Working with WMA and Liquid Audio Downloads

An MP3 file is straightforward. You download it, and you play, copy, give it away, whatever you can do with any other ordinary computer file—a least as far as technology goes. Intellectual property law forbids doing some things with copyrighted songs. The laws of physics and computing couldn't care less. Anything you can do with any other computer file, you can do with an MP3.

WMA and LQT are different. Along with lesser-known formats such as a2b, WMA and LQT are vying to be the standard copy-protection for digital music— any form of digital expression, really. This is an enormously important market because the same compression and swapping of songs will inevitably be used with movies and video. Both formats are designed to be flexible because, at this early stage, the record companies, Microsoft, and Liquid Audio are experimenting with different marketing schemes. Some WMA and LQT songs have a built-in timer that renders them unplayable after two weeks or a month. Other songs can't be played if they're copied to another computer. When you try to play them, you are taken to the Web, where you can register like a proper music listener and a *token* is placed on the computer to authorize the song's playing. MP3 files are not immune. At an increasing number of brand-name sites offering MP3s of BYAHO, scripts first download a small—1KB—MP3, which in turn, downloads the real song.

Jeez, could they make it any more difficult? Of course, they can. And they will as the record labels try different combinations of copy protection to find one with which they feel comfortable and which customers are willing to put up with.

The upshot today is that right-clicking is likely not to work with non-MP3 songs. Resort to the left-click instead. The files will sometimes download without giving you a clue as to where they're going. The trick is this: They are being saved in the directory folders set up as the default download folders for players such as RealJukebox and MusicMatch Jukebox because those programs have registered with Windows the extensions .LQT and .WMA, so that they're the default programs for opening those files. If you haven't yet installed any media players, the Save As box will function normally, giving you a chance to say where you want the files to reside.

It would be convenient if we could ignore Windows media and Liquid Audio files altogether, but unfortunately many of the new songs by hot bands are in those formats. Fortunately, in Chapter 7, "How Do I Play MP3 Files? And How Do I Keep Track of 1,000 Songs?" we'll encounter some ways to convert .LQT and .WMA songs to the more tractable .MP3 format.

Organizing Downloads with Go!Zilla

If you want to download files by only using left mouse clicks, that's fine. Whatever gets you through the download. But with the tools supplied on this book's CD-ROM, you can take as much or as little control as you like. You can have a laissez-faire attitude toward your digital songs, letting them scamper about in meaningless clumps. Or, you can be the master of the digital universe, organizing your songs to the *n*th degree.

Whatever audio player you use, it will to a great degree insulate you from the locations of songs. But for backup or uploading, it's still a good idea to be able to find your songs without the aid of your players. If you use more than one program to download songs, you'll find that none of them necessarily agree on where to save the files. You need to supply the organization. Start off with a folder in your hard drive's root directory. Call it "My Music" or "Songs," whatever—although the shorter the better.

Within that folder, create folders with the names of performers you want in your collection—Madonna, Led Zeppelin, Tiny Tim, Smelly Hedgehogs, and so on. Then, throw in a couple of folders—Various Artists or Misc.—to cover stray downloads that don't rate their own folders. On the other hand, you could create folders for different music genres. You will be able to wring a good deal more organization out of your songs with album names, release dates, and even track order. But you don't need directories to do that. Both MusicMatch and RealJukebox take such anal-retentiveness to a new level.

Decide on a naming scheme. The combination of Artist-Album-Title, such as

`Joe Cocker-Greatest Hits-You Are So Beautiful.mp3`

works well with most songs, and MusicMatch and RealJukebox can be set to use the same strategy.

No matter what scheme you decide on, you can bet that few of the files you find online will be as thoughtfully named as yours. If a download link lets you trigger the download with a right-click and Save Target As, you'll have a chance to rename the file to your own scheme. Left-clicking usually results in oddly named songs, but that simply goes with files of suspicious origins put on the Internet by people obviously lacking your high degree of neatness.

Included on this book's CD-ROM is the free program Go!Zilla. It should be in the Startup folder of anyone who does a lot of downloading—of songs, shareware, or anything else found on HTTP sites. Go!Zilla automatically detects when download links are clicked in both Internet Explorer and Netscape Navigator, and helps make sense of what you have and where.

Accept No Substitutes

Some sites have their own version of download "helpers" they might force on you without giving you a choice. DownloadsDirect and Real Networks, for example, use a program called NetZip. If possible, avoid it. It provides far less of the convenience and organization you'll get from Go!Zilla. In addition, NetZip can interfere with Go!Zilla's operations.

You can hand over the downloading task to Go!Zilla by—most times—clicking and dragging a link to a big red eye that sits on your screen as Go!Zilla's *Drop Target*. Just taking over the download is merely one way in which Go!Zilla helps. You can gather files for batch downloading and see their estimated download times. Go!Zilla also searches for other sites that offer the same file and shows you how fast the different connections are, letting you chose which one to use. If a download is interrupted, Go!Zilla usually can pick up from where it left off. In addition, it keeps a complete record of where you've obtained files, should you want to revisit one. It's designed to work with FTP sites too, but that's not its forte. On the book's CD-ROM, you'll find CuteFTP, which does a better job with FTP downloads.

Buy Off the Advertising

The version of Go!Zilla on the book's CD-ROM is completely free and fully functional. It will not nag you or stop working after a month. But you can pay a registration fee of $25 and get priority tech support, free upgrades, and a version of the software that doesn't have advertising on it.

If you're not the impetuous type who has already installed the software on this book's CD-ROM, now's the time to demonstrate utter disregard for all the legal gobbledygook we've put on it, break out the disc, and install Go!Zilla. The installation's simple. Click on through the installation wizard and when it offers to launch the program immediately, go for it. Then we want to change a few settings and just get a tour of the territory for now.

Setting Up Go!Zilla

When Go!Zilla launches, the first thing you'll see is the setup screen. The most important item is the speed of your Internet connection. Choose one from the list. If you're using DSL or a cable connection, which aren't on the list, select T1. That's a bit of exaggeration, but better to have Go!Zilla overestimate your speed than underestimate it. You'll also see the usual dial-up and proxy information, which you've already gone through before, in which case you simply enter the same information that's in your dial-up and Internet connection settings.

After you finish with the setup screen, you're presented with Go!Zilla's main screen, which is really a view into the database the program maintains on files you've downloaded or pegged for future downloading. Right now it's blank because you haven't yet used Go!Zilla to download any files. And even when you've worked with Go!Zilla for a while, you don't need to be all that concerned with the database unless forget where you stashed a file or you need to dig up its origin for a redownload. We'll get back to it later.

For now, let's click Go in the main menu and select Options. You'll see a screen that looks similar to the ones in Figures 4.3, 4.4, and 4.5. You'll see that nine tabs are at the top of the form. They lead you to myriad changes you can make to how Go!Zilla works. Fortunately, you can safely leave most of the option settings as they are, but you need to make the changes shown in the screen shots.

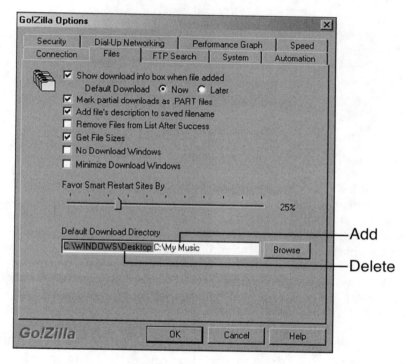

Figure 4.3: *Set Up Your Download Directory.*

Located under the Files tab, the Default Download Directory that Go!Zilla installs with is your Desktop, which is already so cluttered with icons you really don't need to add a bunch more for the collected works of Elvis. Delete the default location and replace it with something such as C:\My Music. (Of course, you should make sure you actually have a folder called My Music before you tell Go!Zilla to save files to it.)

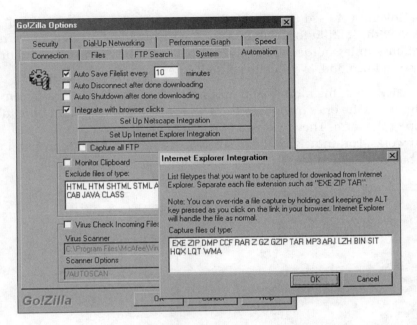

Figure 4.4   *Set Up Go!Zilla to Work Automatically with the Browser.*

Under the Automation tab, check the box next to Integrate with browser clicks. Then click Setup Netscape Integration or Setup Internet Explorer Integration, depending on which browser you use. That will open up the Integration window shown at the lower right. This tells Go!Zilla that anytime you click on a download link that leads to a file with any of the extensions listed in the window, Go!Zilla should take over the download process. We've added LQT and WMA to the list so Go!Zilla will automatically work with Liquid Audio and Windows Media Player files if it gets half a chance. Finally, uncheck the boxes labeled Capture all FTP and Monitor Clipboard. Later in this chapter, we'll have a better way to handle FTP downloads.

After you've finished with the basic settings, find the Go!Zilla eye icon that the installation has placed on your desktop, and drag and drop it into your Startup folder so Go!Zilla will always be running and ready to take on any spur-of-the-moment file mining. Now you're ready to do some serious downloading.

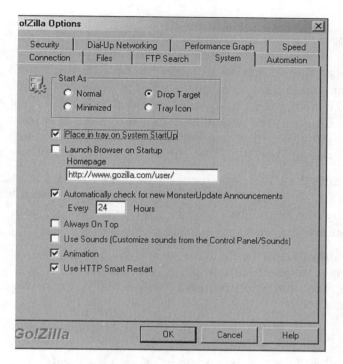

Finally, under the System tab of the Option dialog box, click the radio button next to Drop Target and check the box next to Place in Tray on System Startup. The Drop Target is an icon of a big red eye, presumably belonging to an Internet version of everyone's favorite Japanese rubber supermonster. When the target is showing on top of the browser, you can click and drag download links to the eye to pass them on to Go!Zilla automatically.

Downloading with Go!Zilla

Launch Go!Zilla and your browser. The drop target appears as a bigger-than-average icon in the upper-right of your screen. You can position the target anywhere on your screen. Occasionally, the target gets lost behind other screens. When that happens, right-click the smaller eye icon in the system tray at the lower-right of your screen and choose Drop Target to make the monster's eye reappear.

In your browser, head for any site likely to have downloads. Any of the music download sites discussed in "The Top 100 Internet Audio Sites," at the back of the book should do nicely. (This book is about MP3s, but Go!Zilla works with any type of file—well, almost. In a bit we'll discuss what to do when Go!Zilla gets bamboozled by tricky Web pages.) Find a file download link and left-click it. You may simply go to another Web page that asks you to hand over some simple information about yourself, such as the thing you fear most in your dreams. Sooner on later, though, you'll hit pay dirt.

Here. Watch me do it. Using the HTML search engine at `look4mp3.com`, I launch still another quest for "`idol`." I get only one hit—"White Wedding"—and it turns out to be a funnel leading to a site where I have to send some email to gain access to his cache of outlaw files.

Too much trouble. Perhaps I'll try someone more *au courant*. So, I enter "Alanis." Incoming! Eleven Morissette hits, and they all look good. I choose a link for "Uninvited." I already own it on compact disc, and I figure you can't steal something you already own.

Always Drag

Go!Zilla is good at detecting when you left-click a legitimate download link. But it's not perfect. The best way to make sure a download and Go!Zilla connect is to click and drag the link to the drop target. Even when I accidentally launch a download without going through Go!Zilla, I cancel the download and drag the link to the big red eye so I can keep track of all my downloads.

I hover over the link with my pointer, and in the lower-left corner of the browser it reads "Shortcut to Alanis-Uninvited-ao-vivo.mp3." I lock on and fire—but fall into a CGI script. Luckily, the gRoBot program at `look4mp2.com` intervenes. It analyzes the site and extracts a valid link for the song. I drag the link to the Go!Zilla drop target and release. The result is the screen shown in Figure 4.6, Road Map to Go!Zilla's Download Form.

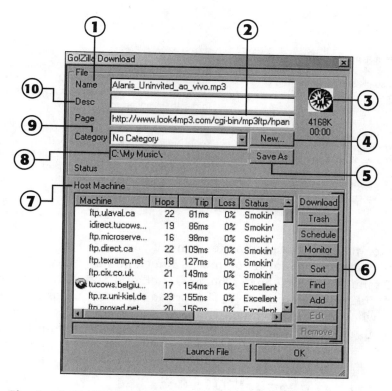

Figure 4.6 *Road map to Go!Zilla's download form.*

① **Name:** The name of the file as it appears at its download site.

② **Page:** The URL of the site where the file is located.

③ **Smart Restart:** Files with this symbol identify FTP and HTTP sites that support interrupted downloads. The feature is particularly helpful on slow or noisy connections.

④ **New:** Click this button to open the Category dialog box. Give a name to a category to which you expect to be adding songs in the future. In the Directory box, enter the folder in which you want files from this category to be automatically saved. Later you can select this category from the Category drop-down list.

⑤ **Save As:** This button opens a normal Windows Save As dialog where you can change the filename and browse to different folders.

⑥ **Control Buttons:** These enable you to download the file immediately, schedule it for later when traffic is likely to be lighter, trash it all together, and otherwise play with the Host Machine list.

⑦ **Host Machine:** Go!Zilla will automatically search for mirror sites, which are other locations that have the same file. It *pings*—sends a short signal to—each site to determine how many connections the file has to pass through and the time of the trip in milliseconds. It notes any data lost as a percentage and ranks the speed of the site as Smokin', Excellent, Good, Average, Little Slow, or No Response. The fastest download may not be the one that you found originally. So, use this list to select the fastest site, which is usually sorted to the top of the list.*

(8) Download Folder: This is whatever you've picked as the default download directory. But the folder for the current download can be changed using Categories or Save As.

(9) Category: The arrow on the right drops down a list of categories you've created by clicking the New button. Categories can be artists'

names, genres, or however you choose to organize your music. Associate different categories with different directories, and the Download Folder will automatically point to the folder that's linked to a category.

(10) Desc: Anything you want to help identify a song, such as "Live" for a live performance. You can set up Go!Zilla so that whatever you enter here automatically becomes part of the filename when you save the file.

All this may be too much record keeping for some of you. Fair enough. You don't have to use categories to download music. You can dump every MP3, WMA, and LQT song in the same folder, helter-skelter, and both RealJukebox and MusicMatch Jukebox do excellent jobs of sorting them all out for you. But there are times—when you're burning a CD or editing a set of songs—when it's handy to have your music organized so you can find specific songs outside the jukeboxes.

When Go!Zilla Goes Bad

Some audio files—usually WMA and LQT—have links that are so convoluted Go!Zilla simply can't handle them if you're using Microsoft Internet Explorer. Go!Zilla's creator, Aaron Ostler, says that with Netscape Navigator Go!Zilla is "practically infallible." But Internet Explorer is designed to hide from Go!Zilla exactly where a URL will take it. I know. I myself was shocked, shocked to learn that Microsoft puts out buggy software. Ostler is working on a way to make Go!Zilla more compatible with Explorer, but if you find Explorer is set on handling a download it's own way, forget about Go!Zilla for the moment and resort to the right-click/Save Target As method to start the download.

---

* Just to get a lot of sites off the hook, the download locations shown here aren't actually for an Alanis Morissette song. There was only one HTTP location for Alanis, and I wanted to show you what the Host Machine list looks like when it strikes a major vein. The sites shown here are actually mirror sites for downloading Go!Zilla. Other screen shots in the book have been doctored for pedagogical purposes. So, don't be concerned if you can't make your computer do some of the things you see here.

If you do use Go!Zilla for your downloading, from the Download form, select the fastest download site and click Download. The form is replaced by a progress box, shown in Figure 4.7. You can hide the box if you want to get on to other business, but if you leave it floating on top of your other screens, the progress box provides a wealth of information about how the download's going.

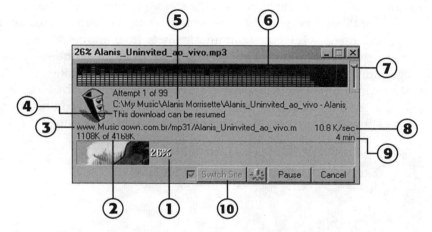

Figure 4.7   *Road Map to the Go!Zilla Progress Box.*

(1) Visual Progress Bar: Graphically shows how much of the file has been downloaded by gradually unveiling some tasteful graphics.

(2) Amount Received: These figures tell how many kilobytes out of the total size of the file have been received.

(3) Download Site: Where the file is coming from.

(4) Resumability: Tells whether the download can be resumed from where it left off in case it's interrupted.

(5) Location: Where the file is being saved.

(6) Progress Gauge: A running visual profile of how fast the download has been progressing. The taller the indicator bars, the faster the transfer.

(7) Throttle: Allows you to slow down the transfer. If you want to continue browsing, lowering the throttle makes the download take longer, but your browsing is faster.

(8) Transfer Speed: Measured in kilobits per second.

(9) Time Left: Approximate time before the download is complete.

(10) Switch Site: If the file's available at mirror sites, use this button to switch to an alternative location if the current run begins to slow down.

When Go!Zilla completes a download, it announces the fact with a monstrous roar that will wake up anyone napping in the next cubicle. In the same vein, Tom Hanks announces, "Houston, we have a problem," if a download crashes. Fortunately, you can turn off the sounds from Go!Zilla's main menu by choosing Go, Options, System tab and unchecking the box next to Use Sounds.

Using the Go!Zilla Database

After you place a song in the Go!Zilla Download form, it's automatically entered into the permanent database of downloads. If doesn't even matter if you haven't actually downloaded it yet. The crucial information about the song is stored so you don't have to find its download site again. All the songs are grouped by the categories you created for them, and you can drag and drop a song from one category to another. A special category is created automatically to hold all files whose downloads were interrupted. Right-clicking any of the titles in the database gives you a choice of actions to take, from downloading the song to launching an FTP search for it. Most commands are also launched by clicking icons in the toolbar above the database listing. (No text accompanies the icons, but you can get a tip about what they do by hovering over them with your pointer. See Figure 4.8.)

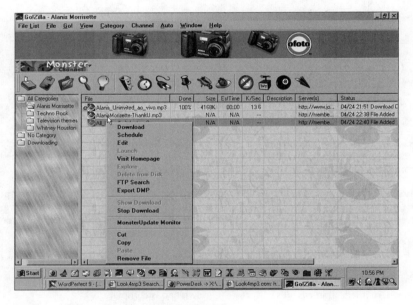

Figure 4.8   *The Go!Zilla Database.*

All files that have been downloaded or marked for possible downloading are automatically added to the file list for later reference or downloading at a more convenient time or when the Web's less congested.

Step-by-Step Go!Zilla

The wonder of Go!Zilla is that so many operations are auto-mated; you really don't have to do much at all. But the follow-ing are some handy step-by-step directions to refer to until you get used to the program.

1. If Go!Zilla's drop target isn't visible, right-click the Go!Zilla icon in the system tray and choose Drop Target.

2. Left-click the download link, drag it to the drop target, and release the button.

3. If you get a message similar to the one shown in Figure 4.9, you can try to continue, but it's generally better to send the downloading operation back to the browser.

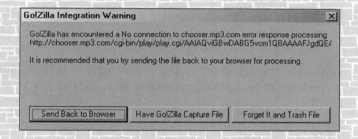

Figure 4.9 *Integration Warning.*

When Go!Zilla encounters a file it cannot handle for some reason, it displays a warning box similar to this. The best bet is to send it back to the browser. In that situation, the browser often takes you to a link that Go!Zilla can handle automatically.

4. When Go!Zilla's Download form appears, enter any additional information you want to record about the download, such as album name, in the Description box.

5. If you already have created a category under which you want to save the song, jump to step 8. If you have not already created a category where you want to put the song, click the New button.

continues

continued

6. In the Category dialog box that appears, enter a name for the new category. Then, finish the file pathname in the Directory box so that it is the location on your hard drive where you want the file saved.

7. Click OK. If the directory doesn't exist, you'll be asked if you want to create it. You do.

8. If you've previously set up a category for the song, click the arrow at the right end of the Category box and select the correct category from the drop-down list.

9. If the correct folder for saving the file doesn't appear in the box directly under the Category box, click Save As, browse to the proper folder, and click OK.

10. Look at the download sites in the Host Machine list. Choose the fastest site, usually at the top, by clicking on the Machine name.

11. Click Download to begin the transfer or Schedule to have the transfer take place when connections are less crowded.

Other Go!Zilla Features

The program also includes a Super Link Leech to grab all the file links on a page. It's a really groovy feature, because it lets you raid hundreds of files from a Web page without the tedium of downloading them individually.

Here's how it works: You see a Web page that has a lot of promising links—so many that you don't want to spend all day clicking and saving and clicking and saving. Instead, click the Leech Files button, which looks like a red file folder with a blood-sucking parasite attached to it. A dialog box appears as Go!Zilla explores all the links on the Web page you're viewing and presents the results in the left-hand pane. You can see if the so-called song files really are downloadable MP3s or misleading links. Select the songs you want to download and click the Add button, then click OK. Go!Zilla will add the entire batch to its download list, and you can suck them all down while you continue your Web explorations.

Another feature, Monster Update, watches for updates to your favorite programs. There are also channels that lead to various Web sites. Additionally, Go!Zilla has a built-in search of FTP locations, although I prefer the search in CuteFTP.

Downloading from FTP Sites with CuteFTP

It is possible to download files from FTP sites with Internet Explorer and Netscape Navigator. This is possible in the same sense that it's possible for me to pour sulfuric acid on my head. It's not something you want to do simply because you can. Stripping songs off FTP really requires a program designed for just that task. Many FTP downloaders are available as shareware, but the best and easiest of them is CuteFTP. Don't let the name fool you into thinking this is some girly-man program. It's robust and powerful enough to make any FTP site surrender its goodies.

If you haven't already installed CuteFTP from the book's CD-ROM, now's the time to do so. The first thing it presents you with when you launch it is the Site Manager. Remember back in Chapter 3 when we uncovered the crucial information needed to gain access to an FTP site—the URL, username, password, port number, and then the *real* username and password you get only after navigating a site filled with banners for things you wouldn't want your mother to see you doing? (And that you wouldn't want to see your mother doing, for that matter.) Well, this is the form where you finally put that information to use.

Ready to Roll

Actually, one of the helpful touches in CuteFTP is that is comes already configured for several dozen FTP sites, grouped neatly into ecological sites, hobbies, government sites, hardware, Internet help, music, literature, operation systems, sports, space, and software downloads. But the ready-rolled music sites aren't that good for bagging MP3s although AOL's FTP music site is an excellent source of lyrics.

Generally it makes sense for the Site Manager to pop up right away if you've already stored the settings for several FTP sites. Then, you just open one of the sites and sail away to download nirvana. But at this point, you haven't added any sites, so we need to use some of the information we gathered in Chapter 3, "Where Can I Find MP3 Music?" I'll use as an example an FTP site whose operator responded to my email plea for a username and password. He seemed like a nice guy, and so I'll be using some *noms de Net* in the screen shot illustrations.

Entering FTP Connect Information

In the Site Manager screen, click New to open a blank FTP form. (See Figure 4.10.) In the box named Label for Site, enter a descriptive name that will remind you what's available at the site, such as "Military Marches."

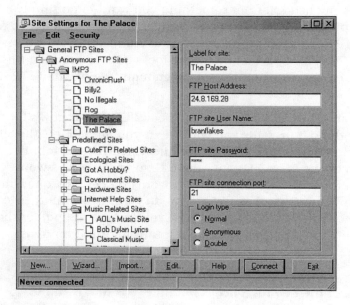

Figure 4.10 *CuteFTP Settings for a New FTP Site.*

When you have the information—the real information—that gives you access to an FTP site, click New on CuteFTP's Site Manager to open a form to store that info.

In the FTP Host Address field, enter the FTP site's location—a series of four numbers separated by periods. (If you don't have this information, you must have skipped Chapter 3. Go back and read it, and this time there may be a quiz.) Enter the user ID in the box labeled FTP site User Name and enter the password in the FTP site Password box. Next, enter the site's port in the box labeled FTP site connection port. If you're not sure what it is, try "21." Leave Normal selected under Login Type.

The descriptive name appears at the bottom of the list of sites on the left side of the form, where sites are saved automatically as they're created. You can click and drag the new site to any of the groups of sites listed above it. Or, you can click on any of the categories and choose New Folder to create a new grouping for the same type of sites. But, you should take note of the fact that if you drag and drop, the site is copied rather than moved to the category. To avoid duplicates, left-click on the new site's description to select it and then right-click and choose Cut from the features menu. Then, right-click on the category name in which you want the site to reside and select Paste.

A Whiz of a Wiz

I should apologize. I could have saved you all that work figuring out and filling in the Site Manager form if I'd told you just to click the Wizard button on the bottom end of the form. The Wizard steps you through filling out all the information one item at a time, and it's accompanied by a good explanation of what's needed. But it's character building to learn how to work with the Site Manager without any mollycoddling wizard.

After you have all the information filled in, but before you try to connect to the site, you need to tweak just one more thing—by which I mean two more things. Click the Edit button at the bottom of the Site Manager. In the Settings box that opens, make sure you're looking at the page with the General tab. In the third box, Default Local Directory, enter the same directory—C:\My Music, or whatever you entered for Go!Zilla. (It's important to have that certain synergy among your MP3 programs.)

Before you leave the General page, take a glance at the large box labeled Site Comments. Because you haven't contacted a site yet, it might be premature to make comments. But the box is a good place to paste those instructions you had to follow to get the site's *real* instructions. Later, you can come back to it to enter telling notes such as, "Best site for Lambada, the forbidden dance."

Next, click the Advanced tab. In the advanced settings section, enter "45" in the box labeled Delay between retries. You can also increase the number of attempts to connect from the 2 that's the default in Connection Retries, but it's the delay that's important. An FTP program that repeatedly tries to log on to a site without a pause between attempts is guilty of *hammering*. This is bad etiquette in the FTP world, and many sites are set up to block the IP address of any computer found to be hammering. A 30-second interval is reasonable.

The reality is that if you can't get on a site right away, you might as well wait a half an hour or so before trying again. Even if you have the *really* real top-secret user ID and password, many reasons could cause you to fail to hook up with an FTP site. The site may have a limit on how many computers can connect to it at the same time, which often is 15–25. Also, remember that some of these FTP servers exist on some college sophomore's laptop. They could simply be turned off.

So, after you change the delay time, click OK. Now you're done. You don't really need to be concerned with the rest of the settings, which get too esoteric for anyone but the committed hacker.

Connecting to an FTP Site with CuteFTP

Hey, we're a mouse click away from violating the United States copyright laws and Berne Convention for the Protection of Literary and Artistic Works! In fact, unless you're a resident of Hasta Della Fuego, you could in a few minutes become a criminal—a music-lovin', computer-literate criminal—but a criminal nonetheless. Ready? I've warned you. I've got witnesses. You asked for it.

With all the information for the site filled in, click Connect at the bottom of the Site Manager. Now the manager is replaced by CuteFTP's main screen—a claustrophobic blending of four separate windows, tools bars, and an advertising banner that is the reason this version of CuteFTP is free. (See Figure 4.11.)

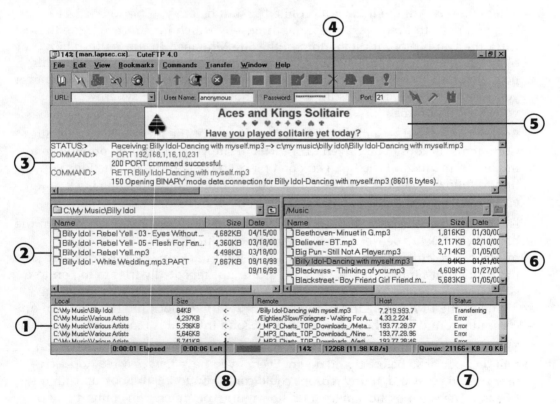

Figure 4.11 *Road Map to CuteFTP.*

(1) Queue: This window lists the files being transferred and those waiting their turn. This screen shows that "Dancing with Myself" is being downloaded. Attempts to download the four other songs in the list ended in some sort of error.

(2) Files in Local Folder: Lists files that have already been added to a subfolder in the local, default download direction, in this case C:\My Music.

(3) Log: This window maintains a running account of commands issued by your computer and the responses from the FTP host. The log contains important clues to why attempts to connect to a site are unsuccessful. The log scrolls to show the complete text, which can be copied and pasted into a word processor for less cramped examination.

(4) Quick Connect Bar: By filling in the URL, username, password, and port number, you can connect to an FTP site without creating an entry in the Site Manager.

(5) Space-hogging Ad: Registering CuteFTP gets rid of the ad and gives you more room for the four main windows. Any of the windows can be toggled off to make more room for the remaining windows.

(6) Files in Host Folder: This is the mother lode: music MP3s the FTP site offers in its \Music directory. You move up and down through folders and subfolders just as you would folders on your own computer using Windows Explorer. Here you can see the long elusive "Dancing with Myself" has been selected for a download, which, in fact, the Queue shows is already taking place.

(7) Progress Bar: Track the progress of a download with the information supplied in this discreet bar. Left to right are the time that's elapsed during the download; the time left; a bar graph that shows download progress; progress expressed as a percentage; how many kilobytes have been downloaded and the transfer speed; and the total size of files waiting in the queue.

(8) Direction of Transfer: Arrows point in the direction of the file transfer. These arrows pointing to the left indicate that the file is moving from the *host*—the FTP site—to the local Billy Idol folder. If the transfer were an upload, the arrows would point to the right.

Of course, because this is your first voyage into the uncharted, dark waters of the FTP sea, chances are you're going to come up empty. Between sites that aren't working and those that want you to go through some more rigmarole before they tell you how to *really* connect to them, you're going to have to kiss a lot of FTPs before you can download a Prince ditty.

And when you do connect successfully to a site, be prepared for long download times. Many of the FTP sites aren't on some powerful file server on a high-speed Internet connection as most commercial Web sites are. FTPs are more likely to be running off someone's two-year-old Pentium II with at best a cable or DSL connection. Make sure you have a good book handy while you wait for the downloads to trickle in. Of course, with CuteFTP's ability to schedule downloads for later, you can download in the middle of the night as you sleep—provided CuteFTP can get through to the FTP sites that a bunch of other PCs are trying to get to as their owners snore.

Can Someone at the FTP Site See My Computer?

No. it's a one-way connection for the FTP server. It cannot ordinarily see your hard drive. An FTP operator may monitor your connection to make sure you're not doing something fishy. And ways do exist to get to your machine if a site operator knows the right commands and your Internet protocol (IP) address. But relax. Hacking's not the norm for FTP operators. And really, why would a hacker trash your three-year-old Pentium when they can bring eBay and Amazon to their knees?

Downloading from an FTP Site

Once you have a solid connection, downloading is so simple that it's anticlimactic. In the host's file list window—the one on the right—scroll through the song names and click the folders, if you find them, to check out the songs in other directories on the hosts. When you find a song that is too tempting to be denied, check first to make sure that the file list in the local window, on the left, is open to the folder in which you want to save the new song. In the example you saw in Figure 4.11, the local window opened into the C:\My Music\Billy Idol folder.

Everything's in place now. It's time to take a step from which you may never return. Highlight the song in the host file list that you want to download. Click and drag the file to your local window, and then release. That's it. If you look at the lower part of the screen, you'll see that the song has been added to the queue of files to be transferred, and in fact, "Dancing with Myself" has already begun the trip. In the row below the queue window are more ways to track the progress of the download—time, percentage, kilobytes—than any sane person wants to deal with.

Browse as You Download

Want to browse a site with CuteFTP while you're waiting for a file to finish an agonizingly long download? Choose the Commands menu and select Session / Spawn Session. Another instance of CuteFTP will load that you can use to browse.

At this point, you can drink a cup of java, go about your work, or do whatever. You're no longer needed, unless for some reason the transfer breaks down. If that happens, the song will remain in the queue, and the name of the song's unfinished file will have the word "PART" appended to it to mark it as a partial download. (Check out the filename for "White Wedding" in the local window in Figure 4.11.) When you reconnect to complete the download, the transfer will pick up at the point it was interrupted so that you don't have to download the entire file again.

Uploading to an FTP Site

We encountered ratio sites in Chapter 3. These are FTP sites that require you to upload some MP3 songs before you can download them. So we need to look at uploading as well.

Paying for Cuteness

The free version of Cute MP3 on the book's CD-ROM is fully functional for 30 days. After a month, it will still work, but the Cute MP3 Search function will be disabled. Also, you can have only one file at a time in the download queue. I frankly feel it's worth the cost of a couple of store-bought CDs—to be exact, $39.95—to have the search function, have multiple downloads, get rid of the advertising, and eliminate the opening nag screen.

Of course, you're probably way ahead of me on this one. *Uploading* is the opposite of downloading. Instead of dragging songs from the host window to the local window, you drag songs from the local window to the host window.

You should know two other points, however. One is to plan ahead of time what songs you want to upload. Create an Upload folder and move or make copies of the songs to that folder. Also, some FTP sites allow you to upload only to a certain folder, usually named—surprise—Upload. Some of these sites are fussy, asking you to put the songs in appropriate subfolders in the Upload folder, but if you upload a song by Martha and the Vandellas to the site's Technorock folder, it's not going to affect your upload ratio. Other sites ask you to not upload certain types of music, such as country or jazz.

You should also remember that the ratio is based on the number of megabytes you upload, not the number of songs. So for the easiest uploading, choose a few songs that are really, really long. In addition, upload credits don't carry from one session to another. So after you log off, any remaining credits are history.

Ratio or Racy?

So what's better—ratio sites or banner sites? Sites that make you upload MP3s before you can download any MP3s? Or the site that will give you *leech access*—unfettered freedom to suck down every song on the FTP site—provided you first go to a Web page and click your way through a bunch of photos of naked women, remnants of which will remain on your hard drive to be found by your spouse and children?

If someone has a site worth leeching, it's faster to trudge through banner sites than upload MP3s. Many FTP sites are not on powerful computers or fast connections, and uploads are slow, even if you're on a fast—cable or better—Net hookup. Banner sites often change their passwords, forcing you to revisit their affiliated porn patches. Also, some of the link sites are wise to the trick and require you to sign up for a trial membership before you see the password. This means giving your credit card number and then having to remember to cancel so it won't be charged.

It's either larceny or lechery. Take your pick.

Automating Downloads with CuteFTP

CuteFTP is about as simple as it gets to manage uploads and downloads. All you have to do is double-click a song listed in the local or host folders. And yet, I'm starting to feel like one of those idiots running around on infomercials shouting, "But wait! There's more!!"

At CuteFTP's main screen, choose Edit, Settings and then click Advanced. On the Advanced Setting screen, most of the boxes should already be checked. But the box we want to make sure is checked is Monitor Clipboard for FTP URLs. This feature saves time and avoids the perils of typos by pasting the correct connection information into CuteFTP whenever you use the Windows clipboard to copy a URL address.

This works only with anonymous logins, which often give you look-only access until you've gone through whatever banner/upload ratio initiation the site requires. If the URL redirects you to still another URL, this won't work. It's a good feature to have turned on, though, especially if you're finding songs using sites such as Audiogalaxy.com. Audiogalaxy searches return all the information for an anonymous connection in a single string of IDs, passwords, site addresses, and port numbers, such as `ftp://mp3:mp3@24.48.97.112:21`. With other search engines, such shortcuts may not look exactly like this, but the ones that provide the service will point you to it proudly, and CuteFTP is adept as translating a wide variety of FTP links no matter how they're put together. MP3 Fiend also creates ready-rolled directions that Go!Zilla and CuteFTP use.

To use CuteFTP's clipboard monitor, simply select the connection information and press Ctrl+C, or you can use the menus for Edit, Copy. CuteFTP constantly checks the clipboard, and as soon and anything appears that has the constituents of an FTP logon, CuteFTP parses the information into its components and pastes them into a logon script. If a filename is part of the clipboard contents—such as `ftp://www.globalscape.com/pub/cuteftp/cute2632.exe`—CuteFTP automatically tries to download it. This also works if you right-click a link and choose Copy Shortcut or Copy Link in Netscape.

Using CuteFTP and Go!Zilla Together

Go!Zilla also has an FTP clipboard monitor I didn't tell you about a few pages back. That's because of the two, CuteFTP is so much better at handling FTP connections. You can have both programs running in the background with this arrangement: If you left-click download links that lead to HTTP sites, Go!Zilla monitors the links and takes over when needed. CuteFTP gets all the links that are copied to the clipboard. If you're using both programs, be sure that Go!Zilla's clipboard monitor is turned off by clicking the Go menu and choosing Options and Automation. Make sure the boxes next to Capture all FTP and Monitor Clipboard are unchecked so that Go!Zilla and CuteFTP don't battle over clipboard contents.

Finding Music Files with CuteFTP

Okay, now you're probably going to be really pissed I didn't tell you about this back in Chapter 3, when we were looking at all the nefarious ways of tracking down MP3s with `Audiogalaxy.com` and MP3 Fiend. But now I'm telling you— CuteFTP has its own built-in Cute MP3/File Search. It is absolutely the best tool to search for MP3s. It has the ability to compile the results of several search engines at several sites into one metasearch, as MP3 Fiend does. It uses Lycos, MusicSeek, FastAstra Web, DeepDance, and four other MP3 search engines. But this is not just another metasearch machine. It also has wonderfully intelligent integration with the downloading functions of CuteFTP.

To launch a search from CuteFTP's main screen, click the Files menu and select Cute MP3/File Search. You also can click the toolbar icon that looks like Earth with a magnifying glass over it. The result is a screen similar to the one shown in Figure 4.12. Because I have what I want of Billy Idol, I've decided to test drive the Cute MP3 search with a more obscure performer, Joe Jackson. Cute MP3 finds a lot more matches than I would have guessed. Take a look at it, and then I'll explain how this all gets even better.

My day job is as a senior editor for a magazine, *Ziff-Davis Smart Business for the New Economy*, which formerly was *PC Computing*. In two decades of testing and writing about software, the one-two punch of CuteFTP and Cute MP3 Search is the cleverest programming I've seen. It might not be the most useful or important software ever written, but it's damn clever.

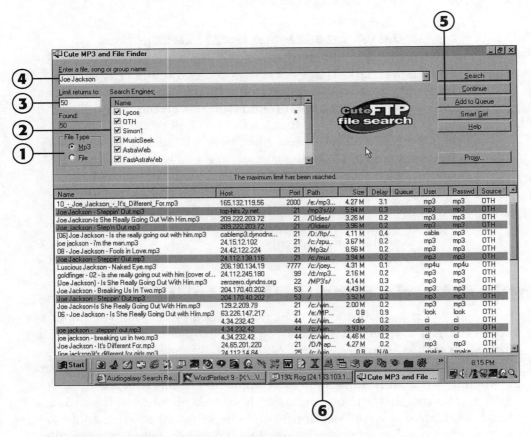

Figure 4.12 *Road Map to Cute MP3/File Search.*

① File Type: Usually set to mp3. Choose File if you want to include WMA and Liquid Audio files.

② Search Engines: These are the external search engines that Cute MP3 Search uses. Exclude sites by unchecking the boxes next to them. When the Search begins returning results, a small x beside a search engine's name indicates a search in progress. A large X indicates a completed search.

③ Limit Returns To: Enter the maximum number of results you want the search to return from all search engines. Default is 50, which for some searches is completed after only one or two search engines have been queried. The actual number of results returned is shown in the box just below this one.

④ Search Terms Window: Enter a song, artist name, or album name. You can use Boolean combinations, such as "Ross OR Supremes" to find all songs by Diana Ross. Not all the search engines recognize Boolean queries, but it won't hurt to try. Other Boolean possibilities include

"Simon AND Garfunkle" and "Lennon NOT Yoko".

⑤ Control Buttons: In addition to the obvious Search button, two other buttons are important. Add to Queue lets you grab files and add them to your queue to be downloaded later. Smart Get searches all the results for matches to any song you've selected. Then, Smart Get attempts to download each of them until it finds an anonymous site and successfully snags the song.

⑥ Search Results Window: The bottom window displays results of the metasearch. Information for each result includes the full name of the MP3, its host address, port, user ID, and password—all of which you need to connect. You also receive the size of the file, the delay that exists at a particular host—the higher the number, the slower the site—which songs have been added to the queue, and which search engine came up with that particular result. Clicking on any of the column titles sorts results based on the information in that column.

First, use the advanced Find function to narrow your search. Right-click anywhere in the search results and select Find from the drop-down menu. This opens a small dialog box in which you can type another search term. This Find searches only the files that are already in the results list and selects those that meet this second criterion, too. In Figure 4.12, the results from a search for "Joe Jackson" are narrowed by a second find for "Step". The results turned up nine MP3s of Joe's "Steppin' Out," including one variant spelling, "Step'n Out."

To download any of Joe's songs, you must click on them. You know the routine. You select more than one at a time by holding down the Ctrl key, yadda yadda yadda. Then, you have your choice: Double-clicking sends them all to the transfer queue. Right-clicking gives you other options, such as Connect for a single download and another way to send them to the queue. Or you could just use Smart Get.

Smart Get makes it all so easy you'd think it'd be against the law. Click to select any song in a list of search results. Make it a song you'd want to download while you're at it. Then, choose Smart Get from the right-button menu or click the big Smart Get button above the listings. Cute MP3 Search then highlights every file with the exact same filename and puts them all in the queue. Because a lot of title information ultimately comes from the same sources, there are more duplicates than you might at first imagine. Anyway, Smart Get then puts all the matching results in the queue, which feeds them to the downloading machine. If CuteFTP encounters an error trying to download at one of the sites, it goes on to the next one. Once it downloads the song, it stops the assault.

Size Does Matter

A wide-ranging search is likely to come up with results that seem to be the same song, but the sizes of the MP3 files are all over the place. Either one of two things is happening. There may be different versions—live versus studio—that have different lengths. That would explain one being bigger than another. Springsteen has nearly a dozen different versions of "Thunder Road." Really.

Another reason the files could be different sizes is that the exact same version of a song has been recorded at different bit rates. We'll get into the nitty-gritty of bit rates in the next chapter. But, in a nutshell, songs recorded with higher bit rates sound better but use more disk space. The only way to avoid poor recordings entirely is to stay away from sites where you've received them in the past.

Other CuteFTP Features

CuteFTP isn't only a program for downloading MP3s. It has a lot of tools for Webmasters who frequently need to upload to their sites. And it has the power to do just about anything you could want, along with a macro language to automate it all. The slightly crazier cousin to CuteFTP is CuteMX, but that will have to wait until the next chapter.

Downloading from Newsgroups

Let's not spend a lot of time on this, okay? If you've read Chapter 3, you already know this is the desperate way to find a song. (And if you haven't read Chapter 3 or had your own experiences with newsgroups, the rest of the chapter isn't going to make any sense to you. You might as well skip ahead to the next chapter, which is about a real fun type of software. You'll really like it.) But let's say, oh, that your life depends on you finding an obscure bootleg of the Grateful Dead's concert at Red Rocks in 1978—especially day four, which is the really good version recorded by a stock broker with a ponytail who was strung out on acid.

Not Just for Music Files

MP3 files aren't the only binary files distributed via newsgroups. The same downloading methods discussed here also apply to graphics, videos, and *warez* (bootlegs of commercial software and games) you'll find in other newsgroups.

So, you can post a message on a newsgroup somewhere devoted to the Dead asking someone to *PLEASE* post an MP3 version of the concert. Pitifully, you check back each day to see if anyone has responded. And then, let's say someone has recordings of that concert and such a sympathetic heart that he uploads the recording as a newsgroup message. What you'd get would look a lot like Figure 4.13.

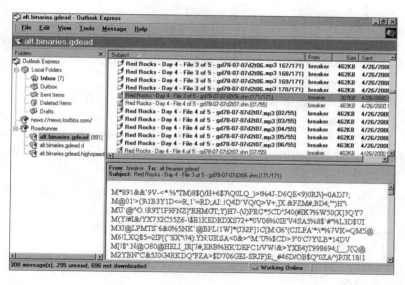

Figure 4.13 *Newsgroup File Transfer.*

Files transferred via newsgroups are encoded and spread across several messages that are posted to a sort of electronic bulletin board.

Anatomy of a Newsgroup File

In the Folders column, on the left of the screen, you see that we're hooked to a newsgroup hosted at a news server operated by Roadrunner, which supplies my cable Internet service. The name of the highlighted newsgroup, alt.binaries.gdead, indicates that this is a newsgroup using an *alternative* format—simply one that's not bound by a lot of rules—offering *binaries*, which is another way to indicate non-text files, and that it's devoted to the Grateful Dead (gdead).

At the top right of the screen is the Subject window with a list of messages that have been posted to the newsgroup. From the titles on the messages, you can figure out what they are. Because these messages involve the Dead, there's a lot more information than you'd find for most other recordings. Let's dissect one title: Red Rocks - Day 4 - File 4 of 5 -gd78-07d206.mp3 (02/55).

"Red Rocks" refers to the Red Rocks Amphitheatre in Colorado. "Day 4" says this recording is the one you were looking for. "File 4 of 5" tells you Day 4 is so long it's divided among five separate recordings, of which this is the fourth. "gd78-07d206.mp3" is the name of the file, also giving clues to the Dead and concert dates. Finally—and here comes the interesting part—"(02/55)" tells you that the MP3 file is made up of 55 newsgroup messages; this message is the second of them. You can see that the third message is just below, then the fourth, and so on. If you look to the top of the list, you see that "File 3 of 5" for the same performance is made up of 171 messages.

Notice that the file sizes are almost invariably the same: 462KB. That's the largest size the newsgroup can handle because, after all, it was designed for text messages, not concerts. So large music files are distributed among several messages. Files that take up as many as 171 messages—or even 55—are unusual. Most songs created to fit between radio commercials will fit in 10–20 messages.

Finally, in the preview window in the lower right, there's a look at part of the MP3 file after it's been translated in a code that uses only alphanumeric characters and punctuation. Interesting to look at once, but of no practical use whatsoever to carbon-based life forms.

Extracting the MP3

Because the recording is split among, in this example, 55 messages, your newsreader must not only translate the alphanumeric code back into MP3 language, but it must piece the 55 parts of the MP3 file together in the correct order. The newsreader in Outlook Express does just fine on its own when it comes to decoding. And you'd think that would be the hard part. But, no, Outlook Express is an idiot when it comes to getting the numbered parts back together properly.

When newsgroup downloads work as they should, all the messages should already be in the correct order in the list you see in the Subject window. But for reasons that we needn't go into here—I have no idea why—once in a while a couple of messages are out of order or one of the messages is missing. If the problem's the latter, then move along. There's nothing for you to listen to here.

But if the order of the files is merely scrambled, Outlook Express gives you—the more primitive form of intelligence—a chance to descramble them. First, select all the messages that make up one file. If the messages are all adjacent, click a message at one end and then, holding down the Shift key, click the message at the other end of the group. If the messages are intertwined with messages that belong to a different file, that's okay, but then you'll have to keep the Ctrl key pressed as you add scattered messages to the selection. (See Figure 4.14.)

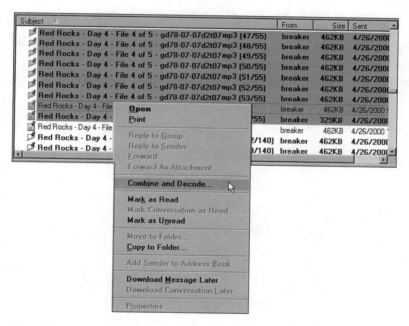

Figure 4.14 *Decoding a Song.*

First, select all the members of a message carrying an encoded tune. Then right-click and choose Combine and Decode.

With all the message parts of the file selected, right-click and choose Combine and Decode. Outlook Express responds with the little, cramped dialog box Order for decoding that's shown in Figure 4.15

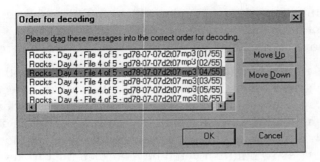

Figure 4.15 *Order for Decoding Dialog Box.*

Move 'em up! Move 'em down! Move 'em up! Move 'em down, disco lady.

You can move the messages up or down using the buttons on the right. The only trick is remembering that 02 is not the same thing as 2. If 11 messages were numbered without the leading zeros, the message would sort like this:

(1/11)

(10/11)

(11/11)

(2/11)

(3/11)

(4/11)

(5/11)

(6/11)

(7/11)

(8/11)

(9/11)

Once you're sure the messages are all in the correct order and have all the leading zeros they need, click OK. In remarkably short time Outlook Express translates the messages and pastes them into a single file, which appears as an attachment in what looks for all the world like a newly arrived email from someone named Breaker. (Handles are *de rigueur* in newsgroups. No one, simply no one, passes along bootleg music without a handle.) In the case of the 55 messages making up part of Day 4 of the Dead, the attached file turns out to equal 18.4MB.

The only thing left to do is right-click the name of the file in the Attach window and select Save As. Lead the file to its new home among your music folders, click OK, and fire up the MP3 player.

There you have it: Three more or less equally complicated and confusing ways to download music that you could copy off your CDs without worrying about things like crossing state lines. Three ways to exchange Ricky Martin songs without having to actually listen to them. Three ways to set the music free!

But wait! There's more!! It'll just have to wait for the next chapter, though, in which I clue you in to one little program that has caused almost as much controversy—and as many lawsuits—as the entire MP3 phenomenon: Napster.

5

What's This Napster? How Can I Use It to Swap Music with Others?

♪ *Setting Up Napster* ♪ *Finding Songs with Napsters* ♪ *Finding the Secret Napster Servers* ♪ *Downloading with Napster* ♪ *How to Bypass Napster Watchdogs* ♪ *Other Distributed Swapping Software*

Shawn Fanning's roommate was always bitching. Specifically, he whined about how hard it was to find MP3 music on the Internet. There was only one thing for Fanning to do: Write a program that makes swapping music with others as easy as a panty raid.

Fanning, a 19-year-old computer science student at Northeastern University in Boston, had to buy a book on programming, but before too long, he'd developed not only software for the blithesome exchange of music files, but a fundamental change in the way information is maintained and transmitted over the Internet. The program was named Napster, after Fanning's own nickname, which he earned from his nappy hair. Napster is at once the most democratic and subversive software I've ever seen. It places distribution of information in the hands of the people using it, which fundamentally undermines the traditional structure of the entire Internet.

Napster turns the top-down mode of the Internet upside-down. Generally when we connect to the Internet, we immediately go to some large repository of Web pages, files, and information —something such as Yahoo, AOL, C-Net, or Mp3.com. There we download news, software, statistics, email, advice, and just about anything else you can imagine from genealogical records to the most recent share price of Cisco stock. All this has been located in *servers*, powerful computers with fast Internet connections built for dishing out files and information. For this we may pay a monthly subscription fee or buy whatever it is with a credit card. More often, though, it's free, supported by the ubiquitous banner ads. But the point to realize is that we, sitting at our personal computers, are on the receiving end only. No one from, say, Slovenia, is going to connect to my PC sitting in Texas looking to download stock quotes, shareware programs, or MP3 music.

Hold it. That's no longer true when it comes to music and Napster. Fanning's program allows someone in Slovenia and me in Texas to swap anything we have on our hard drives. And there's only the minimum contact with any centralized repository. Napster works only with MP3 files, but the concept has already been broadened in programs such as Gnutnella and CuteMX to include any type of file. That is a major change in the organization of the Internet and a change in who controls the distribution.

Naturally, many people consider Napster the Great Satan of Software. These are the people who run the big servers and control the storage and distribution of information. Who you won't find upset are the millions of students, 30-somethings, and baby boomers who use Napster to exchange music MP3s like business cards at a sales convention. Easier, really, when you consider that you don't even have to leave home for a Napster swap meet.

And naturally, Napster has become both a Silicon Valley startup attracting venture capitalists and a target attracting attorneys from the music industry. As of now, there's no business plan for making money off Napster, although the new execs at Napster (the company) are looking for ways to exploit it. Subscription? A promotional media for the record industry? None of the money plans mentions the fact that the overwhelming use of Napster is for outlaw trade of copyrighted music. But that, of course, is exactly what the music attorneys are screaming about.

The Recording Industry Association of America (RIAA), rap artist Dr. Dre, and Metallica have all filed suits against Napster, calling it a copyright "infringement machine." They say Napster is aiding in copyright violations by its users. And that, in itself, is illegal. The musicians want the titles of their records removed from the lists on Napster's servers, and RIAA is asking for damages high enough to bankrupt the infant company.

Napster v. John Law

You've probably heard that the RIAA obtained a court order that could effectively shut Napster down. The decision led to a flurry of download activity as the deadline approached, but a last-minute stay gave Napster a reprieve for several months. As this book goes to press, Napster is still active, and it looks like this situation will continue while the case drags on in the courts.

Napster replies that the program itself is legal because it has legitimate, legal uses despite how some people—people over whom they have no control—choose to use it. The company compares its program to the videotape recorder, which the movie industry attacked at first because it could be used to make bootleg copies of movies. The courts ruled then in favor of the VCR makers because there are legitimate uses for video recorders, and videotapes have since become an important source of revenue for movie studios.

Help from the Other Side

Not all performing artists are opposed to Napster. Rap-metal band Limp Bizkit has embraced Napster. Napster in turn is putting up $1.8 million to be a sponsor of a Limp Bizkit tour.

Some colleges have followed the multiple-use theory in allowing Napster to be used through their computer networks. Many of those colleges that have banned Napster have done so on the basis that the students using it were eating up the college network's bandwidth—the amount of data it can transmit at any one time. Some colleges relented on the Napster ban after students took to the streets in protest. Other colleges, including Yale and UCLA, are now facing their own lawsuits by musicians. The music lawyers have even threatened to name some college students as defendants, a move that would solidify the RIAA's image as a musical bully.

What's important to note at this point is that Napster does not have any of Dr. Dre's or Metallica's or anyone's music located on its computers. All it has are the addresses and contents of music directories that Napster users are making available to one another—but only for the moment and only while a Napster user is logged in to the Napster network. Napster says it's willing to remove any user it knows is distributing copyrighted material. But the lists that users create on the servers are there one minute and gone the next as users log in and log out. It's the guerrilla warfare of the Internet.

While the Jury's Out

The battle of the bands, record companies, students, and software makers will continue long after this book is published. The best source of the most recent news about the controversy and other music industry news is Webnoize.com, which provides thorough, detailed daily reports.

Know what? It really doesn't matter what the courts decide. It's too late for the record industry to kill off Napster. Like MP3, Napster's a hydra. They might succeed in shutting down Napster's own servers. But that will still leave millions of Napster users out there. Because one of Napster's features is a live chat mode, it's not hard to imagine some of the more entrenched users getting together, virtually, and establishing which one's PC becomes the server of the week. That, in fact, has already happened with the appearance of unofficial Napster networks, such as Opennap and MyNapster. (See "Finding the Secret Napster Servers" later in this chapter.) Tracking down users or servers would be as effective as stomping on ants to kill the nest. Napster is a system, and a system can live on even when the members that make it up are replaced or eliminated. And even if the RIAA could eradicate every instance of Napster, similar, often more powerful programs are already vying to be the next bigger, better Napster.

Turn-About

When Stanford student David Weekly published on the Web his reverse-engineered dissection of Napster, the tables were turned on Napster. Executives of the company asked Weekly to remove the information, which, at the time of this writing, he has not done. Links to whatever of Weekly's postings survive, along with other links to open-source Napster, can be found at `www.MP3under.com`.

Already, the inner workings of Napster have been made public. You'll find source code at `http://opennap.sourceforge.net/`. A detailed explanation of the Napster protocol—the rules for computers to exchange information with each other—are at `http://david.weekly.org/code/napster.php3` and `http://opennap.sourceforge.net/napster.txt`. This is all part of a tradition in computing called *open source*. Originating, significantly I think, in the early '70s, when the days of hippies and communes were still a strong influence, open source's essential tenet is this: Information wants to be free. The underlying philosophy of open source is largely idealistic, not commercial. In the early days of computing, visionary idealists saw a world in which computers made all data freely available to everyone. Today, open source is enshrined in Linux, an operating service whose core code is owned by no one and improved upon by and for everyone. And because data covers everything from software code to digitized music, MP3 and Napster are naturals for the open source movement.

The results are Wrapster, CuteMX, Gnutella, Scour Exchange, Gnutmeg, Macster, and on and on until now at least one Napster-like program exists for every type of computer since the Atari 2600. Many of these programs are trying to make changes that would eliminate some of the problems Napster has faced legally. Gnutella, for example, eliminates the servers that maintain the filelists of users currently online. It is Napsterism taken to its most extreme: All information is distributed. There is no center.

We'll take some short looks at those programs at the end of this chapter. Right now, let's take a detailed look in Figure 5.1 at the program that started the landslide: Napster.

Figure 5.1   *How Napster Works*

1. Setup: As a Napster user, you decide which MP3 files on your hard drive will be open to others when you're logged on to the Napster server. These files become your Napster library.

MP3 List

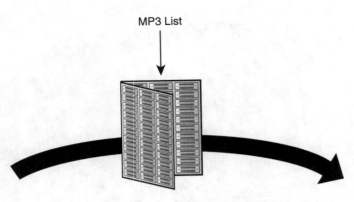

2. Log on: When you log on to one of several Napster servers, your Napster sends the server a list of MP3s in your library.

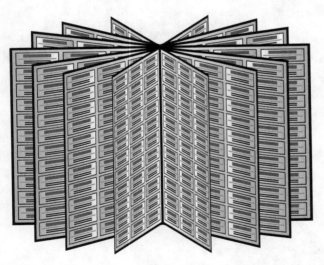

3. Posting: The Napster server posts your filelist in a database where it can be searched by other Napster users. None of the songs are stored on Napster's own servers.

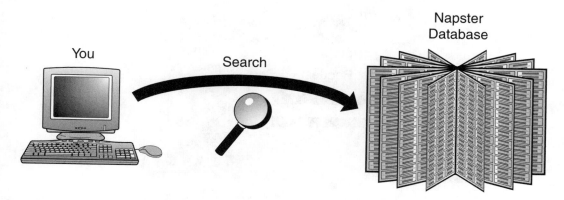

4. *Search: You—and other Napster users—enter a search term. This term can be the title, artist's name, or any other phrase you would expect to be in the filename of the MP3 file you're looking for.*

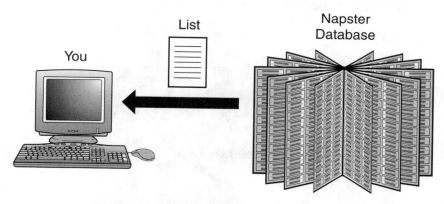

5. *Results: The search looks at all the library records on the server and returns its results—a filelist—to your local version of Napster. The results include the filenames, the type of Internet on-ramp, the Internet address where they can be found, the handles or nicknames of the other users, the type of Internet connection, and other assorted trivia.*

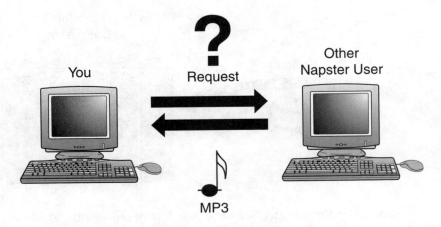

You   ? Request   Other Napster User

MP3

6. Transfer: When you select one of the files for transfer, your copy of Napster sends a request to download the file directly to the computer identified by its IP (Internet protocol) address. The remote Napster obliges by sending the file to your computer.

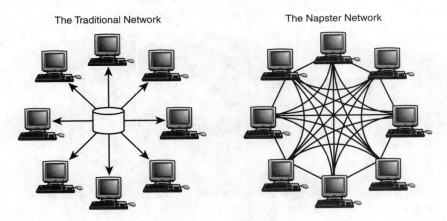

The Traditional Network   The Napster Network

7. Reversal: At the same time you are downloading a file, other Napster users are finding files on your hard drive that they want and are downloading them. Several uploads/ downloads can run simultaneously by taking turns sharing the Internet connection.

The traditional structure of the Internet has been *server-concentric*. Data and programs are stored at a relatively few centrally located servers, or *hosts*. All data requests from PCs (*clients*) go to one of the servers. The host also handles all replies back to the clients.

The Napster structure, on the other hand, is *distributed*. Except for consulting servers to get digital driving directions, each computer using Napster's protocol communicates directly with other clients. A PC can be a host and a client at the same time.

Setting Up Napster

Bummer! For legal reasons, we cannot include Napster on the book's CD-ROM. Download the latest version at www.napster.com or through the link at www.mp3under.com. If the file has "beta" in its name, that doesn't necessarily mean there are later copies. Napster seems to be perpetually called a beta for reasons that may have as much to do with legalities as code testing.

The first time you run Napster, you must perform a few housekeeping chores. In the Connection Information screen, select your Internet connection (see Figure 5.2). If you're plugging in to the Net from a college campus or a decently sized business, select T1 or T3...if you want to tell the truth. (See the sidebar to learn why honesty might not be the best policy.)

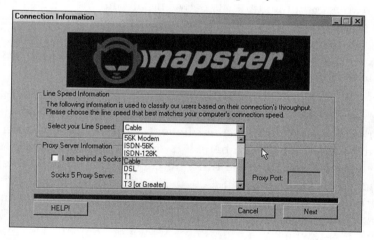

Figure 5.2: *Connection Information.*

Tell Napster what type of Internet connection you have—unless, of course, you're going to lie about it.

It Pays Not to Brag

Napster doesn't really know what kind of Internet connection you have. It relies, instead, on whatever you enter when you fill out the Connection Information screen. If you're a callous, unrepentant bastard who'd steal songs off the Internet, then you'll like this trick: Tell Napster you have a 33.6 modem or simply choose "Unknown." Although other users could guess at your speed from the ping time, they're still less likely to download files from your library because they'll favor known, faster connections such as cable and T1. Your computer will run more smoothly. Also, if you have an extensive MP3 collection, you'll attract less attention if you just put a few songs into a folder you designate as your upload folder. Sure, it's not neighborly. Do you care?

If you are behind a Socks 5 Proxy Server, check the box on the same screen. A *proxy* is a fast, capacious computer that sits between you and the Internet and saves the Internet pages that are sent to you and other people using the same proxy. Then, if the same pages are asked for again, the proxy delivers them from its own *cache*—local storage—rather than waste the time it takes to send the request to some distant server and wait for a response.

If you aren't behind a server, or if you don't know whether you are, leave the box unchecked. If you're behind a different proxy than a Socks 5, Napster may not be able to work with you. If proxy servers haven't surfaced in your other use of the Internet, don't worry about them here. If a proxy becomes an issue, ask your Internet provider or the people who run your college's or company's network. (For the latter, I suggest concocting a good cover story if they ask you why you need the information. Tell them you need to know the proxy so you can look at porn.) If you find out you're behind a different proxy than a Socks 5, check www.napster.cjb.net, which maintains an FAQ where someone else may have supplied a solution to just your problem.

If you're behind a Napster barricade—a scheme some colleges are using to block only Napster traffic—you might have to use some bogus proxy information to get through. You'll see how to storm those bastions later in this chapter.

After you provide all this basic information, Napster connects with its central server, where you must register for access to the Napster databases. Fill in your name—or if you're feeling particularly jaunty, an imaginative handle such as

Phatal-Err. Enter a password and email address. The handle is how others will see you in the Napster databases. A second screen gathers more information about you, but it's not required.

After you get past the registration, Napster offers to scan your hard drives for MP3 files it can add to your library. Unless you want to limit which songs you make available, let it. Finally, there's an Audio Information screen (see Figure 5.3). It lets you choose to listen to MP3s with Napster's built-in MP3 player or the player you normally use. Either RealJukebox or MusicMatch Jukebox on the book's CD-ROM is a better choice.

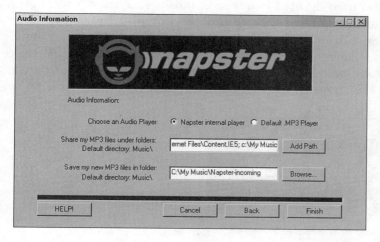

Figure 5.3 *Audio Information.*

Two important settings—what folders you're willing to open to the world and where you want new songs saved—are hidden in the Audio Information dialog box.

If you let Napster search for your MP3 files, the screen shows all the directories in which it found files. Edit out any folders you don't want included. On my PC, for example, Napster found MP3 files in my Recycle Bin and Temporary Internet Files directories. If you didn't allow Napster to find MP3s, enter the directory that has the songs you want to share. Also, give the name of a folder where you want incoming MP3 files to be saved. The two directories can be the same or separate—your call.

Next, Napster attempts to find your port for sending and receiving data. If you are on a local area network or behind a firewall that regulates incoming connections, Napster might not be able to identify your port. In that case, you'll see a screen asking if you're behind a firewall. If you don't know, this time assume you are and click OK. You also might fail to connect if the server is too busy. (I've had difficulties connecting with Napster's server, but usually if I persevere, I've been able to make a connection.)

Identifying the Hot Connections

Getting through the Napster setup can be a hassle, but once you've found a configuration that works, you shouldn't be bothered with it again. Instead, whenever you log on, Napster presents a warning, in stern red text, about legalities—yawn—and a list of the 50-odd channels available (see Figure 5.4). A *channel* is simply an area devoted to a type of music, such as '80s rock, grunge, or hip hop. Next to the name of each channel is a number that shows how many Napster users currently are tuned in to that channel. The more users there are, the more likely you are to find songs you want. You can select several channels at the same time by holding down the Ctrl key as you click on channel names. Select the channels that sound most promising and click OK.

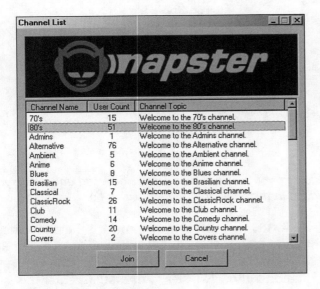

Figure 5.4: *Napster Channels.*

Use channels to ferret out songs you didn't know you liked because you didn't know they existed. Channels let you focus on a few genres of music.

The first thing you see is the Chat screen. This is where typed conversations can carry on in real time, although I've not noticed a lot of chatting when I've been using Napster. The chat screens are used mainly to ask whether someone has such-and-such songs. If you want to chat, type your message in the unlabeled, shallow, wide box toward the bottom of the screen. Whatever you type will appear in the large screen area above the box, both on your computer and any others tuned to chat on the same channel. The chat feature is largely unused. Most Napster users are more interested is snagging songs than chatting.

A more interesting feature of the screen is the list of users who are logged in to the same channel you are. Their handles are presented in a column along with the number of songs each is sharing and the type of Internet connection each user has. Look for cable, DSL, T1, and T3 connections for the fastest downloads. By right-clicking a handle and choosing Information, you can see the *Finger Information*—more details about a user, including other chat rooms the person is using and the number of files he or she is uploading or downloading. Another right-click choice is Add to Hot List. To qualify for Hot List membership, a site should have a fast connection and a good selection of songs. By creating a Hot List, you easily can check to see whether your favorite MP3 libraries are online and available for browsing and downloading. Remember that all Napster connections are transitory. If you can find a good library that always seems to be logged on, it's prime Hot List material.

Double Firewalls

If you're behind a firewall, Napster checks any library you add to your Hot List or try to download from to see if it's also firewalled. If it is, Napster pops up a Window to announce that both you and the other library are behind firewalls and can't transfer files to one another. In this situation, delete the library from your Hot List and put it out of your mind, even if it has every song you've every wanted. There's no known workaround.

Finding Songs with Napster

But enough about chat! Click the Search button on the toolbar located at the top, just below the menu. Now we're arming Napster for a full-force search of all the libraries listed as being online. Figure 5.5 explains the features in Napster's search form.

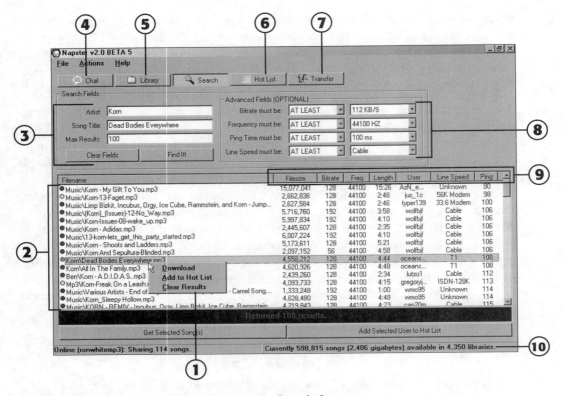

Figure 5.5: *Road Map to the Napster Search Screen*

① Right-Click Menu: Download a song, add a user's library to your Hot List, or clear the search results. A new search also clears off old results.

② Search Results: Songs found by search, including other information useful in deciding which songs to download. A green bullet to the left of a title means cable speed is faster. A yellow bullet means 56K/sec modem to ISDN-128K. A red bullet means 33.6K/sec and slower, or unknown speed.

③ Search Fields: Searches by artist, song title, or both. The default value for maximum results, 100, works out fine most times. The maximum is 250 hits, at least in the beta version.

④ Chat Button: Switches to the chat screen and list of libraries that are currently logged in.

⑤ Library Button: Displays the files you're offering as downloads to others. This is also the place you find Napster's built-in MP3 player. Gives you something to do.

⑥ Hot List Button: Displays the list of libraries you've marked for your Hot List. By clicking any of the libraries—provided it's online—you can then browse all the files available in that library.

⑦ Transfer Button: Displays the progress of downloads and uploads and files waiting in queue.

⑧ Advanced Fields: These let you filter out any files or connections that don't meet your standards of quality and download speed. They are not, however, entirely functional in the beta of Napster.

⑨ Other Result Details:

Filesize: Most pop songs are in the 2–6MB range.

Bitrate: How many data bits are used to record each second of audio. Higher numbers are better. Your minimum for quality should be 96kbits/sec, roughly the quality of FM radio. 128kbits/sec or better is considered more or less compact disc quality.

Freq.: Frequency, in this instance, refers to how often each second the audio is sampled as it's digitized. (See the illustration of how MP3 works in Chapter 1, "What Is MP3 Internet Audio and Why Should I Care?") Most songs are captured at 44KHz.

Length: Measured in minutes and seconds.

User: The handle used by the song's owner.

Line Speed: The type of Internet connection as reported by the Napster user. Before selecting songs, click the heading for this column—twice— to sort the connections by speed. T3 is best, and T1 is second best. DSL and cable connections vary in speed, but you can consider them roughly equal to each other. For cable and DSL connections, note that *upstream* data (moving from a PC to the Internet) does not transfer as quickly as *downstream* data (coming from the Internet to a PC).

Ping: The time in milliseconds to bounce a signal off the other person's computer and get it back to your computer.

⑩ Status Bar: Shows you how many songs, their total size in gigabytes, and the number of libraries currently available.

A search with Napster has the advantage of simplicity. Type in, at the least, the name of a song or a performer. Or include both, especially if the last time you heard some song was on a hazy night in the '70s that you don't remember all that well. Boolean search isn't fluent here, although entering two artists' names will yield only results that include both. When I typed in "Cher or Elton John" to test whether you could get results at once on two artists—whom I didn't expect to have ever recorded a duet—I was surprised when Napster came up with a song that has both artists performing, along with Tina Turner. "Cher or Black Sabbath," however, turns up neither Cher nor Black Sabbath.

When filling in a title, use as few words as possible. There's no guarantee of accuracy on the part of all these strangers who named the files. If you enter "The Taxi Song" to find the song by Harry Chapin, you get no results at all. "Taxi" by itself finds Chapin's song as well as songs by artists as different as Joni Mitchell and Herb Alpert.

Usually, you can skip the Advanced Fields part of the search. The overwhelming majority of MP3 files Napster finds already meet what should be your minimum standards—a bit rate of at least 128, which is roughly the quality of a compact disc, and a sampling frequency of 44KHz. Between Ping Times and Line Speed, line speed is the better indicator of speed. A ping is how long, in milliseconds, it takes your computer to send a message that essentially says, "Hello," to a another Napster user's computer and to receive an echo of the same message—the smaller the ping, the better—in theory. Generally, the shortest ping times should correlate to the fastest connections, such as T-3, T-1, and DSL. But so many factors, such as the Internet path and switches the ping travels, influence ping time that the same connection can register a blistering ping time one minute and a narcoleptic speed another minute. If you're looking for the fastest connections, make your choice on the basis of line speed, not ping. But remember that your actual results are influenced by the number of Napster users trying to download from the same host PC.

Considering that typically there are a half-million or more songs to search in thousands of library lists, Napster searches are remarkably fast, even if you narrow the search by including a song title. Results are automatically sorted by ping time. But because ping results are not reliable, the best way to inspect the search results is to first click the Line Speed column header. Click a second time to bring the fastest locations to the top of the column.

Then, search the titles for likely songs to reel in. Double-clicking any title sends it to the queue to be downloaded. You also can select several songs at once by holding down the Ctrl key as you click them. Click Find It!, or right-click and choose Download, to add all the selected songs to the queue.

The obvious choices for any song would seem to be the T-3 and T-1 connections. But it's not that simple. By default, Napster is set to allow only three simultaneous uploads—songs headed *away* from your PC. In other words, no more than three songs can be ripped from a single computer at one time. This is to safeguard your PC from being overwhelmed by other Napster users latching onto your music library like sharks in a feeding frenzy. While three uploads are taking place, subsequent requests for a song are put into a waiting queue until one of the three uploads completes. T-3 and T-1 connections are tempting because of their speed, but they're tempting to everyone. A site with a fast connection and a good selection of songs is likely to have several Napster users in its queue. You, of course, would be placed at the end of the queue. A modest cable or DSL connection that only has one song by the artist you're looking for is often the best choice.

There is an advantage in selecting more than one song at a time. Your success in getting any one file downloaded depends on the speed of the connection, how many others are trying to download from the same library, and how many simultaneous connections the other Napster user permits. If you put a half dozen or so songs in the queue, some of them will download before others and still others will never make the trip, but there's no way of predicting which. In fact, if I want a particular song, I frequently select it simultaneously from multiple sources. Then I check the Transfer screen, and when one of them begins downloading, I cancel the others. If a file hangs on "Getting Info..." for more than a minute, the chances are poor that it will ever turn into a download.

Moderation in All Loads

In Napster's Preferences screen (choose File, Preferences from the main menu) you can change the Transfer Settings to modify the maximum number of files you want your system to download at the same time as well as how many simultaneous uploads (other people's downloads *from* your library) each user can attempt. The default for both is 3, which works well. The more songs you download at one time, the longer each of them will take. In the end, you'll have spent about as much time downloading as if you had done them one at a time. But if your connection is broken while more than one download is happening, you lose all of them. If you request more downloads than you allow yourself in these settings, the excess will wait in your queue until one of the working downloads ends. The restriction on the downloads *from* you is more a courtesy to other Napster users by preventing any one user from hogging your library.

Finding the Secret Napster Servers

Ordinarily when you launch Napster, it connects you to the Napster metaserver, run by Napster, Inc. The metaserver, in turn, assigns you to one of the many servers in the Napster network that store the actual lists of songs available at other Napster users' PCs. These servers run in cooperation with Napster, Inc., but are not operated directly by the company. The metaserver tries to assign Napster users so that the load is more or less distributed evenly throughout the Napster network. You have no say-so in which server you wind up using.

But with a program called Napigator, included on the book's CD-ROM, you can choose to which server in the Napster network you're assigned. Even better, you can choose from servers outside the official Napster network when you find fewer users clogging the same server, faster downloads, and servers that specialize in types of music, from rap to gospel. (As this book went to press, a new version of Napigator was being readied for release. It has a new look that's easier to use. The instructions here for the older version should give you a good idea of how Napigator works. The newer version can be downloaded through a link at www.mp3under.com.)

When you launch Napigator, it displays a screen similar to that in Figure 5.6. Napigator displays the text name of each server, its IP address, the network it's a part of, the number of Napster users attached to the server, the total number and size of MP3 files available from the server's users, and its ping speed. (Napigator doesn't provide the statistics for servers associated with Napster, Inc., at Napster's request. At the same time, Napster, Inc., doesn't object if you use Napigator in conjunction with Napster.)

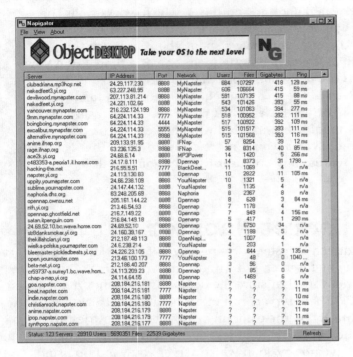

Figure 5.6: *Choose Your Napster Server.*

Napigator has only one screen, but it's packed with information on the secret servers Napster doesn't tell you about, much less connect you to without Napigator calling the shots.

To choose any one of the servers for your Napster host, simply double-click it. If Napster is already running on your computer, it will disconnect from any server it's already using and create a new connection with the server you chose. If Napster isn't running, Napigator will launch Napster and immediately hook it up to the server you selected.

You can tell whether you've connected to an official or unofficial Napster server by reading the welcome message on Napster's chat screen. If it's the standard message, you're using a standard server. If the message is worded differently— usually including a lot of anatomically impossible threats aimed at anyone who misuses the system—you've latched onto a rogue server.

The number of users and songs at each server varies from less than 10 users and a couple hundred MP3 files to thousands of users and hundreds of thousands of files. Some of the servers with few songs are used primarily for chatting. Others are devoted to specialty music. After you explore some of the servers, you can recognize the servers and networks that tend to handle the types of music, or chats, you prefer. But the big advantage to Napigator's server listings is that they let you tailor your search for speed or thoroughness. If you're looking for a current Top 40 hit, chances are good it will be on many of the servers; so choose one with few users and avoid cybercongestion. If you're looking for a particular rare cut, choose one of the monster-sized servers; it won't be as speedy, but it will give you a better chance of finding less popular songs.

Even with the bigger independent servers, your download success is likely to be higher when you go through Napster's own servers. Napigator is too new a program and too many factors are at play for me to make a technically valid judgment on the speed and reliability of the unofficial servers Napigator finds. But my seat-of-my-pants verdict is that, using the independent servers, far fewer MP3 downloads get hung up endlessly "getting info." More downloads begin immediately rather than keeping you hanging for results that never materialize. Plus, the downloads are faster and encounter fewer transmission errors.

Napigator is also handy if you're using a university or business network that has banned Napster. The chances are good that the network administrators haven't blocked access to the alternative Napster servers.

Napigator is free and takes about a minute to learn. If you're going to use Napster, the best way to increase your successful download count is to also use Napigator. It's become a permanent feature of my MP3 arsenal.

Downloading with Napster

By using official or renegade Napster servers, choosing songs for downloading is as easy as double-clicking them in the Search screen. This sends the MP3s to a

Transfer screen, such as the one in Figure 5.7. The Transfer screen gives a running account of both your downloads in the top window and other users' uploads in the bottom window.

You can safely ignore all the information in either window. That is, except for the Status column. Napster has no way to alert you when the library from which you're downloading suddenly disappears because the library's owner goes offline. Search result pages don't update themselves. Left to its own devices, Napster will just sit there for eternity waiting for downloads in its queue.

The secret is in interpreting the Status column. It should be fairly straightforward. It has about eight phrases it uses to tell you how things are going. The first message you'll see is Getting Info… Your Napster is checking to see if the file is really where the library says it is. If Napster can't find the song, probably because that library is already offline, it displays Unavailable! If the song's there, and if you're not jammed up with a lot of other downloads, the Status column will tell you it's Downloading, and you'll see the nice graphs and other information out to the right—the Progress, Rate, and Time Left columns. They tell you the same thing in three different ways.

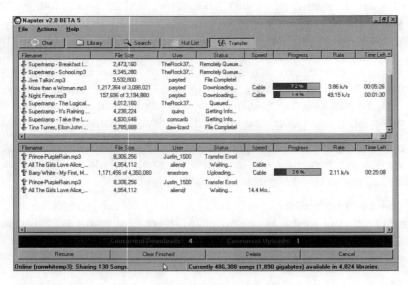

Figure 5.7: *Napster's Transfer Screen.*

When you see this screen, it's all downhill from here on. Well, almost.

By default, Napster will download only three songs at the same time. You can change that, but don't unless you have a very cranky connection. Then, set allowable downloads to one at a time. If you already have tossed a lot of songs into the Transfer queue, the new song will be given a Queue status until some other downloads end and one of the three default download slots opens up.

If you see a Remotely Queued... status, it means your request is waiting its turn at some other Napster user's computer. Napster also lets you say how many simultaneous downloads any one person can perform. The default is three, which is fair. Other statuses are Transfer Error!, Waiting in the Upload window, Cancelled, and File Complete!—all of which I'm sure need no explanation.

(Okay, the Transfer Error! could be due to a lot of things, none of which you have the slightest control over. Don't worry about it.)

The trick to it all is to look for songs where the Status seems stuck on Getting Info..., Queued, or Remotely Queued. What this really means is that there hasn't been a message from the remote library since the latest Status announcement. And there's not going to be a message. Right-click the stuck songs and choose Delete/Abort Transfer to clear the clutter off your screen.

That's it. This little program that could change the Internet is simpler to use than a pencil sharpener. Unless, of course, you're behind a proxy.

How to Bypass Napster Watchdogs

Several colleges have banned Napster, not for ethical reasons, but because Napster fans were chewing up enormous amounts of bandwidth. (Businesses can't be far behind with their bans.) Get a few thousand students downloading "Bohemian Rhapsody" at the same time they're letting others download from them, and it leads to traffic jams that set off all kinds of alarms in those little rooms where the college's computer staff spends their time reading *Popular Schematic*. In case you don't realize it, the network folks know who's using the Internet and how much they're using it, and could probably figure out where they're going. It's all information no one's really interested in unless whatever you're doing makes you a Webhog.

The colleges must know that something such as a Napster ban is simply waving a red flag in front of some very smart geeks just looking for an excuse not to read their History assignment. One such person is David Weekly, a student at Stanford University who figured out a way to trick his college's computer into thinking he wasn't connected to a Napster server. The explanation here is based on the solution at his site, `http://david.weekly.org`. I'm indebted to David for letting us include it.

Fooling the Blockade

Napster's Preferences dialog box allows you to type in a proxy so you can access the network if you're behind a *firewall*, which is a software barrier to block attempts to use the network mischievously. If you use a proxy, Napster will connect to the proxy and ask the proxy to connect to the Napster network on your behalf. Then, when the proxy receives information, such as a list of songs on a remote computer, the proxy passes it along to you. In this way, your computer is accessing only the proxy instead of talking to the Napster network directly, an arrangement that generally makes for faster responses.

Local network administrators are just that: *local* network admins. Specifically, they only have the power to filter out packets that leave your computer destined for some other specific set of computers. So when they say, "We've blocked Napster," what they really mean is, "We've shut off direct access to the Napster servers."

So, if you can convince the network administrators that you're communicating with some proxy server, they won't be able to see past the proxy to the Napster server you're really connecting to.

Now all you need to do is find a proxy computer. (There are several at `http://proxys4all.cgi.net` that you can piggyback on.) This proxy must be on a network that can directly access Napster. You can't just run a proxy on a computer on your local network and expect this to work.

The best way to do this is to ask a friend who's not behind a Napster blockade and who's willing to make his computer a proxy. Preferably you want a friend with a high-speed Internet connection. Ask the friend to install Socks 5, the most common style of proxy. Once your friend has his Socks 5 proxy server running, on your computer just type the proxy's IP address and port number into the proxy section of the Napster preferences. Off you go into Napsterworld again!

If you're having trouble connecting to the proxy, try setting the proxy up on port 80 or port 21.

The free Socks 5 proxy software is available at `http://www.geocities.com/SiliconValley/Heights/2517/sockserv.htm`. Installing it is pretty straightforward.

Check http://david.weekly.org/code/napster_proxy.php3 for a more complete list of sites offering proxy programs. Red Hat has a Socks 5 proxy software, RPM, for Linux you can download from http://ftp.redhat.com/pub/contrib/libc6/i386/socks5_1.0r10_5.i386.rpm. Visit http://david.weekly.org/code/napster_proxy.php3 for detailed instructions for installing RPM. Even better, there are some lengthy configurations settings you can simply copy and paste into RPM. The configuration will allow connections to the Napster metaserver and to each of the known Napster servers as well as allowing direct connections to another Napster client. You also will get instructions for debugging the setup if something about it doesn't work.

Other Distributed Swapping Software

The concept behind Napster—everyone's a client, everyone's a server—is such a potent idea that it hasn't even taken a year for people to write similar programs. Napster is not a complex or big program. After someone has explained the concept, it's not hard for some cowboy programmer to churn out the code to fulfill the concept.

The following are some of the more interesting Napster pretenders. For links to these and others, see the book's Web page, www.MP3under.com.

Gnutella

The story behind this program is as interesting as the program itself. The beta version of it was written by the creators of Winamp, a popular MP3 player, after the Winamp company, Nullsoft, was bought by AOL. Gnutella's creators posted the new program on the Internet—for less than a day. That's how long it took the AOL honchos to find out about it and order the program stricken from the Net.

Of course, by that time enough people had downloaded Gnutella to ensure that it will be circulating the Internet until the next millennium. In addition, programmers intrigued by the promise of Gnutella have continued its development, and a few Web sites devoted to it have popped up. (Check the book's Web site, www.MP3under.com, for links to the latest places you can find Gnutella lurking.)

The promise that so intrigues people about Gnutella is that the program carries to the logical extreme the concept of distributed databases, which Napster started. Napster uses centrally located servers to keep records of Napster users who are logged in and what songs they have available on their own PCs, which then become ad hoc Napster servers. Gnutella does away entirely with the centralized database. Gnutella running on one PC scours the Net for other Gnutella users, and gets its information directly from them. There are no centralized servers. This process is more time-consuming than Napster and more of a drain on a computer's resources, but the concept—complete democratization of the Internet—is enough to keep programming idealists going.

Also, Gnutella doesn't limit itself to MP3 files. Any type of files can be exchanged using it. This is a tack other Napster would-bes have followed.

CuteMX

This is Napster done right. Napster is a fine program for what it does, but its design shows all the hallmarks of quick-and-dirty programming. Its menus are practically useless. And a lot of the right-click features you'd expect in a Windows program aren't there.

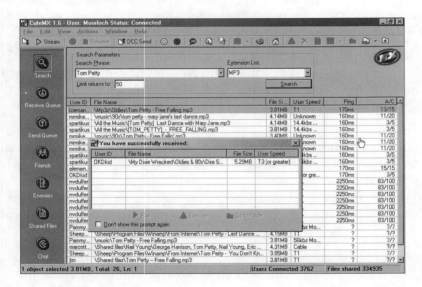

Figure 5.8: *CuteMX.*

While doing the same job as Napster, CuteMX does it with a look and feel that's easier to work with.

Sure, Napster is okay. But CuteMX does the same thing Napster does—and more. First, it is like Gnutella in that it isn't limited to MP3 files. More importantly, it adheres to the rules for how a Windows program should look and operate. (See Figure 5.8.) The most serious question about CuteMX is this: Does it have the *reach* that Napster does? Both programs depend for their success on a lot of people using them. Otherwise, your chances of grabbing a particular song dwindle. Napster has the established user base, but CuteMX isn't far behind. In my informal testing of CuteMX, I routinely found 300,000 to a half million songs from 3,000–5,000 users. It's really worth a look, and we've put it on the book's CD-ROM.

Others

Creating Napster-like programs seems to be the current fascination of program-mers. There are at least a dozen such programs available for download. Macster is, naturally, Napster for the Mac. Wrapster, like other post-Napster programs, opens up file exchange to any type of file. SX is ScourExchange, a program put out by one of the more famous Internet MP3 search engines, scour.com. And Freenet claims to take Gnutella's stealth swap one step further. It hides the sources of downloads on the Freenet network. You'll find links to these and other exchange programs at the book's Web site, www.MP3under.com.

How Do I Convert My Music CDs to MP3 Files?

♪ *What's the Best Format to Use?* ♪ *How Do I Rip Songs Off TV, Radio, and Cassettes?* ♪
Is There Any Way to Change Windows Media and Liquid Audio Files into MP3s and Waves?
♪ *Can I Record Webcasts or Streaming Audio?*

Maybe you still feel a little queasy, guilty, or just plain chicken when it comes to downloading MP3 files from anonymous partners in crime. I don't blame you. Not everyone is cut out for a life of digital crime.

Happily there is a sin-free, felony-free way to get superb MP3 files of the music you already love—from your own collection of music compact discs that you've spent thousands of dollars on over the years. Using MusicMatch Jukebox—provided on the book's CD-ROM—you can copy your music CDs, convert tracks to MP3s, and create a virtual jukebox on your hard drive. When you download, you get what you get. Most downloaded MP3s are fine, but occasionally you get one that sounds as if it were recorded in a cavern or where the person who recorded it mixed in his own guitar solo for "Stairway to Heaven." When you convert tracks yourself, you have total control over the quality, the compression format, and how you name the song files. Plus you have the ability to edit the songs to add your own creative touches. In this chapter we'll see how to *rip* tracks from compact discs and transform them into MP3 files. ("Ripping" is another one of those cool words you get to use if you play with MP3s.) And CDs are not your only source of MP3 tracks. In addition to ripping, you'll see how to capture music from anything from an 8-track to cable TV.

What Do I Get If I Buy MusicMatch?

The free version of MusicMatch Jukebox on the book's CD-ROM may be have all the power you need. But for $30, you get a jukebox that's faster and smarter. MP3 encoding is 20 percent faster, and CD recording works as fast as your writable CD drive allows up to 6X (one-sixth the time it takes to play a CD). The paid version also prints custom CD-R jewel case inserts with album art and track titles, prints the inventory of your music library and playlists by track and artist, and has an enhanced equalizer with custom presets. You can also create custom genre classifications, such as "kick-ass" and "Southern rock."

We'll do all this using MusicMatch, one of the two MP3 suites on the book's CD. MusicMatch can really do a lot more than merely rip. Like the other suite, RealJukebox, MusicMatch organizes your song files, plays them, creates playlists for your every mood, plays streaming audio straight off the Net, and burns your tracks onto writable compact discs. For most of those operations, RealJukebox is far easier to use. But Real's product doesn't match MusicMatch Jukebox when it comes to converting songs to high-quality MP3s and to wave (.WAV) and Windows media audio (.WMA) formats. You need wave files if you want to edit the audio, and .WMA files are a serious contender for your attention because they are smaller files with the same sound quality.

The free version of MusicMatch Jukebox on the CD is the only free MP3 program that records audio at up to 160 kbits/sec. RealJukebox—included on the book's CD-ROM because it's easier to use once tracks have been converted to MP3s—records MP3 at bitrates only as high as 96 kbits/sec. (We'll get into bits

later. For now, that means that MusicMatch's MP3 files are closer to CD quality.) And we'll look at the important features of MusicMatch and see how to use
them to create better-sounding MP3s—or waves or .WMA formats, too.

If you've been following along with me so far, you know I think MusicMatch is
painfully awkward to use and that you're better off using RealJukebox for everything except ripping music tracks and converting among audio file formats. But I
don't want to be dogmatic. Software tastes vary as widely as musical tastes. If
your mind has not been as enslaved to the Windows way of doing things as mine
has, you might find MusicMatch's idiosyncratic look fresh and charming. You
might even want to use it for all your MP3 needs. Take a look at Figure 6.1. It's a
road map to MusicMatch Jukebox to give you the general lay of the land. Then
we'll get to the tasty details about converting music CDs to MP3 files.

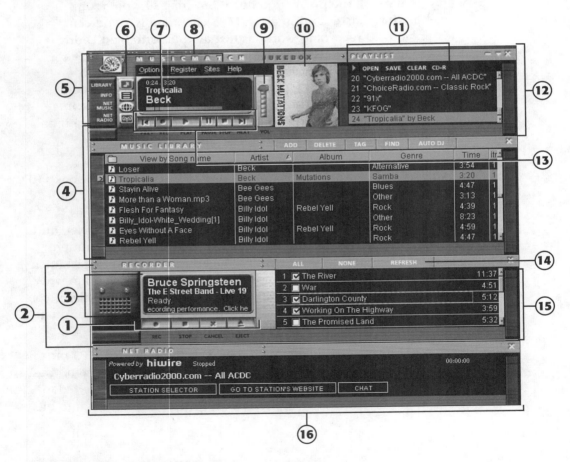

Figure 6.1   *Roadmap to MusicMatch Jukebox.*

(1) Controls: Record, Stop, Cancel, Eject CD.

(2) Recorder Module: The recording unit. It can be detached from the other modules.

(3) Current Track: Name of the artist or band and the CD currently being recorded, along with the percentage recorded, the bit rate, and the speed of the recording. (1X is standard CD speed; a 4X speed means it's taking one-fourth as long to record the song as it would to play it.)

(4) Music Library: A list of songs already added to your music library, along with artist and album name, genre, and length of song. Songs can be sorted by any of the information by clicking the label at the top of a column. Change what information the columns display and the order in which the columns appear by clicking Options, Settings, Music Library.

(5) Player: Plays the songs that are selected from the music library.

(6) Module Buttons: Click the buttons to the right of the labels, not the labels themselves, to activate the different modules and features in MusicMatch.

    Library: Toggles Music Library module.

    Info: Toggles information about the song currently being played, including other songs that you're also likely to enjoy.

    Net Music: Opens a link to search for music on the Internet.

    Net Radio: Toggles streaming audio module to play music from traditional radio stations and cyber Webcasters.

(7) Player Read-out: Tells the name and artist of the song currently being played from the playlist.

(8) Menus

    Options: All the vital operations of MusicMatch are accessed from the Options menu. It would be the File menu in a standard Windows interface.

    Register: For upgrading and buying the full version of MusicMatch.

    Sites: Link to MusicMatch's home page, CD Database, and other Internet sites.

    Help: Local and online help and tips.

(9) Volume Control

(10) Media Window: Displays graphics of the CD cover or other image associated with a song.

(11) Playlist Controls: Govern actions on songs in Playlist windows.

    Open: Opens a previously saved playlist, which is a collection of specific songs played in a specific order.

    Save: Saves a playlist collection to a file on the hard drive.

    Clear: Removes all songs from the current playlist. (To remove a single song, highlight it and press the Del key.)

    CD-R: Records the songs in the current playlist to a writable CD.

(12) Playlist Window: Songs are dragged here from the Music Library. The collection of all the songs here constitutes a *playlist*. Playlists can be saved to disk and opened later to listen to those particular songs. Playlist collections can also be transferred to CD-recordable discs.

(13) Player Controls: VCR style—Previous track, Record, Play, Pause, Stop, Next Track.

(14) Recording Selection Controls: Select all songs, Clear selection of all songs, Refresh information on CD currently in the CD-ROM drive.

(15) CD Contents: List the titles and time lengths of songs on the CD being recorded from. Check boxes indicate songs you choose to record to the hard drive.

(16) Net Radio Module: Tunes in streaming MP3 Webcasts.

What's the Best Format to Use?

In the free version of MusicMatch Jukebox, alone, there are 11 choices for sound quality. Songs can be recorded in MP3 format, as Windows media audio (WMA), or as wave (WAV) files. And for MP3 and WMA files, you can set the *bit rate* to control size and quality. The bit rate is the number of bits the recording uses for each second of sound. The higher the bit rate, the better the recording quality but the larger the resulting file size.

With wave files, you record with no compression at all. The resulting WAV file is the same size as the original track on the compact disc. If fact, with some minor differences, wave files are identical to audio tracks although WAVs will not work on an ordinary music CD player. You should record to wave format if you plan to edit the tracks before converting them to MP3s.

Editing Song Files

Use the wave format if you want to manipulate the files with an audio editor, such as Sound Forge XP, included on this book's CD-ROM. For example, you might record an hour-long concert off the TV, cable, or satellite video sources. With an editor, you can break the single, hour-long file into files for each song it contains.

Using MusicMatch, you can convert an MP3 file to a wave file, edit that, and then convert it back to an MP3. But some audio information will have already been lost in the original compression. Although the differences might be unnoticeable to the casual listener, a wave file created from an MP3 will not have as much information as a first-generation wave file.

Microsoft claims that its Windows media audio (WMA) compression produces better sound, bit for bit, than MP3 compression. Listening tests by ZD Labs support the claim, and in our own, less formal tests, at the same bit rate, WMA files sounded better. We're not talking the difference between tin cans with a string and a Bose sound system. The differences are so minor you won't notice them unless you're one of those really weird audiophiles who use amps with vacuum tubes. MP3 files sound as good as WMA files if they use a higher bit rate.

If file size is an issue, well, first, get a bigger hard drive. If that's not in the budget, use WMA format. But keep in mind that few portable MP3 players—one is the Diamond Rio—can play WMA songs. MP3 is the standard, and you'll have the best selection of software and hardware to use with your computerized music library by sticking to MP3.

And, to tell the truth, the paranoid part of me doesn't like the fact that copy-protection is such an integral part of Windows media audio. It's not that I don't trust Microsoft. It's just that I don't trust monopolistic, multi-national bullies. Just because Microsoft wants to call the shots on format standards, you don't have to go along with them. MP3 has the momentum. It's the place to be, dude.

Setting Bit Rates

To select bit rates for either the MP3 or WMA format, from the Options menu, choose Recorder, Settings. The result is the screen shown in Figure 6.2. The radio buttons along the side allow you to choose preset bit rates for all the formats. (Wave files are recorded only at 411.1 kbits/sec.) The more bits used in any format, the better a digital song will sound. But the more bits you use, the larger the file will be. Unless you have a hard drive so large—or a CD collection so small—that you don't care how much space you use, you must decide on the best trade-off between quality and size.

MusicMatch provides four preset MP3 bit rates and three presets for Windows media audio. You can also pick any bit rate between 8 and 320 kilobits a second for MP3 and between 5 and 160Kb/sec for WMA. *For general all-around, high-quality recording, click the radio button next to MP3 128Kbps.* Avoid 160Kb/sec. While most other bit rates convert a song faster than it takes to play it, 160Kbps will make recording take longer than simply playing a song. It's really only for those bragging perfectionist types you avoid at parties. If you're cramped for space, 96Kbps MP3 files make acceptable music recordings. If you have a portable MP3 player with limited memory, 64Kbps is a good compromise between quality and the number of songs you can take with you. Because the voice does not have the range music does, it's fine to run lower bit rates for speech, such as a teacher's lecture.

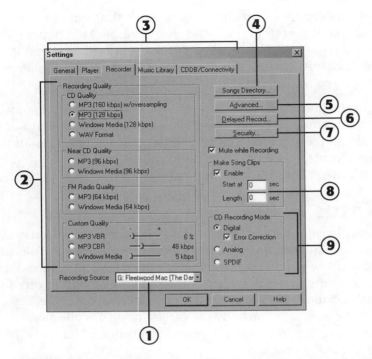

Figure 6.2: *Roadmap to MusicMatch Jukebox's Recorder Settings.*

(1) Source: Choose among CD-ROM drives, line-in, and sound mixer audio sources.

(2) Recording Quality: Choose among wave and WMA and MP3 compressed audio formats. The higher the rate, the better the sound and the bigger the file. *VBR* is *variable bit rate*, which adds to ripping time, but produces a smaller, truer recording. *CBR* is *constant bit rate*. Don't use it.

(3) Other Settings Tabs: These take you to other setup screens, but most of their default settings will work for you.

(4) Songs Directory: Click this button to open a dialog to tell MusicMatch where to save ripped files and to create a filenaming scheme.

(5) Advanced Recording Options: A lot of settings so esoteric that you can ignore them unless you're a fanatic perfectionist with nothing else to do.

(6) Delayed Recording: Set the date and time for unattended recordings.

(7) Security: Lets you set up digital rights management. Don't go there unless you're having problems downloading to portable MP3 players.

(8) Song Clips: Record only part of a track by specifying the number of seconds into the track recording should begin and end. Not a lot of demand for this.

(9) CD Recording Mode: Digital is the fastest ripping of CDs. If you do not have a CD-ROM drive capable of digital extraction, MusicMatch won't let you make this selection. Checking the Error Correction box lets MusicMatch double-check on the accuracy of its recording and fix errors. It adds a small amount to the time it takes to rip a track.

Or you can choose a *variable bit rate (VBR)*. The variable method does a quick analysis of the upcoming music and determines the optimum number of bits needed to record it. For quiet, simple parts of a song—such as a dramatic pause—there is less information to record, and so MusicMatch gets by with fewer bits. The bits saved there are used later for a complex passage that needs the extra bits to capture it faithfully. Overall, the ups and downs average out to an acceptable bit level. The only drawbacks are that variable bit rate recording takes longer, the files are larger, and not all players support variable bit rate encoding. However, the MusicMatch Jukebox, Real Jukebox, and Winamp players do.

Use VBR encoding when consistent audio quality is the top priority and file size is not critical. Choose a VBR setting from 1 to 100. The low end—1—is the lowest quality/highest compression, and the high end—100—is the highest quality/lowest compression. A good setting to start with is 50.

Table 6.1 shows the approximate quality and compression ratios for various formats and bit rates.

Table 6.1:   *Bit Rates, Audio Quality, and File Size*

Format	Bit Rate (Kb/sec)	Quality	Compression Ratio
MP3	160	Being there	9:1
MP3	128	CD	11:1
MP3	96	Near CD	15:1
MP3	64	FM radio	22:1
WMA	128	CD	11:1
WMA	96	Near CD	15:1
WMA	64	FM radio	22:1
WAV	1411.2	CD	1:1

I'm sure there a really good reason that some audio engineer understands as to why MusicMatch includes *constant bit rate (CBR) encoding*. It lets you choose any rate from 8Kbps to 320Kbps. Because the bit rate stays the same throughout, it can hurt audio quality and the efficiency of the encoder. Use CBR encoding only when you need to limit the size of the MP3 file or, as MusicMatch says, "produce consistent file sizes." Setting the bit rate higher than 128Kbps makes for little or no improvement in sound quality.

If you figure out a good use for CBR—why it was worth some programmer's time more than a usable set of menus that would eliminate some of the mystery of using MusicMatch—drop me an email. My address is on the back cover. For now, pick MP3 at 128Kbps, and we'll move on.

Setting Up a Painless, Yet Sensible, Way to Save MP3s

Before we actually start ripping, we must take care of another important setup task: telling MusicMatch where and how to save the MP3s you'll be ripping. MusicMatch has a very smart, flexible approach. Are you still at the Settings/Recorder screen? If not, from the main screen click Options, Settings, Recorder. Now click the Songs Directory button, and you'll get the screen shown in Figure 6.3.

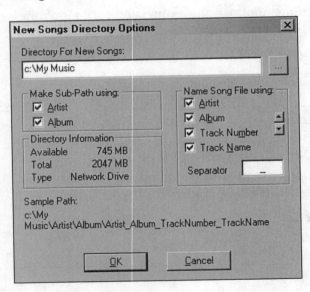

Figure 6.3: *New Songs Directory Options.*

The selections you make here determine how MP3 files are named when you rip them from CDs and where they wind up on your hard drive.

At the top of the form, fill in the main folder in which you'll be saving all songs. Make it one just off the root directory as I have here with C:\My Music. Now, it would be nice and organized if we had a different directory for every artist, and inside those, separate folders for each album you rip. To make that happen, be sure both Artist and Album are checked in the space labeled Make Sub-Path Using. This automatically creates a directory in C:\My Music with the name of the artist, and inside that directory, MusicMatch will create another folder, this time named for the album title.

To the right is the Name Song File Using box. The default setup of MusicMatch is to create filenames based solely on track names. My preference is to check all the boxes and use the little arrows to make sure the filenames are made of the items in the order Artist, Album, Track Number, and Track Name. Then MusicMatch will use each of those pieces of information to create a filename with this scheme:

```
C:\My Music\Artist\Album\Artist_Album_TrackNumber_TrackName
```

Or in a real-world example:

```
C:\My Music\Beck\Mutations\Beck_Mutations_06_Tropicalia.mp3
```

Yes, the artist and album names get repeated, which is redundant. But you won't ordinarily see the filename if you're using either MusicMatch or RealJukebox to play your MP3s. Both suites filter out all the redundant information and display neatly organized titles, albums and artists drawn from the files' tags, which we'll look at in a moment. And this scheme is handy if you ever need to move or copy the files somewhere. Then you'll appreciate having all the crucial pieces of information about a song in the filename.

But Where Does All This Information Come From?

About now you may be starting to wonder where all this album and title information is going to come from. You've sure got better things to do than look up all those details and type them in. So don't. You don't have to. There is a Web site that anyone converting songs to MP3s should bow down and praise. It's Gracenote, located at www.cddb.com—the Compact Disc Database. Starting off as an all-volunteer operation, Gracenote has gradually accumulated information on more than 6.5 million tracks from nearly 550,000 albums, accurately identifying different versions of the same song by the same performer and providing more information than any sane person wants to know. The most recent expansion of the database includes nearly two dozen information items. Just to name a few, there are artist name—which can change from track to track—album name, track name and number, label, year recorded, and Web URLs for artist or fan sites. There are more than 20 *metagenres*, such as rock, classical, new age, jazz, and more than 200 *subgenres*, such as goth punk, baroque, meditation, ragtime, and some I have no idea what they are—like ska and ambient. CDDB has been upgraded recently to let Web browsers prowl through the database to find band credits, composers, and other minutiae of music.

When you put a compact disc in your computer's drive and run MusicMatch Jukebox, the software looks at the start and stop times of all the songs on the disc. Jukebox sends that information to Gracenote's server on the Internet. There the database identifies the CD recording. Some other factors help narrow it down, and at its worse, Gracenote might ask you to choose between a couple of albums by the same artist. When the CD's identity is confirmed, Gracenote sends back to MusicMatch all the basic information you want to store. MusicMatch uses that data to create the folders that hold the songs. It also uses that information to fill in another identifying element of an MP3 file—its *tag*.

Tips for Ripping CDs with RealJukebox

Although the free version of RealJukebox is limited to recording MP3s at 96 kilobits a second, you'll want to use it instead of MusicMatch Jukebox if you spring for the registered version, which records at up to 320 Kbits/sec. Either version of RealJukebox is as mindless to use as MusicMatch once you have set it up by clicking the Tools, Preferences. You can leave most of the settings at their defaults. RealJukebox automatically creates folders named for the artist and album, and includes the track number and title in the filename. It's a good idea to change this under the tab for Music Files, Change Filenames so that the files' names also include artist and album.

Under the Recording tab, run the test to determine if your CD-ROM drive will permit ripping of tracks digitally, which is both faster and more accurate. On the same tab is an empty checkbox for Eject CD when Done Recording. Check it. If you're working on other computer tasks the CD's popping out is a good way to let you know it's time to rip the next CD. Similarly, under the General tab, you may check the box for CD AutoRecord so that RealJukebox begins ripping as soon as it detects a CD has been put in the drive. This is handy when you're ripping mass quantities, but when your rip marathon is through, uncheck the box if you plan to use your PC to play CDs without converting them to MP3s.

RealJukebox also supports ripping to wave files and the proprietary Real format. The latter is the default when you install RealJukebox. It's quite good, but not supported by all players. Change the default to MP3 before you begin ripping.

Branding Your Song Files with Tags

A tag is an integral part of all MP3 files. The MP3 format sets aside several of a file's bytes to contain information that identifies the file in terms of music tracks. The tags in older MP3 formats include only such items as artist, title, and album, track number, and playing time. The tag feature has been expanded in the last few years to include more esoteric information, such as a graphic image of the CD cover, multiple genres, Web sites, and your own comments. The result is similar to the tag information displayed in Figure 6.4. (Other formats, such as WMA, also contain tags.)

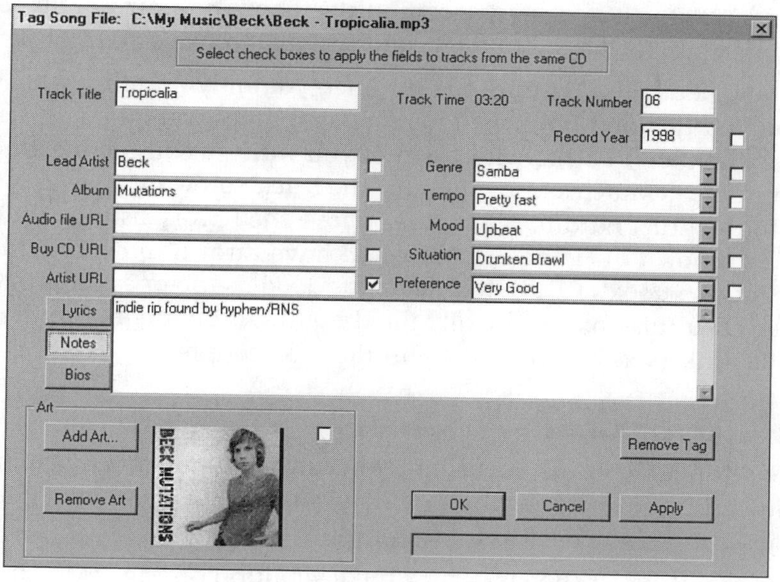

Figure 6.4:   *Tag Is It.*

MP3 tags contain all the details behind a song, and the great part of them is that MusicMatch automatically fills in the tag for you using information from the Web's Gracenote.

The result is that you're not reduced to organizing your MP3 tracks solely on the basis of the filename. Most software MP3 players read the tag information and build a database of songs that can be searched and sorted based on any of the fields included in the tags. Software players—and some hardware players—also display the track information as a song plays.

MusicMatch, RealJukebox, and other MP3 ripping software, using the data from the Web's Gracenote, automatically enter the basic information—artist, album, title, and so on—into a song's tag as it's being ripped.

Gracenote doesn't include information for all the fields in the tag. You have to find, for example, album covers and lyrics on your own. (Amazon.com is a treasure house of cover art. For lyrics try, what else, www.lyrics.com. Because of copyright restrictions, the lyrics are incomplete, but it's the closest thing we have to a library of lyrics.) Some tag categories, such as Situation appropriate for the music—say, Drunken Brawl—depend on your own inventiveness. Unless you have nothing else in the world to occupy your time, you don't need to fill in all the tag fields. But if you're obsessive-compulsive about organizing, the tags will give you an excuse for not getting out and socializing like a normal person.

And if you've downloaded MP3s from the Internet, you may find that whoever ripped them originally didn't have the tagging capabilities you do in MusicMatch, or else didn't bother with them. If you want to edit tag information, highlight in MusicMatch's Music Library the track you want to work with and click Tag in the little, hard-to-see buttons above the library listing. That will give you the form shown in Figure 6.4. We could have thrown individual tagging programs on the book's CD, but none are as good as the ones built into MusicMatch and RealJukebox—especially the drag-and-drop tagging in the latest version of RealJukebox, which we'll see in the next chapter.

How Do I Rip a CD?

Aside from the settings we've just looked at, you can pretty much leave all the other MusicMatch Jukebox settings the way they come. Now you're ready to actually rip those tracks off your CDs.

If the recording module isn't showing, click the Rec button on MusicMatch Jukebox. The recording section opens at the bottom of the other MusicMatch modules. Then make sure you're connected to the Internet so that you can suck down the tag information from CDDB. If you use a dial-up connection, dial up. You have to be connected to the Net to get the tag information only when you stick a new CD into your computer's drive to rip it.

When you do insert a CD, there are a few seconds when nothing much seems to be happening. This is when MusicMatch is checking your disc against the CDDB. In less than a minute, the CD Contents window you saw back in Figure 6.1 becomes populated with track names and their lengths in minutes and seconds. The other tag information doesn't show up at this point. You'll see it after a song is added to the Music Library. Check the box next to the name of each song you want to rip. Or, click the All button to add all the songs from a CD-ROM, and then click Rec.

And that's it. Really. The only troublesome job was setting up MusicMatch Jukebox in the first place. But once you do that, you can practically rip CDs in your sleep. And audio CDs aren't the only things you can rip.

How Do I Rip Songs Off TV, Radio, and Cassettes?

Music CDs aren't the only source of MP3s, you know. You can transfer music from your turntable, tape player—8-tracks, even—TV, cable, and satellite. All you need to do is create a connection between whatever your sound source is and your PC's sound card.

Wiring a Sound Source to Your PC

Recording MP3s from other sound equipment takes only two things. One is a Y-adapter audio cable. It has plugs on opposite ends that look like the ones in Figure 6.5. You can get the cable at RadioShack for five bucks. Ask for part number 42-2481, which is the longer, six-foot cord.

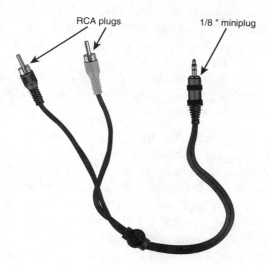

RCA plugs

1/8 " miniplug

Figure 6.5: *Y-adapter Audio Cable.*

On one end is a stereo 1/8-inch mini plug that fits into the line-in jack on your sound card. The other end of the cable splits into two larger plugs, one of them red and the other either black or white. These are commonly called RCA plugs, and they go into the stereo out jacks on whatever you're ripping songs from.

The second thing you need is a radio receiver, tape deck, TV, or any other audio source that has two jacks to fit the RCA plugs into. Most recent electronics equipment will have these jacks. If you can't find them, look for any type of connectors that are labeled "Audio out." These include the lines from a tape deck or turntable that normally would go to a sound system's amplifier.

Run the Y-adapter from whatever source you're using and push the mini-plug into your sound card's line-in jack. Now you need to tell MusicMatch Jukebox, which usually expects to record off a CD drive, to listen to the line-in source. In MusicMatch, click Options, Recorder, Source, and then choose the Line In selection. (Another way to do the same thing is by clicking Options, Recorder, Settings. At the bottom of the screen, in the same dialog box you saw in Figure 6.2, a drop-down list labeled Recording Source shows all the possible sources for sound input. Click the arrow at the right side of the list and choose Line In. Click OK to return to the Jukebox's main screen.)

What we're doing here is the same thing we used to do when we made 8-track or cassette tapes from a radio or turntable. It's analogous both technically and legally—or so it seems to me. But remember, I'm not a lawyer and you certainly shouldn't depend on anything I write that sounds like legal advice. Still, what's the difference, eh? Although you wind up with a digital MP3 file, what you're recording must pass through an analog stage as it travels over the cable to the sound card. This is true even if the source is a digital TV signal such as you get with satellite and some cable receivers. That analog stretch puts the kibosh on the record industry's fear of digitally perfect recordings. And, really, if the music police were going to object to this method, they should have said something 20 years ago, back when we were taping FM broadcasts.

Here are some practical tips. Before you start recording the one-night-only return of Jerry Garcia, test out your rigging to make sure it works. For some reason unknown to the best minds in the universe, some software mucks around with the settings on your sound board's mixer control. It does this without telling you. The change it likes to make most often, it seems, is to mute the line-in source. Whenever your sound goes awry, first check the volume controls. Right-click the little loudspeaker in your system tray down in the lower-right corner of the screen. If it's not there, click Start, Accessories, Entertainment, Volume Control. Make sure there's no check mark next to the Mute label for the line-in control. Then retest to make sure that fixed it.

Ripping in Absentia

Use MusicMatch's scheduling feature to capture audio from a TV or radio program that will be on when you're away from your PC. Click Option, Recorder, Settings. On the right side of the screen—the one you saw in Figure 6.2—click the Delayed Record... button. In the new form that appears, check the box labeled Active. Then fill in the dates and times an event is schedule to begin and end. Use military time. Click OK until you're back at MusicMatch's main screen. Finally, click the Rec button on the recording module.

Despite the analog segment, I've made recordings this way with spectacular results. I use a satellite receiver for two reasons. The first is that the signal is analog only between the receiver and sound card, which results in a clear, clean signal. The second is that a lot of concerts are on satellite, and it has its own audio channels for dozens of types of music. (The TV tells me the artist, title, and other information I wouldn't learn recording from a radio.)

Another trick you can do is record the output from a sound card in one PC to the input on a sound card in a different computer. All you need is a cable with mini-plugs on both ends. I've been told you can actually do this with two sound cards in the same computer. But that way, madness lies. Expansion card conflicts are too common even when the cards serve different functions. (Fortunately, we have a perfectly sane way to play and record a sound at the same time, but I'm getting ahead of myself.)

Starting a line-in recording session to capture one song is tricky. You'll never start it early enough or end it fast enough. This line-in technique is better used for concerts that you can record as one long track. Or tune your digital cable or satellite to one of its music channels and just capture everything it broadcasts for an hour or so. Then use an editor, such as Sound Forge on the book's CD-ROM, to extract and convert to MP3 only the songs you want to keep.

Recording So You Can Edit

If you're recording a concert or just a stream of songs from satellite, the radio, or the Internet, chances are that you'll want to break the audio file into tracks so they will be more manageable or just to get rid of the junk at the start and end. When you know you'll want to edit the audio files you're recording, it's best to make the original recording in wave format. You can't directly edit MP3,

WMA, and Liquid Audio files because of the way they're compressed. You can convert those formats to waves, edit them, and then convert them back. But MP3, WMA, and LQT files use *lossy compression* to achieve their small sizes.

Lossy means what it sounds like. You lose some information during the compression that you don't get back when you restore any of the compressed formats to a wave. Most often, the compression algorithm discards information about sound that is beyond the range of human hearing, so the difference won't be obvious to a casual listener. (And let's face it, the speakers connected to your computer probably aren't as good as the ones on your stereo anyway.) But lossy compression is the factor that makes MP3 music *near* CD-quality but not *quite* CD-quality. Although your music tracks may eventually wind up as MP3s, if you anticipate editing them, rip the tracks initially as waves, edit, and then convert to MP3.

Be aware, however, that an hour of wave audio takes up more than 600MB on your hard drive. Make sure you have the disk space, and as soon as you can, do your editing, convert everything to smaller MP3 files, and zap the massive wave file.

To save in wave format using MusicMatch Jukebox, choose the WAV Format radio button on the same Recorder Settings screen that we used in Figure 6.2 to set the bit rate. When you're set up properly for line-in recording, the window on the left of the recorder will display a scrolling message that says, "Press (Start) to begin line-in recording."

Well, there is no Start button. (See what I mean about MusicMatch's design having little thought behind it?) You'll need to press the Rec button—not the one you used to display the recorder, but another Rec button on the recorder itself. But don't do this yet. Before you start recording, go to the window on the right side of the recorder and give your recording session a name—anything you want. Now, click Rec. MusicMatch saves the incoming audio as an editable wave file until you click the Stop button.

Later, to convert songs from wave back to MP3, click the Option menu, then File, Convert. You'll see the screen shown in Figure 6.6. Make sure Source Data Type on the left is set to WAV, and for the best results, that the Destination Data Type is set to VBR or a constant bit rate of at least 96kb/sec. (128 is preferable.) Then browse through the file lists on the left until you find the wave files you want to convert. Highlight them and click Start. MusicMatch does the rest. Just don't forget to delete the waves before they clog your hard drive like digital kudzu.

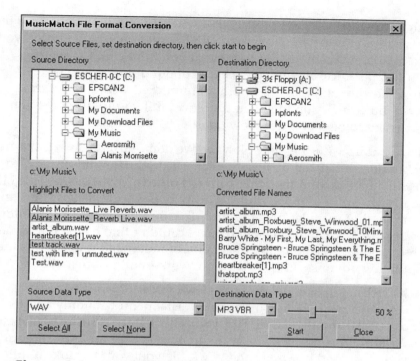

Figure 6.6: *MusicMatch File Format Conversion.*

Scroll through the Source and Destination Directories to find the files you want to convert and where you want them to wind up. With Source Data Type set to WAV, the window labeled Highlight Files to Convert will show all wave files. Highlight all the songs you want to change to MP3s and click Start. MusicMatch also converts from MP3 and to WMA, constant bit rate MP3, and variable bit rate MP3. But all it can do with WMA files is change their bit rates.

Is There Any Way to Change Windows Media and Liquid Audio Files Into MP3s and Waves?

It's not that Windows media audio isn't a splendid, fine compression format. It's just not standard. The standard is MP3, and you can do more with your music if you have it in the MP3 format—and sometimes in the wave format. Non-MP3 formats, such as WMA , LQT, and Mjuice, also tend to put little time bombs in files that cause the songs to stop playing after 30 days, to not play at all if you copy them to a different computer, or to prevent you from editing their tags. I've only seen two instances in which I was told about a time bomb before I wasted my time downloading. I've seen other gimmicked WMAs that have already expired, but which don't tell you that fact until you try to play them after what turns out to be a pointless download.

Are we going to put up with the bull? No way. We don't have to. Two programs for just this situation are linked at www.MP3Under.com, both free and uncrippled. One file zaps time bombs, and the other converts among WMA, wave, and MP3 formats. The first program, the one that sniffs out booby traps, is based on an unfortunate name that includes a word purported to make women and children swoon and computer book publishers nervous. I couldn't find a clue to the identity of the program's author. So I took the liberty of modifying it to change the name to a similar word: unsuck. (This does not work in all instances.)

Install Unsuck.exe by simply copying it to its own folder on your hard drive. Launch it and you get a small dialog box and a File menu with only two choices: Exit and File. When you click File, your only choice is Unsuck. Click it. The dialog box that appears displays an unexpurgated verion of the original name. Avert your gaze and browse to the WMA file you want to make a little more cooperative. Double-click the WMA file. If it's too late and the song's life has already come to an end, there's no resurrecting it. Unsuck displays the message "error: reading file." But if you've made it in time, just sit there while the software does its job. The result will be an additional WMA file in the same folder as the original and with the same name as the first, to which has been added one word that indicates it has, indeed, been converted.

Converting Among MP3s, WMAs, and WAVs

In the previous example, you can delete the old WMA file and keep the new, uncrippled one. But the new file would, of course, be more malleable to the host of MP3 utilities for tagging and organizing if it were an MP3. That's where Shuffler comes in.

Shuffler Music Converter, on the CD, easily converts among WMA, MP3, and WAV formats. From Windows Explorer, right-click a file in any of those three formats and choose Convert To. Shuffler opens a screen—one of two in Figure 6.7—that lets you add other files or entire folders to your selection. Click the green arrows in the upper right to go to the next screen, which is shown at the lower right.

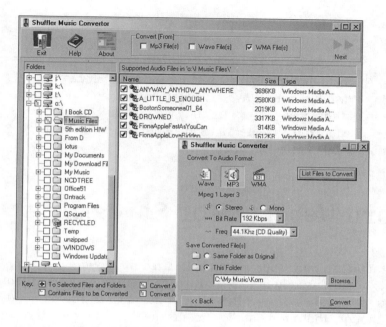

Figure 6.7: *Shuffler Music Converter.*

Using Shuffler Music Converter, it takes only a few clicks to select songs in one format and a few more clicks to convert them to MP3, WMA, or WAV formats. Have a good book handy. The process is slow, and your PC's not much good for multitasking while Shuffler is running.

In the second screen, click a button to choose what format you want the songs to wind up in: WMA, MP3, or WAV. You can choose bit rate, frequency, and the folder you want to hold the convertees. Click the Convert button, and Shuffler takes as long to convert each file as it would to listen to it.

To use Shuffler with Windows media audio, you must have installed the WMA CODEC (*compression/decompression*). If you're in doubt about having it, run wmaudioredist.exe, available through a link at www.MP3Under.com. Shuffler can't convert WMAs that still have time bombs in them. If Shuffler gives you an error message that says, "Unable to load CODEC to convert..." followed by the file's name, run the file through unsuck.exe first, and then use Shuffler to covert it.

That leaves us with Liquid Audio files and Mjuice. But where there's a will, somewhere there's a sleep-deprived programmer who can crack any protection. Read on.

Faster Compression

Shuffler is most helpful doing something MusicMatch can't: Changing WMA files into WAVs, a format you can edit. But then to compress those waves into nice, tiny MP3s, MusicMatch Jukebox is faster. You'll create MP3s in less than a tenth of the time Shuffler takes to create them.

Can I Record Webcasts or Streaming Audio?

Sure. Streaming audio is a good source for music. Streaming audio consists of *Webcasts*, which is audio—usually music—that's sent over the Internet in real time. You tune your software to any of these Webcasts much as you'd tune a radio. Be aware, though, that many audio streams are mono because that way less information needs to be sent over the Internet. See Figure 6.8.

You get two programs on this book's CD that receive streaming audio. MusicMatch Jukebox receives streaming MP3s, usually from a server running the program ShoutCast. RealPlayer, the older sibling of RealJukebox, plays audio Webcasts in streaming MP3 and Real's own, proprietary format. (Real also does streaming videos. Many Web pages give you a choice between Real and Windows Media Player to see a streaming video. Choose Real.) Real has the capability to broadcast different audio streams at the same time, each tailored to different Internet connections. If you have a 33.6bps connection, you should choose a stream that doesn't sound the best, but which won't drop out parts of the Webcast because your connection's slow. If you have a cable or faster connection, you can choose a stream that sounds better without dropping out. Windows Media Player is also designed to handle streaming format, and Microsoft has been working on a version 7 with added capabilities. But in version 6, at least, it sucks.

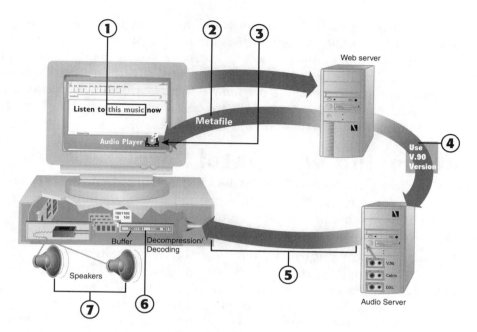

Figure 6.8: *How Streaming Audio Works.*

(1) When you click on a word or picture linked to an audio source, the *Web browser* contacts the *Web server* holding the current Web page.

(2) The server sends your browser a small file called a *metafile*. It tells where your browser can find the sound file, which doesn't have to be located on the first server. Your PC also gets instructions on how to play that type of audio.

(3) The metafile tells the Web browser to launch the appropriate *audio player*. The most popular is RealPlayer, included on this book's CD. MusicMatch Jukebox, also on the CD, can receive streaming MP3 audio.

(4) The audio player contacts the audio server providing the sound file and tells this server how fast your Internet connection is.

(5) Based on the speed of your connection, the audio server chooses one of several versions of the audio file. It sends higher-quality sound, which requires a wider bandwidth, over faster links, and lower-quality sound over slower con-

nections. The server sends the audio files to the PC as a series of packets in a protocol that permits the occasional packet to get lost without critically disrupting the transmission.

(6) When the packets arrive at your PC, your system decompresses and decodes them, and sends the results to a *buffer*, a small portion of RAM that holds a few seconds-worth of sound.

(7) When the buffer fills up, the audio player starts to process the file through your sound card, turning file data into voices, music, and sounds while the server continues to send the rest of the audio file. This process can go on for several hours. The buffer can temporarily empty if it doesn't receive enough data to replenish it. This happens if you access another Web page, you have a poor connection, or Internet traffic is heavy. If the buffer empties, the audio replay pauses for a few seconds until your PC accumulates enough data to resume playing. If the sound source is live, the player will skip portions of the audio program.

There are thousands of these Webcasters. Some are simply audio feeds from ordinary FM and AM radio stations. Others are heard only over the Internet. The real-time factor makes this perfect for distributing news, sports scores, and stock prices. The closing price of Cisco isn't something you'd want to record, but the streaming music and the audio portion of videos is. Here's how to capture streaming audio, the audio portion of videos, and a lot more—such as Liquid Audio and Mjuice tracks—to files on your hard drive.

Stream Ripping with Total Recorder

Among the files on this book's CD is Total Recorder, which captures streaming audio to a file. For that matter, it captures *any* audio your computer produces— music; sounds from other programs; even the explosions, monster roars, and Nine Inch Nails music tracks from Quake. (It works with other games, too.)

Total Recorder manages this by sticking its own driver between the software, such as Real Player, and the driver for the sound card. A *driver* is software code that translates the general instructions from software into the specific commands needed to work with a particular piece of hardware. If it weren't for drivers, your computer would be able to work with only a small number of sound cards, printers, video cards, and other components because those would be the only devices the operating system knows how to control.

The Total Recorder driver intercepts the commands from the software and makes a copy. It sends the copy to the Total Recorder program, which translates the audio stream into wave format and saves it to a temporary folder. The driver sends the duplicate version of the audio to the regular driver for the sound card, and everything works normally from that point. See Figure 6.9.

The method Total Recorder uses is interesting compared to unsuck.exe, which converts WMA files to waves. Unsuck works by playing the WMA file and capturing the file's analog output as it comes out of the sound card. Then it translates the analog signal to a digital wave file. You still have that analog phase where some sound quality will be lost. But Total Recorder works entirely with digital signals. The sounds it captures never go through an analog stage.

The version of Total Recorder with this book is free. But it's got a small catch. The free version lets you record only up to 40 seconds of audio from any source. It you want to record anything longer—from a song to a movie soundtrack— you have to pay $12 to uncripple Total Recorder. If there were a free solution as good as Total Recorder, we'd give that to you. But there isn't. And $12 is a small price for a program that opens up as many possibilities as Total Recorder does.

There's one other hitch in using Total Recorder. It has a look and feel that isn't simply user-unfriendly. It's user-hostile. When I first ran Total Recorder, I didn't have the slightest idea how to use it. I even resorted to reading the help files, which I usually consider cheating. The help files weren't much help, and I had to fall back on trial and error. There are still some fine points I'm not sure about, but the basic use of Total Recorder is really simple once you figure it out.

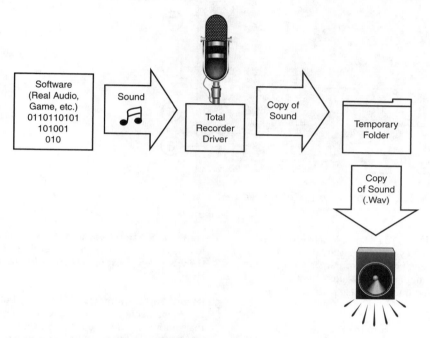

Figure 6.9: *Capturing Audio—Any Audio.*

Total Recorder sets up its own driver between the audio software and the sound card's driver so it can copy incoming audio to a wave file.

When you install Total Recorder, it sets itself up so that it integrates automatically with your PC's sound system. If the default settings don't work, Total Recorder has only a few settings that you can play with, as I did to get it working. I really do recommend reading the help files, and the road map to Total Recorder in Figure 6.10 shows you the important buttons to push.

The best way to learn how to use Total Recorder is to play around with it a bit. Just make sure Total Recorder is running and in record mode before you begin an audio stream. Don't be confused because nothing seems to happen when you click the Record button. Total Recorder waits until it detects incoming audio before it starts recording.

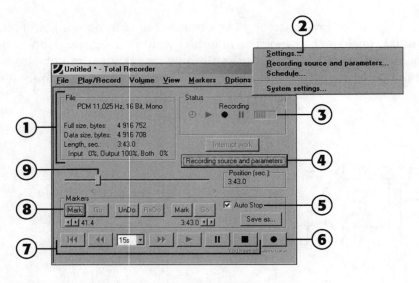

Figure 6.10: *Road Map to Total Recorder.*

(1) File Information: You'll know Total Recorder is recording when you see the numbers in this box start changing. (The program is on automatic pause until it detects audio input.) The numbers keep track of the file's size and length in seconds.

(2) Options Menu: Next to the File menu's Save function, the Options menu gets the most use. If Total Recorder is not working, experiment with the two Settings and the Recording Source and Parameters dialog boxes. Schedule lets you set up Total Recorder to begin and stop recordings at specific dates and times.

(3) Status Box: Tracks whether the program is scheduled to record, or is already recording, playing, or paused, and volume.

(4) Recording Source and Parameters: Before you begin recording, click this button and in the dialog box it opens make sure the Software radio button is pressed and the boxes are checked for Generated (Output) and Requested (Input). Change other settings only as a last resort if the program won't record.

(5) Auto Stop: Check this box to make Total Recorder stop recording when an audio stream

ends. This is a good way to do it. If you plan to manually stop a recording and get distracted, the wave file will eat up disk space like potato chips.

(6) Record Button (Important): Press this button *before* you begin a stream or another program that produces audio you want to capture, such as a DVD player. Remember: Recorder has already diverted the incoming audio through its own driver. If the sound is already playing when you click the Record button, the stream may ignore Total Recorder. When you click Record, actual recording doesn't begin until Total Recorder detects audio input.

(7) Controls: This is the standard set of buttons issued for any music player, plus a control to let you decide how far the jump buttons jump. It is set here for 15-second leaps.

(8) Marker Controls: Allow you to place markers in a recording for rapid access or for extracting just the selected portion of the audio track to be saved as a separate file.

(9) Progress Indicator: Works only when playing back a recording.

MP3 as soon as you can to save space. The fastest way to convert them is with And don't forget that Total Recorder creates only wave files. Compress them to MusicMatch Jukebox.

7

How Do I Play MP3s? And How Do I Keep Track of 1,000 Songs?

♪ *Setting Up RealJukebox 2* ♪ *Creating Playlists* ♪ *Editing Tags with RealJukebox* ♪ *Sure, My Ears Are Having Fun, But What About the Rest of Me? (or, May I Have Some More Eye Candy, Please?)* ♪ *How Can I Listen to My MP3s on the Go?*

Finally, after collecting MP3s from the Internet, CDs, and all the various electronic media that bombard our homes, we now are ready to listen to them. And to do this, we're going to abandon MusicMatch Jukebox and use a more versatile and easy-to-use audio player: RealJukebox.

There are a few ways in which RealJukebox doesn't have the power of MusicMatch Jukebox. MusicMatch gives you more controls and options while recording, making it worth occasionally laboring with MusicMatch's eccentric interface. After all, you only rip songs once. Playing them is for a lifetime.

When you want to listen to your music or be your own DJ by creating playlists of favorite song combinations, you want software that's simple and as much like the other software you use as possible.

That's why we're swapping programs in midstream from MusicMatch to RealJukebox 2, a product that grew from the streaming audio software RealPlayer. It's included on the book's CD as a part of the Real Entertainment Center. Real's products have been consistently the easiest to use but a bit straight-laced. With the upgrade to RealJukebox 2 in the summer of 2000, the software is getting the pizzazz of players such as Liquid Audio and Sonique and the muscle of MusicMatch and WinAmp, long considered the MP3 player of connoisseurs.

The CD with this book has the entire family of Real Network products: the Real Entertainment Center, with RealJukebox 2 Basic for ripping and playing songs in any format, and RealPlayer 8 Basic for streaming audio in MP3 and Real's own widely used format, RA. There's also RealDownload 5 Basic, a product similar to Go!Zilla for tracking all those downloads and MP3 sites. It's less complicated than Go!Zilla, but that's because it doesn't have Go!Zilla's organizing and cataloging features. In fact, if you use Go!Zilla, it's best not to install RealDownload because the Real program usurps Go!Zilla's interception of downloads.

Windows Has Just Begun to Fight

At the time this book was going to press, Microsoft was introducing its beta of Windows Media Player 7 for Windows 98 and later and for Windows 2000. It's Microsoft's attempt to establish a beachhead in a battle where it's a latecomer. It combines the functions of a streaming audio and video player with a jukebox to play sound and visual media. Then it throws in artist and album information from All Media Guide (AMG) and support for portable players and CD recorders. All in all, it's not as slick or versatile as RealJukebox, but it is from Microsoft, which is pushing for its WMA format and player to be the standards for digitized audio. The WMA format is showing up at a lot of the major music sites. And Microsoft has been known to muscle its way to the top of a market. You can check out Player 7 at http://www.microsoft.com/downloads/ search.asp?.

Setting Up RealJukebox 2

RealJukebox 2 is not simply a great music suite. It's also one of the best designed programs I've seen in 20 years of reviewing software. Just about every time I think, "Gee, it'd be nice if it could do this so-and-so," it turns out RealJukebox does it. And often I've found cool and useful features that hadn't occurred to me.

And one not so useful feature.

At some point in the installation, Jukebox will ask you if you want to enable security for Jukebox music. Sounds good. After all, you're supposed to have security on your computer. But think about it. These security features are designed to prevent you from playing music that may seem to have a questionable origin even though you've paid for it. For example, you may have made a second copy of a CD because you lost the original, something that could trigger security restrictions. What is the advantage of security for consumers? None. So the smart thing to do is to make sure security is not enabled. But you knew that, right?

Liquid Audio, Mjuice, and WMA formats usually have some security system of their own that involves a token file hidden on your hard drive or getting authorization from an Internet site. Unless you convert those files to MP3 with Total Recorder or unprotect WMA songs with Unsuck—see Chapter 6, "How Do I Convert My Music CDs to MP3 Files?"—you have to put up with a lot of copy-protection obstacles. I've yet to encounter a file I couldn't play because RealJukebox's security wasn't enabled. Don't enable it if you're not forced to.

When you install RealJukebox, it asks whether you'd like it to find all the audio files on your hard drives. You do. Jukebox plays—last I checked—12 audio and video formats, including MP3, WAV, WMA, and, of course, Real Audio. If it finds a format it's not already equipped to play, it checks the Internet for the right *codec*, which is a hunk of computer code that translates that track's format into music.

At the end of its music search, Jukebox adds the titles, tags, and filename information of the audio and video files it finds to its own database. The actual locations of the files don't change, but it looks as if your music collection were in one large, but extremely organized, group.

Working from this database, you create *playlists*—different collections of songs that represent your favorites, your party music, whatever those songs mean to you. There is only one copy of a track, even though one song can belong to any number of playlists, or even be in the same playlist more than once. RealJukebox automatically creates several logical playlists for you, such as grouping titles by the same performer, genre, album name, and even the songs you've listened to most recently. Could it get anymore mindless? Take a look at Figure 7.1: Roadmap to RealJukebox 2. It presents a guide to one-click access to all but a few of the jukebox's features.

RealJukebox's Secret Song Superintendent

One of RealJukebox's neatest tricks is hidden in the StartCenter, an icon in your system tray that you can right-click to display a menu of jukebox options. One option is Watch Music Folders. Click it and you're presented with a display of file folders in which Jukebox has already found music files. It nicely offers to check these folders every so many minutes or hours to see if they have any new music in them. If they do, the songs are automatically added to the database.

Creating Playlists

Because RealJukebox automatically creates playlists grouped by artist, artist/album, genre, and recently played tracks, you may be hard pressed to think of playlists of your own to create. You can do it, though, and it's a kick to play DJ. Click the New Playlist button on the right, and Jukebox gives you a chance to name the new list. You also can choose all the tracks in the current view to be added to the playlist, or all the tracks you've already selected by clicking track names as you hold down the Shift and Ctrl keys. Or simply tell Jukebox to make an empty playlist. Say where in the program's organizer window the list should reside. Then, at your leisure, drag and drop new songs on the playlist to add them.

AutoPlaylists are playlists based on a set of criteria you provide. First, click the AutoPlaylist button on the Navigation Bar and the New AutoPlaylist button that then appears on the Command Bar. A window similar to that shown in Figure 7.2 opens to let you name the AutoPlaylist and create a set of rules that determine which tracks make it to the AutoPlaylist. In Figure 7.2, I've already added one rule—that the tracks must be from the alternative, blues, or folk genres. In the Track Selection Rule dialog box, superimposed to the lower right, I can choose any other tag field, such as artist, and then select only certain performers. I'll pick only women so I can create my own Lilith Fair. You define the maximum length of any one song and specify the ideal total time-length for every track in the list. This is handy when you want to burn a CD, and you need to find a combination that fits into 74 minutes, the most you can get on a CD in the required, uncompressed form.

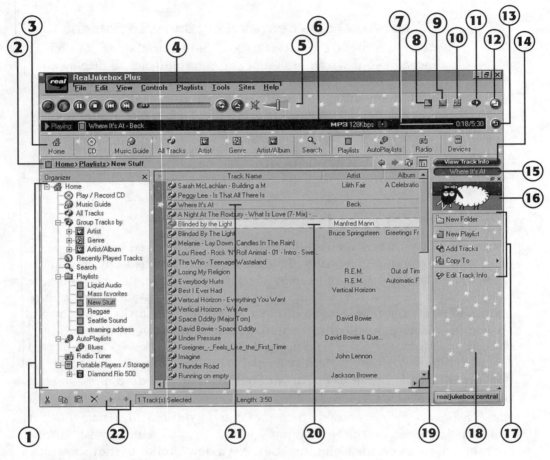

Figure 7.1: *Roadmap to RealJukebox 2.*

The screenshots of RealJukebox are of the paid version, which was the only one we could get our hands on while the program was still in beta. Features that are only in the paid version are identified in the callouts.

(1) Organizer: Many of RealJukebox's features are accessible from this panel, which displays both functions and playlists in a single cascading set of options you navigate as if you were browsing through directories. Many of the selections here are also found on the toolbar and on the Home menus.

(2) Location Bar: Shows where you are and where you've been, browser style.

(3) Navigation Bar: Customizable shortcuts to playlists and features. The buttons shown on the bar here are, left to right:

Home: Displays a list of Jukebox functions with quick explanations.

CD: Displays the tracks of the compact disc in the CD-ROM drive.

Music Guide: Links to Real's own excellent download and music news page.

All Tracks: Displays all tracks in your music collection listed by track name.

Artist: Displays all tracks sorted by performers' names.

Genre: Displays all tracks sorted by genre.

Artist/Album: All tracks sorted first by performers and then album titles.

Search: Another way to activate an Internet or local search.

Playlists: Displays the names of all playlists, the number of tracks in each, and the total playing time of each list.

AutoPlaylists: Displays lists created according to your custom settings, such as all Dylan songs that are ballads. The jukebox automatically updates the playlist.

Radio: A quick way to bring up Real radio for streaming MP3 and Real audio feeds.

Devices: Displays a list of devices, such as portable MP3 players, that Jukebox is configured to work with.

(4) Title: Name of song currently playing.

(5) Play Controls: The usual assortment of remote control-style buttons. Left to right: Record, Play, Pause, Stop, Previous Track (hold for Rapid Reverse), Next Track (hold for Fast Forward), Progress slide bar, Continuous or Repeat, Shuffle Play, Mute, and Volume Control.

(6) Menus: For most functions, using the jukebox's generous assortment of toolbars is easier. But you'll need to resort to menus to print jewel-case covers (registered version only), display *themes*, set preferences, configure portable players, and get to more Web sites and help screens.

(7) Activates Crossfade: The ability to fade out one song while fading in the following song is in only the registered version.

(8) Equalizer: Pops up 2-band equalizer in the free version. In registered version, it's a 10-band equalizer with presets.

(9) iQfx2: Activates an add-on that emulates surround sound. iQfx2 is partially crippled; the paid version provides more controls.

(10) Launch RealPlayer: RealPlayer is a separate program for streaming audio and video over the Internet.

(11) Switch to Skin: Change, radically, the appearance of the jukebox. More later in this chapter.

(12) Return Button: If you've been browsing among other songs and you want to return to the track that's currently playing, click this.

(13) Read-out: Tells the format, bit rate, time played, and total time for the current track.

(14) (15) View Track Info: Replaces the Playlist window with detailed information from a song's tags.

Artist/Song: Identifies the track currently playing.

(16) Visualizations: Animated cartoon and abstract art that moves in time to the music. Visualization is displayed in the small window, or zoomed out to quarter-screen size or to full screen.

(17) Command Bar: Displays buttons for functions that are relevant to whatever's displayed in the Playlist Window. In this example, the buttons all call functions appropriate when a playlist is shown. Top to bottom: create a New Folder into which several playlists can be grouped, create a New Playlist, Add Tracks to a playlist, Copy tracks to a playlist or portable player, and Edit Track Info contained in tags.

(18) Themes: Picture, pattern, and color themes are applied to the surfaces of the Jukebox like wallpaper. The theme here is "Shooting Stars."

(19) Playlist Window: Either a list you've created or that Jukebox has automatically organized, whichever one is selected in the Organizer to the left. In this case, the playlist "New Stuff."

(20) Selected Track

(21) Track Currently Playing

(22) Track Movers: Move selected track up and down the playlist.

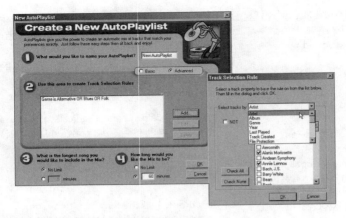

Figure 7.2:   *Creating a New AutoList.*

RealJukebox lays out its dialog box for creating a new AutoPlaylist with one-two-three directness. The feature gives you tremendous power for creating playlist mixes with very little effort.

Now I'll get an AutoPlaylist with tracks sung only by female blues, folk, or alternative artists. In actuality, I wound up with 59 minutes and 13 seconds—pretty close to the 1 hour I asked for—of Joni Mitchell and Linda Ronstadt. After you click OK, don't be surprised if proper mix doesn't show immediately. Go to the new playlist's name under AutoPlaylist in the Organizer, right-click, and choose Remix Now. The new playlist will appear.

In fact, each time you remix a playlist, you'll get a different selection of songs—not entirely different but different enough that the playlist doesn't become old. You can create as many rules as you can think of. And it's interesting to see which artists and songs fate decides should all go for a ride together.

Danger, Will Robinson!

You'll quickly learn as you toy with playlists that right-clicking any track brings up a host of options for moving, tag editing, and copying, adding, and deleting tracks. With most playlists, deleting a song means it's removed from only that one playlist. It still stays in your library, and the disk file that holds the track certainly won't be deleted. Unless...you're in one of the groupings RealJukebox creates automatically, Artist, Genre, Artist/Album. If you lean on delete there, Jukebox asks if you also want to delete the track from your hard disk. Don't automatically reach to check some box. Pay attention!

Other fun and games with playlists include dragging and imaginatively dropping tracks here and there in a playlist. Go ahead—put Manfred Mann's "Blinded by the Light" right before Springsteen's "Blinded by the Light." You still won't figure out what the lyrics are, but it's a good contrast in styles. Why, with playlists alone, RealJukebox provides hours of procrastination and unproductive fiddling. Come on! They're called *play*lists, not *work*lists.

Editing Tags with RealJukebox

The effectiveness of Jukebox's playlist depends entirely on the quality of each track's tag information. Last chapter, as you ripped your music CD collection into a god-awesome mass of computer files, you learned that MusicMatch Jukebox identifies the album and pulls down the information from an Internet database to complete the tag essentials. (Same for RealJukebox's ripper). This makes for terrific automatic lists. But MP3 tracks you obtain from shady sources—we're not mentioning any names, you understand—may have originated from someone who is nowhere near as thoughtful, purposeful, and well-equipped when it comes to software as you are.

This means you must edit tags, which you can do with either MusicMatch Jukebox or RealJukebox and which, with very little effort on your part, makes you appear to be very busy at something obviously important. Usually this involves a lot of cutting and pasting as you disassemble some filename such as "Vertical Horizon_06_It's only ME (Live stages)."

RealJukebox provides a handy way to change the same tag field for several tracks at once. Select the files in any playlist that you want to change. Get them all with the Shift and Ctrl keys. Then right-click and choose Edit Track Info. The jukebox opens a dialog box where all the tags that should *remain* unchanged are blocked from any attempt by you to give every song in the album the same name. But other fields, such as genre and cover art, are subject to your whims. Change an item once and the same field's updated in every track on the album. I've used this to change the genre on all Aerosmith songs from "rock" to "show tunes."

Real also provides well-conceived tag templates for various types of music. Classical, for example, has fields for composer, movement, and the like.

What Do I Get for My Money in the Registered RealJukebox?

For $29.95, you get the ability to print jewel case liners and track lists; crossfade between tracks—a *really* cool effect—a 10-track equalizer; an exclusive pack of five way-cool skins; access to the advanced AutoPlaylist features; the ability to convert among MP3, WAV, and WMA formats; faster performance on a Pentium III computer; phone support; and a manual. There are package deals for registering RealPlayer and RealDownload at the same time; check out www.real.com.

You can add a secret feature to RealJukebox 2 by surfing to www.real.com/rjcentral. This is a site devoted mainly to wicked skins, which we're about to look at. But hidden down at the bottom of the page is an inconspicuous link, almost as if Real doesn't want you to know about it. Click the link and you go to a page where you can download a free upgrade to raise RealJukebox's highest bit rate from 96Kbits a second to 320Kb/sec. Software developers—go figure.

Sure, My Ears Are Having Fun, But What About the Rest of Me? (or, May I Have Some More Eye Candy, Please?)

So there you are, with one of the greatest collections of MP3 songs known to mankind, and the question inevitably arises: What are you supposed to do while you listen to your music? For starters, you could consider working. That's the excuse you had for buying your computer in the first place—you were going to use it for important financial stuff and research, not for playing games and listening to music. Heaven forbid.

Well, you can work if you want to, all the while immersing yourself in an environment of your own, special music. But I think your eyes should be having at least as good a time as your ears. Do you think they're having fun staring at a Word document while your ears boogie to vintage Bowie? With RealJukebox, you have hundreds of different visual treats. Here are just a few of them.

Skins

Among the practical, helpful advantages of RealJukebox are its simplicity and its consistency with a user interface we're already familiar with—Windows. But one of the most pleasurable features of RealJukebox is the ability to destroy utterly the Windows look and feel, all in the pursuit of individuality, beauty, and plain old coolness.

The feature that permits this is called *skins*, aptly named because a skin changes only the surface look of RealJukebox, not how it functions. RealJukebox isn't the only MP3 suite that comes with skins. But it's one of the few that has available more than 600 different skins. Outside of Winamp, it may be the only player with this many skins. I've got other things to do than go around counting the skins used by every MP3 player. But it's definitely the only player that has *animated* skins. Real supports video, live HTML pages, Web links, and *visualizations*, a name for abstract patterns that dance in time to the music.

The Skinny on WinAmp

RealJukebox offers some groovy skin options, but the player that rules the roost skin-wise is WinAmp. You can download thousands of skins that make WinAmp look like a home stereo, give it a futuristic high-tech look, salute your favorite sports team, or let you gaze at Britney Spears while the music plays. Lots of sites are out there—searching for "winamp skins" will get you started, or you could try www.winamp.com.

I could write about skins all day. But you'll get a better sense of them by looking at the skins in Figure 7.3.

One of my favorite skins is in Figure 7.3, called Puny 2. It takes the bare minimum of screen real estate while still giving me access to all of RealJukebox's essential functions. Other skins are downright mysterious, and you only become proficient in using them to control RealJukebox with time and practice. But that's the point. A skin should be your own, not something any doofus who sits at your computer can use. It's private, secret, it's *your* skin.

Now, the very idea of skins is diametrically opposed to the main reason for recommending RealJukebox in the first place: its ease of use and adherence to the Windows interface. But for day-in, day-out listening to MP3s, you need to learn only a few buttons—play, pause, stop, skip, and how to right-click to change the skin back to the traditional RealJukebox look when you need handholding to get through unaccustomed features.

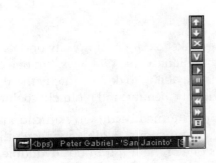

Here's Puny2

Mandara   *and Irem.*

Figure 7.3:   *The Skinny on Skins.*

Various skins for RealJukebox include the minimalist Puny 2, which hides unobtrusively in the lower-right corner of your screen; the ultracool, if slightly obtuse, Mandara; and the Peter Max-ish Irem, which offers little clue about how to use it.

Plus, RealJukebox has animated skins. How cool can you get, I ask you. These are skins that may incorporate RealJukebox's visualizations or have animated images of their own—or both. I'm particularly fond of the golden scarab animation in which a golden bug comes to life and dances to the beat of the music.

If you want to take this individualization to its ultimate expression, create your very own, original skins using the simple skins toolkit that comes with RealJukebox and is on this book's CD. It let's you see the actual *source code* so you can figure out how the skins work. We've also put on the CD SkinsEditor for RealJukebox. The shareware editor, which costs $13 if you decide to keep it, is an easier, cleaner way to create skins.

Visualizations

Can you say, "Acid trip"? Good, then you have the general idea behind visualizations. RealJukebox comes with a half dozen visualizations that combine everything from sheep to flames to cosmic superstring, all moving, pulsing, growing, and dancing to the music.

You can run the visualization in a small window, like the sheep visualization you saw in Figure 7.1 (and which is a lot more amusing than it looks). You can blow them up to about quarter-screen size, or bounce them up to full screen. Of course, the bigger they get, the more halting and jagged they become. They really look better *not* full screen. The rhythmic psychedelics also work with RealPlayer streaming audio and video, which is fun because you can see what Jon Stewart's voice would look like if it were the flames of hell.

Visualization may not be for everyone. With any more than one program running in the background, my slightly dated test systems got the jitters. The visualization and music took turns halting and skipping. Users of Pentium IIIs, which are designed for media, should have no problems at all. (Which is just like Pentium III people. They always have that more-digital-than-thou attitude, and I've really had it with them up to about *here!*)

By clicking the Tools menu and Visualization Settings, you can control the direction, twists, and swelling of the abstract visuals. This in itself is easily good for an entire weekend when you should be mowing the lawn.

Themes

As if there weren't enough visual delights, RealJukebox also provides *themes*. (They're found only under the View menu.) Themes are like Windows wallpaper but for the surface of the standard Jukebox. They don't move or anything. But give them a spin. I like the bees theme on the Jukebox in Figure 7.1 because it also changes the playlist window to show dark letters on a light background, which is easier to read than Jukebox's standard white on black.

How Can I Listen to My MP3s on the Go?

The only problem with MP3 files is that you have to have this 60-something-pound computer to listen to them. Even with a laptop PC, you've got to carry around headphones or speakers that produce audio that sounds like mice wrestling inside your laptop.

Enter the portable MP3 players. These electronic devices the size of a pack of cigarettes and the price of a 35-inch color TV are the ultimate answer to music on the move. I hate to tell anyone who has already bought a portable MP3 player that if he'd only wait a decade, these things are going to be sold in blister-paks at K-mart for $19.99. That's the price you find today for Walkman-style portable tape decks, which have a lot of moving parts that require assembly while MP3 players have no moving parts—just a bunch of etched circuit boards and microchips. They're just crying out for cheap, mass production by slave labor in some Asian country or Kathy Lee's garage.

Only two things are wrong with the players. One is that the memory they use—*flash memory*, sometimes called *compact memory*—is expensive. The advantage is that flash memory doesn't lose what it's storing when a device is turned off. Currently, most users have only one memory chip because 32MB of flash memory can cost $50–$75. Users simply download various playlists to the same memory chip, which gets tedious after a bit. When the memory price drops to $5—and it will—you can have multiple memory chips of different playlists that you plug in depending on your musical mood.

Can I Use My Portable Player with RealJukebox?

Could be, depending on the brand and when you read this. RealJukebox 2 hit the market with support for the Diamond Rio 500, Diamond Rio PMP 300, Creative Nomad, Phillips Rush, and RCA Lyra players, and for storage on Iomega drives. MusicMatch supports Diamond Rio 300 and 500 RCA Lyra, Memcorp Soulmate, and Creative Nomad. You can get to the latest updates for both players from the Internet by choosing Tools, Install Device in Real, and Options, Add New Features in MusicMatch.

The other thing wrong with the players is that, caught between the consumers and the record industry, they haven't yet figured out what they want to be when they grow up. Some players double as radios or voice memo recorders. Most play MP3s, but some also take on WMA songs, and Sony is pushing its own format for both music and memory, in the form of chips that look like a stick of gum. Here are some guidelines to follow when shopping for a portable player.

Memory

The most important feature to check out is the amount of memory that comes with a player and how much you can add to it with removable flash memory. Your player will only remain interesting as long as the music it plays does. The more memory you have, the more music you have, and the longer it takes you to get bored. Make sure that the player accepts standard flash memory cards. Proprietary memory is expensive. Sony's stick memory is cute, but stay with something more conventional. Extra memory for it will be easier to find and cheaper.

Transfer Method

Older players—if you can talk about "older" for a device that's not even two years old—have parallel port connections, which usually require some sort of docking station, and of course we really need more gadgets on our desks. Look for a player with a universal serial bus (USB) connection—provided your PC has USB ports, which it will if it's less than 3–4 years old. The connectors on USB cables are small, eliminating the need for a docking station, and USB makes for quick downloads.

SDMI Compliance

Although some portable players are already claiming Secure Digital Music Initiative compliance, it's more a statement of good intention than fact. As of mid-2000 the SDMI had not really figured out how technology is going to stop humans from turning into a species of music thieves.

But even if the exact workings of copy protection are settled and standardized, this should be clear: SDMI-compliance is not a selling point. You don't get anything from it, and as a rep for one of the portable player manufacturers quipped, "*Not* SDMI-compliant may be the best slogan to have."

Controls

Can you use them without looking at the player? This requires field testing at the nearest electronics store.

Player	Company	Base Memory	Formats	Size	Weight	Price	URL
MPDj MP1000	AudioVox	32 MB	MP3	63.4 x 83 x 18.3 mm	56g without battery	$179	http://www.audiovox.com/mp3/mp3.html
Cabo MP3-64	Best Data	64 MB	MP3	66 x 90 x 18 mm	74g without batteries	$249	www.cabomusic.com
c@mp CP-UF32	HIT	32 MB	MP3	63 x 102 x 11.5mm	78g without battery	$180	http://www.mp3player.co.kr/
Nomad II	Creative Labs	64 MB	MP3, WMA	65 x 93 x 21 mm	88g without battery	$330	http://www.nomadworld.com
Nomad II	Creative Labs	32 MB	MP3, WMA	65 x 93 x 21 mm	88g without battery	$170	http://www.nomadworld.com
Nomad 32	Creative Labs	32 MB	MP3, WMA	58 x 85 x 17mm	64g without batteries	$230	http://www.nomadworld.com
Nomad 32	Creative Labs	32 MB	MP3, WMA	58 x 85 x 17mm	64g without battery	$330	http://www.nomadworld.com
Nomad 64	Creative Labs	64 MB	MP3, WMA	58 x 85 x 17mm	64g without battery	$400	http://www.nomadworld.com
Nomad II mg	Creative Labs	64 MB	MP3, WMA	58 x 90 x 18 mm	64g without battery	$400	http://www.nomadworld.com
Nomad Jukebox	Creative Labs	6 GB	MP3, WMA	127 x 127 x 38.1 mm	397g with rechargable battery	$600	http://www.ondigo.com/home.html
Rio PMP300	Diamond Multimedia	32 MB	MP3	88.9 x 63.5 x 16 mm	46 without battery	$169	http://www.riohome.com
Rio 500	Diamond Multimedia	64 MB	MP3	91.2 x 62.48 x 18.8 mm	54g without battery	$270	http://www.riohome.com
Pocket Digital Audio Player	Dynamic Naked Audio	0 MB	MP3	46 x 53 x 16 mm	30g without battery	$68	http://www3.dynamicnakedaudio.com/html/prod_pda.html
MPMan MP20*	Eiger Labs	32MB	MP3	91.4 x 69.9 x 16.5 mm	68g without battery	$130	http://www.eigerlabs.com/mpman/index.htm
Nex	Frontier Labs	64 MB	MP3	69 x 69 x 21mm	55g without battery	$180	www.nex-player.com
Personal Jukebox PJB-100	Hango	4.86GB	MP3	149.86 x 81.28 x 25.4 mm	278g without battery	$750	http://www.pjbox.com/
eGo	i2go	64 or 96 MB card	MP3, upgradable	69.85 x 31.75 x 114.3 mm	156g without batteries	$189-$499	http://www.i2go.com/asp/pgobject.asp
I-Jam	I-JAM Multimedia	0 MB	MP3	85.73 x 50.8 x 23 mm	71g without battery	Parallel $220; USB $270	www.ijamworld.com
WinJam	I-JAM Multimedia	32 MB	WMA	85.73 x 50.8 x 23 mm	71g without battery	$130	www.ijamworld.com
D'music SM-320V	Pine Technology USA	32 MB	MP3, CDA	85 x 63 x 17.5 mm	62g without battery	$249	http://www.pineusa.com/
Pontis SP 503	Pontis	0 MB	MP3	20 x 110 x 70 mm	90g without battery	$229	http://www.pontis.de/
OmniPlayer	Sphere Multimedia Technologies	32 MB	Line-Out	11.76 x 68.58 x 30.48 mm	97g without batteries	$199	http://www.omniplayer.com
JazPiper* MVR64P	RFC	64 MB	MP3	66 x 90 x 18 mm	74g without batteries	$249	www.jazpiper.com
DAP pro	Right Technology	32 MB	MP3	90 x 60 x 15 mm	70g without batteries	$199	http://righttechnology.com/
DAP 64 pro	Right Technology	64 MB	MP3	90 x 60 x 15 mm	70g without batteries	$199	http://righttechnology.com/products.htm
DAP exe	Right Technology	128 MB	MP3	90 x 60 x 15 mm	70g without batteries	$349	http://righttechnology.com/products.htm
VAIO Music Clip	Sony	64 MB	MP3, ATRAC3	119.1 x 23.1 x 22.4 mm	42.5g without battery	$299	http://www.ita.sel.sony.com/jump/musicclip/#
Yepp YP-E64	Samsung	64 MB	MP3	65 x 87 x 17.2 mm	53g without batteries	$230	http://samsungelectronics.com/products/yepp/yepp.html
MS Walkman	Sony	64 MB	MP3, ATRAC3	119.1 x 23.1 x .22.4 mm	63g without battery	$400	http://www.ita.sel.sony.com
Lyra	RCA / Thompson	32-64 MB	MP3 & Real	114.3 x 63.5 x 23 mm	94g without battery	RD2201 $170 RD2204 with car kit $250	http://www.lyrazone.com
Rome	Unitech	32 MB	MP3	63 x 102 x 11.5 mm	60g without battery	$199	www.romemp3.com

BT=Bass /Treble   P=Pre-sets   LCD=Liquid Crystal Display   SM=Smart Media   MMC=Multimedia Card   CF=Compact Flash
HD=Hard Drive   MS=Memory Stick   WMA=Windows Media Audio   ATRAC3=Proprietary Sony audio format

176

Extras

Some players come with FM radio; an equalizer with presets for classical, jazz, rock, and other music styles; multi-line LCD read-outs; and a memo voice recorder. The most intriguing of these is the ability of the portable players to hold non-musical, regular computer files, such as Excel and WordPerfect documents. That's handy if you have to take some data on the road or simply want to transfer files that are too big for a Zip disk. But generally, in a trade-off among memory and features, you're better off putting the money into larger memory. When the thrill of downloading to a player fades away, you'll spend most of your time listening to the set of tunes on a single memory card. Get as many songs as you can into the memory at once.

The following chart covers the players that are the real players in the market at this time. Use the table to narrow down the search and then head for the discount electronics store that usually has the biggest selection of products.

What Else Can I Use MP3s With?

Not much. For now. One of the problems with MP3 songs, or any format other than WAV, is that you can't play MP3-inhabited CDs on the normal compact disc player you have in the entertainment center, the car, the other car, or any Walkman-type CD player.

Just think. On a single home-burned CD, using MP3s, you could put the equivalent of a dozen ordinary compact discs. Suddenly your car has 10 hours of ever-changing music without you having to carry CDs in the glove compartment. And under the seat, and in the back seat, and in the trunk.

And, to think of it, most PCs are located where the best sound system is and where the family—the adults, anyway—usually listen to music. You've got 1,000 songs on your hard drive. If you could only connect your family room's sound system and your PC, you're talking major party.

You can connect the two by simply running some inexpensive cables from the sound out port on your PC sound card to the signal in jacks on your amp. You'll be amazed how much better the MP3s sound when they're teamed with a decent sound system. Wait till the electronics manufacturers and the record companies—which, in the case of companies like Sony, are both—begin to feel comfortable giving away the family jewels, their entire record catalogs. I imagine the marketing people on the hardware side are chomping to be set loose on a market where they can sell everyone replacements for all the CD players they already have. Already, some early birds are fighting over worms.

MP3s on Wheels

I know that walking among us today are people whose goal is to turn a car into one giant rolling audio speaker. I know because I've been to the Consumer Electronics Show, where a huge area is devoted to auto sound systems that cost more than the cars themselves. That's the equipment that makes you feel a heavy bass beat while the car is still two blocks away. I think auto-obsessions like that are probably a self-image thing, like anorexia.

These are the people who'll buy something like the Mpeg LTD, an MP3 player for the car selling for $1,200–$1,900. For your money you get a Linux computer with 6–36 gigs of hard drive storage, enough at the high end to hold 600 hours of music at bit rate of 128kb/sec. You could go nearly a month without hearing the same song twice.

The player slips in and out of a slot in the dashboard so you can fill it up at your PC using a USB or serial port connection. (Wireless models are in the works.) Last I heard, they were taking back-orders at `http://www2.empeg.com/main.html`.

Nomad Jukebox

Any player that doesn't fit into a shirt pocket has one strike against it. But Creative's Nomad Jukebox—about the size and, for some reason, the shape of a portable music CD player—stores up to 600 gigabytes of MP3, WMA, and WAV files by using laptop hard drives. That's about 100 hours, and if it doesn't fit in a shirt pocket, it still weighs less than a pound and runs on four AA batteries. $600 is also a better deal than the car MP3 player. Look at it as a dollar a gig. And consider that the biggest flash memory is a 224MB CompactFlash card, which only the RCA Lyra player can use, and costs $800. Shirt-pocket size suddenly seems not that all-important.

But here's the cool thing: time-scaling technology. It lets you speed up or slow down the playback without sacrificing audibility. You can get Backstreet Boys to sing a song in a fraction of the time without sounding like chipmunks. It's the same notes, only played and sung really fast. If it's not actually on the market by the time you read this, check out `http://www.nomadworld.com/products/nomad-jukebox`.

MP3 for the Handheld

All you executive-on-the-go types are already carrying Palm computers. Surely there's a way to fill them with a few tunes. And that way is the MiniJam, but it's designed for the HandSpring, which uses the same operating system. Palm users can look for one to come their way sooner on later. Meanwhile, droll at http://innogear.com/start1.htm#.

Haven't graduated to the executive class yet? Then accomplish pretty much the same thing with a SongBoy. It plugs into your GameBoy and plays audio—and video—Windows media files downloaded from a PC. And it doubles as a voice recorder. It costs only about $80, but you need a couple of 32MB memory cards to get the total 90-minute storage capacity.

Home Sound System Player

You know that CD player you bought 10 years ago—the one you thought was so cool because it has a carousel that holds three CDs? Well, throw it out. For $240 you can replace it with a combo CD/CVD/MP3 player. With Karaoke, yet!

Raite's AVPhile 715 and 715K players read the ID tags on MP3 files and display the information on their own displays. They're not widely distributed yet. Try a Frye's Electronics if you're near one. Or check out http://www.raite.com.tw/edefault.htm.

Becoming a Broadcasting Mogul

Or here's another way to get your PC communicating with the sound system. The Radio Webcaster from In House Radio Networks takes the output from your PC's sound card and transmits it over any unused FM band. With a range of about that of a cordless phone, it spreads your own private music to any room in the housewith an FM receiver. It comes with a remote control for $149 and is available on the Web at www.radiowebcaster.com.

All these prices, by the way, are what's called "estimated street prices." What that really means is that the manufacturers don't want to tell you the suggested retail price because they're afraid the prices would scare you off. But the dealers like the SRPs because it lets them boast about the gargantuan discount they'll give you because they like your face. The prices you actually encounter may vary widely. Traditionally, cutting edge technology commands a high price when it's new and scarce. Give it a year or two and the prices will drop to the merely outrageous.

How Can I Create My Own Music CDs?

Of the music compact discs you own, how many are perfect? By perfect I mean that each and every song on the disc is one that you like. Not many, huh? Even the best CD albums have one or two clunkers that have you hitting the next track button each time they start playing. And too often the song that prompted you to buy the CD in the first place is a ringer, the only song on the whole disc that's tolerable.

The obvious solution: Make your own music CDs. You'll need hardware—a recordable CD-ROM drive (CD-R) and some blank CD-R discs, which cost a measly $25 for a box of 20. And you'll need software. RealJukebox will do nicely, and you already have it on the book's CD. Then you'll find there are two ways of recording your own CDs: Quick-and-dirty and slow-and-clean. We'll look at both ways.

Mind you, these are *music* CDs—the kind that you pop into your regular CD player in the entertainment center, in your car, or dangling from your hip. You don't need a computer to play these, but you can. You can even rip MP3s from these CDs and start the whole process over again! But if you do that, chances are you've contracted a serious obsession and need help.

Getting Started

If you have a rewritable CD drive (CD-RW)—one that lets you erase and reuse the space on it—it most likely will also record CD-R discs. With CD-R, you only get one chance at recording. If you change your mind about what songs you want on the CD, want to add more, or if you botch things up, you can't go back and change them. It seems as if CD-RW is a smarter way to go, but it's not.

CD-RW is great for backing up a hard drive's files, which will naturally change over time. You can use its rewritability to keep your backups current. But a lot of ordinary CD players can't read CD-RW discs. You're better off recording to CD-R unless you know exactly what players you'll use the CD with and can run a test of CD-RW discs to find out if the players recognize them. Also note that CD-RW and CD-R both read CD-ROMs. So if you're hard up for space to add drives to your computer system, a single CD-RW can take care of all your recording and CD playing.

Most writable CD drives are basically similar. The less expensive ones use an IDE interface—the same electronics inside your computer that your hard drive and floppy drive are connected to. Some external drives connect to the parallel port or a USB port. There are also writable CDs for SCSI connections, which are faster but more expensive.

The discs you use with CD-R, though, are not all the same. Some brands simply don't perform well with certain CD-R drives. Don't rush out a buy a stack of 100 recordable discs until you tried at least one of the same brand to make sure it and your drive are compatible.

As for software, it's highly likely that recording software came with your CD-R or CD-RW drive. (It didn't? Log on to the manufacturer's Web site to see if one's available there for free. If it's not, it's time for a nasty email!) It's probably a variation on recording software made by Adaptec, better known for its drive adapters. You may simply use that software and follow its instructions, but if you do that, you'll lose the synergy that comes from burning with the same software you use to organize your music. The instructions in this chapter are for using RealJukebox to burn CDs. (That's right, campers—RealJukebox doesn't just take music from CDs, it can put music onto blank ones as well.) The principles hold for any recording program. You can also burn CDs using MusicMatch Jukebox, the other MP3 suite on the book's CD-ROM. But because the first step in recording is assembling a playlist, it's easier with Real's software.

Port Pointers

The people who make PCs simply love to confuse matters by creating new types of connections that would work with half the devices made to connect to computers. Here's a quick guide to the alphabet soup of connectors and their advantages and disadvantages.

IDE (Integrated Drive Electronics): This is an inexpensive connection for floppy, hard, and optical drives that is built into every PC today. It's only middling fast, and can support only four drives, but it's cheap and writable CD drives for it are also the cheapest.

SCSI (Small Computer System Interface): So named in order that computer geeks would have a cute word to banter about— "scuzzy." It is the most expensive and fastest of peripheral connections, and there are many flavors with different speeds. PCs do not ordinarily come with them, and you must buy an SCSI expansion card—less than $100—to use SCSI devices with it. Those devices can include CD drives, hard drives, printers, and scanners. SCSI peripherals are typically faster and more expensive than IDE add-ons. The most SCSI devices that can be connected to one port is seven.

USB (Universal Serial Bus): All new PCs have one or two small, flat rectangular ports to which anything from a mouse to a printer or hard drive can be connected. They are fast enough for most operations, and they can be daisy-chained from one USB device to another so that there is virtually no end of devices you can add to your PC via USB.

Parallel Port: This is the port most printers connect to. It's not your ideal connection for speed, but CD-writable drives designed for the parallel port are among the least expensive, and may be your only alternave if you're using a older laptop with no USB and no way to add a SCSI port.

Faster Burns

The first recordable CD drives were 1X, meaning that it took as long to record a CD as it would take to listen to it. Now any new CD-R or CD-RW will be at least 2X, meaning tracks are recorded in half the time it takes to play them. If burning CDs becomes a habit with you, upgrade to LaCie 12X CD-RW. Not all discs are capable of recording at this speed, which takes only five minutes to fill an entire CD-R. In that case, use 8X discs with LaCie. The drive performs a test to see if the discs are capable of 12X. If not, it downshifts to 8X. LaCie's burn rate for rewritable CDs is 4X. The drive lists for $459 at the time of this writing, when they were brand new. Prices will undoubtedly get better.

You'll need two additional pieces of software to use RealJukebox, assuming they didn't come with your CD recorder. One is an adaptation of the core of Adaptec's Easy CD Creator. It's called engsetup.exe and only works with RealJukebox. Download it at http://www.adaptec.com/realdeal. This version allows you to record CDs at 2X speeds—twice as fast as it would take to play the CD. If you want to take advantage of faster recording at speeds up to 12X—provided your recorder can handle the speed—plus additional features for making data, video, and music CDs, consider purchasing a full copy of Adaptec Easy CD Creator Deluxe. It costs about $90—pricey software just for having fun, but not too pricey for the consummate CD creator. It has really cool features such as the ability to crossfade songs as they're recorded, and it has good functions to use your CD recorder for backup.

When you launch engsetup.exe, directions tell you how to install the software on your system. (Actually, it becomes a part of RealJukebox, rather than a separate program on your PC.) After it's installed, be sure you reboot your system.

The second piece of software is a RealJukebox plug-in. *Plug-ins* are chunks of code that provide added capabilities to software. The only way to get the plug-in is through the jukebox. Run RealJukebox and click the Devices button in the toolbar, or use the menus to select Tools, Add Device. Either way you wind up at a window that shows what you already have, such as a plug-in to download songs to a portable CD player. Right-click anywhere in the window and choose Add Devices. You'll get a screen like the one in Figure 8.1. The list that appears next should include Adaptec Creator Plug-in. If it doesn't, make sure you're connected to the Internet and click the Update List button. Jukebox will contact Real's Web site to get the latest list of devices.

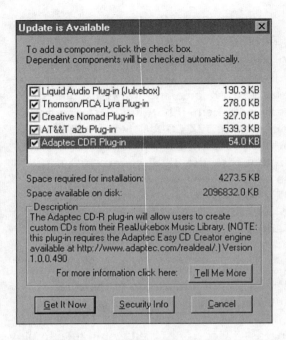

Figure 8.1: *RealJukebox's Add Devices Screen*

Go to this dialog box to add the engines for writing to a CD-R as well as set up RealJukebox to transfer songs to a portable MP3 player.

Select the Creator plug-in and click OK. Nothing much will appear to happen, but Jukebox is actually adding to itself a small piece of software that lets it work with Adaptec Creator. When it's finished installing, you'll see a new addition under the Devices branch at the bottom of the Organizer—Adaptec Creator Plugin. It you click on it without a blank, recordable disc in the drive, RealJukebox complains, "No storage detected. Check connections and press F5 to refresh." The connections are not the problem. It just can't find a disc it can record to.

Now you're ready to record your first CD. Or to be cool, you're set to burn!

Burning Quick and Dirty

The first thing to do is create a *burn list* of the songs you want on the CD. You can choose any of Jukebox's preconfigured lists for albums—not very imaginative—or you can assemble your own list of songs to create a fast, custom CD of tunes.

But first, put a blank recordable CD in your CD-R or CD-RW drive. You won't be able to add songs to the list of files to be burned without a blank disc in the drive. If you have a CD-R that's only partially filled, it can't be used for the remaining space.

Now open the Add Tracks window. To do so, click the View menu and select Go To, Portable Music, Players/Storage. A list of installed devices appears in the main window. Make sure the Adaptec Creator Plug-in is selected. If it is, the main window will list the make and model of your drive, something such as "Memorex CDRW 1622 D3.9," which is the name of the drive I use.

Creating a Burn List from a Playlist

If you've already gathered the songs you want to burn to a single playlist, open that playlist by clicking the plus-sign box next to the playlist's name in the Organizer. The songs in that playlist should appear in the main window. Select all of them and, in the Command Bar on the right, click Copy To, Device. If the Adaptec plug-in is not already selected, click it and then the OK button.

Automatic Timing

Use the AutoPlaylist feature to get the most music squeezed onto CD, so long as you don't care exactly which files you record. AutoPlaylists, discussed in Chapter 7, "How Do I Play MP3s? And How Do I Keep Track of 1,000 Songs?" are files chosen from the playlists and groupings you specify. Set the total time for all tracks in the list to 74 minutes, the most a CD of uncompressed music files can hold. In seconds the automatic feature produces a list that comes to within seconds of the max. Don't like the particular combination? Tell it to remix.

Creating a Burn List Using Add Tracks

If you haven't already prepared a playlist for the songs you want to burn, assemble a burn list with the Add Tracks window. With the Adaptec Creator Plug-in highlighted in the Organizer, right-click the name of your writable drive in the main window and choose Add Tracks. Voilà: An Add Tracks window appears. And, not unsurprisingly, at this point, the list is empty.

You'll fill it by combining songs from anywhere in RealJukebox's song database into a burn list that appears in the Add Tracks window. The window includes a sort of mini-Organizer that lists all the groupings and playlists where you can find songs. Open a grouping or playlist by clicking on the plus-mark boxes. Select all the songs you want to burn by clicking song names as you hold down the Shift or Ctrl key. Add them to your burn list by clicking the Add Tracks button. (If you're not sure whether a track is one you want to copy to CD, first click the Preview button at the bottom of the Add Tracks window to listen to it.)

While you're using the Add Tracks window, the bigger main window of RealJukebox should be visible in the background. By moving the Add Tracks window up a bit, you can see the part of the main window that tells you the total size of all the files you've selected so far and how much room is left on the CD. Each time you add a track to your burn list, the numbers change. The limit is 650MB, or 74 minutes.

What Music Formats Does RealJukebox Burn?

RealJukebox burns all songs to CD in the CDA format (compact disc audio) used by music discs. RealJukebox automatically converts songs from MP3, WMA, WAV, and RealAudio (RA) formats into CDA. If you want to burn Liquid Audio, Mjuice, or a2b music files, you'll need to convert them first to MP3s manually using TotalRecorder. (See Chapter 6, "How Do I Convert My Music CDs to MP3 Files?")

Go to other playlists and groups, repeating the process until you think you have more than enough tracks to fill a disc. When you have finished selecting all the tracks for your CD, click Close to close the Add Tracks window. You're returned to the main screen, which now displays the songs chosen for transfer, something similar to Figure 8.2. If you've selected too many songs, the overflow will be highlighted at the bottom of the list.

In Figure 8.2, we're two files too many to fit everything on disc. After Bowie's "Major Tom," there's only 50MB of room left on the CD—not enough to squeeze in "Band on the Run" and "Bad Boys" both. But notice that "Bad Boys" is only 38MB, easily small enough to fit in the remaining 50 megs of space. By dragging "Bad Boys" so that it comes before "Band on the Run," the burn list now includes it in the tracks ready to transfer. (Actually, we now have 12MB of space left. If we could find a track no bigger than that, we could add it to the list to fill the disc completely.)

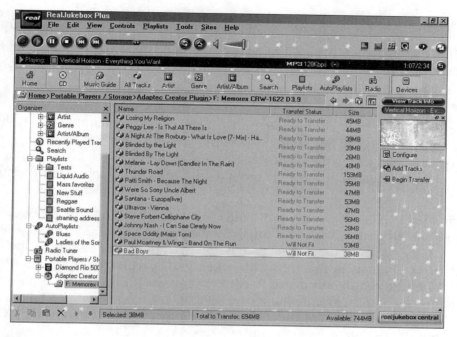

Figure 8.2: *Burn List.*

As you gather songs to be recorded to CD, RealJukebox creates a burn list with a running total of file sizes to keep you within the storage bounds of a CD.

Burning to a Portable MP3 Player

The process of assembling a playlist to record on disc is almost identical to what you do to send files to a portable player, such as a Rio or I-Jam. Instead of selecting the writable CD, choose the player as the device. If your player isn't among those listed, right-click the Portable Players / Storage item in the Organizer, and choose Add Device.

Burning

Once you're satisfied with the selection of songs and the order in which they'll be recorded, click the Begin Transfer button in the Command Bar on the right side of the RealJukebox window. The window displays a running account of the songs as they're transferred to disc. If all goes well, you won't be needed for the next half-hour or so.

Actually, that's a polite way of telling you to get lost. It's not that you're not needed. It's that you shouldn't try to do anything else with your PC while it's burning a disc. The job is very time sensitive, and if you're recalculating an Excel spreadsheet while burning, you could wind up with stutters in the final product. Bring a book.

If you are needed, it will be because of an error message that tells you that burning has halted prematurely. You have a choice of forging on in hopes that it's a momentary glitch or aborting the burn. Give it a try if you want to, but chances are good you're already fried. If you choose to abort, you'll save the songs already recorded. But if you continue, the entire disc may become unusable.

You could, theoretically, record audio tracks in *multisession*, a mode that lets you record some files, stop, and record more files later. But an audio CD player will only play the tracks in the first session. If you need multiple session capability, cough up the money for the full version of Easy CD Creator, the program whose engine does the actual burning in RealJukebox. It lets you add one or more audio tracks to a disc incrementally over several writings *without* closing a session, until you are ready to close it. The disc cannot be played in a normal CD-ROM drive or home or car stereo until the session is closed.

This is why it's a good idea to populate a playlist or autoplaylist and then select all the songs in it and click the Copy To command to send them all to the burn list. If something goes wrong, you can't count on the burn list still being there to try with a new disc. If you haven't created a playlist just for the songs you want to transfer to disc, you'll have to go through the selection process all over again.

Hey! What Happened to All My Tag Information?

It's easy to become too pampered by the wealth of information about the name of a track, the artist, and the scads of other information stored in MP3 tags and especially in RealJukebox's database. When you record your first writable CD, you may be surprised to look at the tracks through RealJukebox and not see the tag data. Although some of that information is stored in an MP3 file in addition to the jukebox's database, it's not retained when a track is converted to CDA, the file format used on music CDs. Not even the song's name is preserved. Using Windows

Explorer, look at an audio CD you've burned. The tracks will be named Track01.cda, Track02.cda, Track03.cda, etc. Even when RealJukebox is playing the burned tracks, the player can't tell you the name of the songs. The only way RealJukebox has to obtain the information from the online CD Data Base is by matching the start and stops times of the tracks against Gracenote. Because this is a custom disc, if its times match those of any album in the CDDB, it's an extraordinary coincidence. RealJukebox takes the best guess it can, but is always wrong. Click the check box that tells RealJukebox not to try to find a match for that disc.

(Curiously, when a wave file is burned as a CDA, some track information is stored with it. And although you'll only see Track01.cda with a file manager, RealJukebox—and other MP3 players—display the tag information while playing the song. Only it's the wrong track information. A King Crimson song, for example, was constantly identified as something from a Michael Jackson 1992 souvenir single. MP3s, WMA, and Mjuice files burned to disc don't do this. I have no idea why.

How to Record Better CDs

As usual with computers, it can't be all this simple. It's not. Here are some guidelines to follow to improve your odds of coming away with usable CDs.

Check Your Disk Space

A CD-R holds up to 650MB of data—74 minutes of audio. Recording to a CD works best as one long, uninterrupted burn. That's why RealJukebox first stores all the tracks to one large, temporary file—or will if you have 650MB of space. And if whatever space you do have is badly fragmented, the process may still be bumpy. If you don't regularly defrag your hard drive—which you should do for better performance even if you aren't recording to CD—run Windows Disk Optimizer or a defragger from Symantec or another utility maker to gather your free disk space into one big field where the temporary file can exist in one piece. For Disk Optimizer, click Start, Programs, Accessories, System Tools, Disk Defragmenter. The first time you defrag, the process may be lengthy because your drive is bad shape. But frequent and regular maintenance defrags will go much faster.

Choose Your Blank Discs Carefully

Many different brands of blank CD-R discs are available. The most common difference among them is the different color dyes that are changed by the heat of the drive's laser so it can record data as bits—0s and 1s, which are recorded as *scorched* and *unscorched* areas. But not all dyes work well with the lasers on all CD-R and CD-RW drives. If you have a fast CD recorder—4X or higher—make sure the discs you get are recommended for faster speeds.

Oh, and don't use CD-rewritable discs. They're more expensive and some music CD players—those that live their lives without being surrounded by a computer—don't read them at all.

Let Up on Using Your PC During Burns

Do not use your computer while burning CDs. The CD burn process is extremely memory intensive, and using other programs may interrupt the process. The CD recorder has a memory *buffer* to protect against interruptions and slowdowns. But if the interruption is so long that the recorder's buffer is drained completely, a *buffer underrun* occurs, recording stops, and most often the recordable CD is irretrievably damaged. If it is playable, you may find flaws in the form of tracks that are too short, muted, or skip within the song. And you thought we left those days behind with our old, scratched vinyl albums!

Turn Off AutoRecord

Disable the AutoRecord feature of RealJukebox. This feature automatically starts recording MP3s from a disc inserted into the drive. That's handy when you're ripping several CDs. On some CD-R drives, the Adaptec plug-in ejects a CD and then reloads it to let you know the burn was successful. If AutoRecord is enabled, RealJukebox will attempt to record your new CD to the hard drive.

How to Record the *Best* CDs

I told you earlier that this was the quick-and-dirty way to record to discs. The symmetry of time and matter in the universe demands that there be a slow and clean way to record. Here it is.

Rip to Wave

MP3 files can't be edited directly, which is a problem if you want to do anything with them, such as extract a sound clip, change the volume, or mix a couple of tracks into one. There is an obvious detour around that problem, though. Just convert the MP3 files to the storage-hungry WAV format, edit away, and then convert the tracks back to MP3.

But MP3 is a lossy compression format. That means the process of making a file smaller involves throwing away some of the data that's in the original, uncompressed file. The loss is irreversible. If a wave track is compressed to an MP3 file and then uncompressed to a WAV again, the newer wave file is *not* identical to the original WAV.

Now, the entire idea behind MP3s is that the compression losses are not supposed to be noticeable. For practical purposes, you can take that as gospel. I cannot detect the differences between a regular CD and its MP3 spin-off played on the same sound equipment. But I'm oblivious to a lot of things. If you have a keen ear, and if you want to record to CD so you capture every nuance of the original song, don't convert the songs to MP3 anywhere along the way.

This means that when you rip songs, whether in MusicMatch or RealJukebox, you must rip them to wave files, which, except for a few file formalities, are identical to CD music tracks. Burn your recordable CDs from the original waves, and the sound quality should be absolutely untouched, regardless of how sensitive or insensitive someone is to music's subtleties. A few other editing tasks require songs to be in wave format. But after you're past all those and the burning session, you can convert the waves to the smaller MP3s and zap the wave files to free up space on your hard drive.

Sounds fine—if you're an audiophile with unlimited hard drive space. In the real world of tin ears and 10-gig drives, we compromise. For all practical purposes, most people won't notice the difference.

Normalizing

When a brand-name music CD is created, the volumes of all the songs on the disks are roughly the same, allowing for deliberately quiet passages and storming finales. But the volume of songs on one CD may be widely different from the sound levels on other discs.

We don't usually notice this when we listen to one complete CD after another. Even with CD carousel changers, there's enough of a pause between the CDs that we aren't comparing two sound levels. And if some CD is a blaring exception, we turn down the volume and it's perfectly fine for the rest of that disc. But when you burn songs from different CDs, the unevenness of the sound levels from song to song is often painfully obvious.

The solution is to set all the tracks to the same volume level, known as *normalizing* the tracks. This is done with software that listens to the sound levels of several tracks you plan to group together and changes the volumes of all the tracks so that they're equal.

This operation is, ideally, performed on WAV files. But that's ideal. We've already agreed to compromise, for convenience, space savings, and for all those MP3s you have where...well, let's just say the original CD isn't easy to put your hands on.

Shuffler, which we looked at in Chapter 7, makes it easy to convert MP3s to WAVs and back again. And RealJukebox has its own ability to transform MP3, WAVs, and WMAs from one to another with fine-adjustment control over things such as bit rates.

But why bother when, as luck has it, there's a program—MP3 Educator—that let's you normalize a folder full of MP3 files without having to translate them to waves in a separate operation. It converts the MP3s to WAVs, normalizes all of them in comparison to each other, and then converts them back to MP3s—all without you having to pay attention to it.

MP3 Educator is fully functional and free for 15 days. After that, it'll cost you $13.50 to register it. You'll find a link to it at www.MP3Under.com.

Skips, Crackles, and Pops Elimination

If you're converting to MP3 the stack of vinyl records that's been gathering memories in the attic, take a look at Wave Corrector, an audio utility on the book's CD specifically designed to deal with the noisiness of vinyl. Working only with wave files, it automatically sniffs out the pops and other noise on an old recording and filters the bad noise out of the good noise. The cost to register it is $45. But if capturing those old records is important enough for you to spend your time ripping them, go all the way.

If the distortions you need to eliminate from a file are more on the order of background noise behind conversation and tape hiss, use WAVClean. It's good at altering the overall, ambient sound of a recording. After WAVClean scrubs a file, it lets you play the original and the cleaned up file. If it needs more scrubbing—or stayed in the tub a bit too long—you adjust the scrubber with a handy slide control. The free version, available through a link at www.MP3Under.com, does only the first 100 seconds of a song, and after 30 days, the length gradually shrinks until it vanishes or you register for $20. (Isn't it amazing, the clever ways programmers create their software to entice you to pay for it? You would think the record companies, instead of carping about MP3s, could be equally clever.)

Labeling and Covering

We did say this was supposed to be the very best CD. So we'll talk a bit about labeling. The best, all-around labeling device is a permanent-ink marker, like you buy in any office supply or school book store. There are programs out there—look for links at www.MP3Under.com—that let you create CD jewel case covers and the labels that go directly on a CD. You add graphics, song titles, make up your own album title, and essentially spend a couple of hours making it look pretty. I've done a few like this, as presents, but otherwise it's a lot of bother.

If you do want to do labeling, though, let me give you two tips. One, get the pre-cut disc labels that have only two labels to a page, laid out identically. Some come with three labels to a sheet, laid out in a little zigzag. On those, you'll never get the label to print in the right place. Two, don't try to apply the disc label to the CD with your bare hands. You'll never get it on without wrinkles, at best. The plastic thingie in the HP CD-Labeler II kit that aligns the label evenly with the disc works just fine.

Have fun.

Epilogue

In the course of researching and writing this book for six months, it's possible some songs I don't have the rights to made it to my hard drive. But most of the songs I downloaded were from CDs or cassettes or records that I'd purchased at least once in my lifetime. I can't help feeling I still have a right to listen to those songs even if I can't find the medium they were on at one time. I'm never going to repurchase the Melanie album I had in the '70s. I'd be too embarrassed to ask for it at Tower Records. But I was happy to meet an old friend in MP3 form: Melanie's "Lay Down (Candles in the Wind)." The sounds of it rushed me back to a particular moment I had forgotten I had forgotten. My son, Michael, who wrote the reviews of Web sites for the book, and I were both sprawled on the living room floor listening to the best white spiritual to make the Top 40. Nothing big. Not a momentous occasion. But just one happy minute that I would never have relived but for MP3s, Napster, and some other Melanie fan on the Internet I'll never meet and never know.

Top 101 Internet Audio Sites

Portal Sites ♪ Outlaw Sites ♪ Big Five Record Labels ♪ Search Engines ♪ Music Genre-specific ♪ Online Music Stores ♪ Independent (Indie) Bands ♪ Resources ♪ Webcasts/ On-line Radio ♪ Miscellaneous Sites

Reviewed by Michael White

There are so many MP3 and other music sites on the Web, you could easily waste a lifetime surfing mindlessly from one to the other. That's fine for most of you, but some people actually have lives. For those of us who do, here are the best 101 MP3 sites we could find.

Some of the choices are obvious. Others get pretty subjective. But whatever you want to get out of Internet music, these 101 sites are the best places to start looking for it. We've arranged the sites into 10 categories:

♪ **Portal**—One-stop surfing for all your MP3 needs and links to other Web sites. Included are *mega-portals*, which do the same, only a lot more of it.

♪ **Outlaw**—Sites that have downloads and links to a curiously large number of songs by bands you've actually heard of.

♪ **Big Five**—Sites run by the major music labels.

♪ **Search Engine**—Specialists in finding song files at other sites.

♪ **Genre**—Sites that concentrate on one or two types of music.

♪ **Music Store**—Sites for buying music.

♪ **Indie**—Launching pads for independent bands and mucho free music.

♪ **Resource**—Good sites to find MP3 and other music related software, hardware, and info.

♪ **Webcast**—Sites providing MP3, Real Audio/Video, or Windows Media streams, which can be audio-only or video casts.

♪ **Misc**—The name tells all: We couldn't figure out where else it belongs.

Each site includes star ratings, from five stars (★★★★★) for excellent to one star (★) for don't-go-there. The real duds where culled out, but a lot of good sites that didn't make the cut are discussed in the reviews for each site. All in all, with other sites referenced in the reviews of the best 101, you'll find information on more than 300 sites. The reviews tell you which audio formats are supported, the quality of BYAHO (bands you've actually heard of) and indie downloads, where to get software and news, a quick best reason to surf each site, and an in-depth review. Updates to these reviews and reviews of new sites are found at the book's own Web page, www.mp3under.com.

To start, we'll look at *The* MP3 site, the one to which other sites owe homage for its leadership in the MP3 community, and the first one the record companies seem to think of when it comes to filing lawsuits: MP3.com.

Guide to Terms

BYAHO = Bands you've actually heard of. **Chat/Msg. boards** = as relates to music and/or potential to share/trade MP3s via email. **Linked** = Feature is not at the site itself, but is offered through a link to another site. **Links** = The quality of a site's links. **LQT** = Liquid Audio format. **N/A** = Not applicable. **RA** = Real Audio format. **Radio** = Streams of real-world and online radio stations. **Webcasts** = refers to usually long, streaming audio and/or video, such as concerts, band interviews, music programs, music videos, or complete album streams created specifically for the Web. Webcasts can also be live or archived. **Wizard** = Search engine that finds songs based on your musical preferences. **WMA** = Windows Media Audio format.

Portal Sites

1. MP3.com ★★★★★ **CATEGORY: Portal > Megasite > Megamegasite**
URL: **www.mp3.com**

Best reason to surf this site: This is a great starting point for all MP3 explorations.

Audio file formats: MP3 **Streaming audio formats:** MP3, RA, WMA **Free BYAHO songs:** ★★★ **Indie songs:** ★★★★★

Music variety: ★★★★★ **Speed:** ★★★★★ **Webcasts/Videos:** ★★★★ **Radio:** ★★★★ **MP3 software:** ★★★★★

Music/MP3 news: ★★★★★ Chat/Msg. boards: ★★★★★ How-tos: ★★★★ Links: ★★★★ Search engine: ★★★★

Search:	
This site	

Search by:

Artist	Song
Genre	Alphabet
Region	Radio
Hardware	Software
News	Wizard

Buy music: Yes

Ships CDs: Yes
Price: $5.99–$9.99
Custom CDs: No
Pay per track: No

The mother of all MP3 sites, MP3.com, started by audio innocent Michael Robertson in late 1997, offers a lot for music fans and indie artists. It has *so much,* here's a quick rundown. At MP3.com, you read tons of MP3/music industry news and software and hardware reviews. Download lots of MP3/music software; post messages and chat about music, artists, software, hardware, and news in various chat rooms and forums; look up concerts and events in your city and around the world; listen to MP3.com's own online radio station, which randomly streams songs from their database; or create your own station and stream the songs *you* like from their database. Watch featured Webcasts of concerts and videos; go to www.mp3radio.com (an MP3.com and Cox Interactive Media collaboration) for more radio, Webcasts, and MP3s by bands you've actually heard of (**BYAHO**); check out MP3.com's own **E-zines** for more reviews, photos, artwork, songs, and station links; and get great deals on classical music—$4.99 for each classical CD assembled by MP3.com's experts. Buy, sell, and swap MP3 software, hardware, musical instruments, concert tickets, and more at MP3.com's partner site www.webswap.com; send MP3 greeting cards via email; and even have MP3.com send you recommendations of songs you might like based on your favorite genres.

MP3.com is one of the premier places for **solo musicians** and **indie bands** to post their MP3s, make some money, and promote themselves. You have to offer at least one free MP3 to get your own band page at MP3.com, and you sell your CDs through the site's own store. MP3.com splits 50-50 with indies for manufacturing, selling, and shipping the "Digital Automatic Music," or DAM CDs which include the ordinary music tracks plus MP3 versions. Indies can also make money and **promote themselves by taking advantage of some of mp3.com's more popular programs**. These include the **Payola** program, an auction for bidding on good song placement within mp3.com so the song will get more noticed; the **Payback For Playback** program, in which the most listened to artists get cash every month—similar to www.amp3.com's **Pay For Play** program; and the **New Music Army** program, in which indies earn 5% of CD sales from artists they've enlisted at MP3.com (MP3.com takes 45% of this). Lots more stuff. Just click the **New Artist Sign-up** link on the home page to find out how to create your own band page, upload your music, and upload artwork to be on your CD cover.

This is by far the best known MP3 site, getting more than **500,000 unique visitors a day**, making it the best site for bands to gain exposure—if they don't get lost in the crowd of over **40,000 artists.**

BYAHO have been known to post some of their music at this site, including **Alanis Morissette, Tori Amos, Tom Petty, The Eagles, Ice-T, Danzig, Billy Idol, Willie Nelson,** and **Tom Green.** In general, though, MP3.com is really geared more toward the indie musician/band.

Ironically, even though MP3.com has always gone out of its way not to violate copyright laws, MP3.com has been the target of many lawsuits, and lost a legal battle brought by the **RIAA** (Recording Industry Association of America) over the site's My MP3 service. MP3.com purchased more than 80,000 CDs, converted them to MP3 format, and placed them in a database at **www.my.mp3.com**. Prove you already have one of the CDs in that database by *beaming* your CD to My.MP3.com, and you can stream them anywhere, from any computer. At the time of this writing, MP3.com had lost suits by two record labels and was working to resolve other cases out of court. A recent judgement against the company could cost it millions of dollars and potentially put it out of business, so stay tuned to your favorite news source for further developments.

2. FindMP3.org ✮✮✮✮✮ **CATEGORY: Portal**
URL: `www.findmp3.org`

Best reasons to surf this site: This is a very easy-to-use site where you'll find lots of great links to MP3 sites in many different categories with no porn ads.

Audio file formats: MP3 **Streaming audio formats:** MP3 **Free BYAHO songs:** Linked **Indie songs:** Linked

Music variety: ✮✮✮✮ **Speed:** N/A **Webcasts/Videos:** Linked **Radio:** None **MP3 software:** Linked

Music/MP3 news: Linked **Chat/Msg. boards:** Linked **How-tos:** ✮✮ **Links:** ✮✮✮✮✮ **Search engine:** ✮✮✮

Search:
Web sites

Search by:
Artist
Song
All Words
Any Word
Phrase
Buy music: No

Not to be confused with the search engine **FindMP3.***com*, FindMP3.*org* is similar to *Pure***MP3.org**. Sound confusing? Then think this: No porn. FindMP3.org promises you will encounter no porn banners or links. And, like PureMP3, FindMP3 is a treasure of links to all sorts of MP3 Web sites in several genres and other musical categories—particularly **MP3 trading** sites, **full album downloads**, and '50s, '60s, '70s, and '80s music. The "Top Rated" section features links to MP3 sites voted best by the site's users. Using FindMP3's search engine pulls up links to sites that have MP3s by whatever band you've typed in. You won't find the BYAHO here, but you'll find links to pop-up-free sites where the name bands are.

3. AudioDreams.com ✮✮✮✮ **CATEGORY: Portal**
URL: `www.audiodreams.com`

Best reasons to surf this site: Lots of free indie MP3s, tons of MP3/music news, and links to partner and other MP3 sites. Good range of MP3 forums for posting messages.

Audio file formats: MP3 **Streaming audio formats:** None **Free BYAHO songs:** ✮ **Indie songs:** ✮✮✮✮✮

Music variety: ✮✮✮✮ **Speed:** ✮✮✮✮✮ **Webcasts/Videos:** Linked **Radio:** Linked **MP3 software:** ✮✮

Music/MP3 news: ✮✮✮✮ **Chat/Msg. boards:** ✮✮✮✮ **How-tos:** ✮✮ **Links:** ✮✮✮✮✮ **Search engine:** None

Search:
This site only

Search by:
Artist
Song
Genre
Buy music: Linked

AudioDreams.com is part of the **EatSleepMusicNetwork** and representative of a lot of MP3 sites you see—the way **MP3Yes** and **MP3Park** are representative of sites that belong to the **Change Music Network**. At AudioDreams you get lots of fast downloading, free indie MP3s, and can post messages in many MP3 forums to get site recommendations and share MP3 files. You also find lots of MP3 and music industry news and many good links to other MP3 sites. Indie artists can post their music. Similarly good partner sites: **www.cybertropics.com**, where you search FTP sites for MP3s, download *lots* of good MP3 software, read MP3/music news, participate in music forums, and more; **www.mp3shack.dk**, in Denmark, which has links to MP3 software, hardware, MP3 radio, forums, MP3 search engines, and a link to open an X-drive account to get free MP3s by BYAHO; and **www.mp3aus.com** which is an Australian partner site that is not up at the moment, but should be soon, unless, of course, they can't get it up. Go to **www.mp3.com.au** to visit another popular site from Australia with MP3 downloads, chat, charts, forums, MP3 software, lots of MP3 news, and more; **www.bigmouth.co.uk** claims to be "UK's No. 1 Music Information Station." You can check out tour/concert information, including the "Top Thirty Tours," and read lots of music headlines with links to the full stories; at **www.mp3illusion.com** search for music to buy with the Bottom Dollar search engine, read MP3 news, and get MP3 software, including a good selection of Linux/UNIX and Mac programs.

4. Music.ZDNet.com ★★★★★ CATEGORY: Portal
URL: `music.zdnet.com` or `listen.zdnet.com`

Best reasons to surf this site: Get great MP3 how-tos, post questions in widely used forums, get lots of MP3 software, and find music downloads on the Web with a search engine powered by Listen.com.

Audio formats: MP3, WMA, RA, LQT **Streaming**: MP3, RA, WMA, LQT **Free BYAHO songs**: Linked **Indie songs**: Linked

Music variety: ★★★★★ **Speed**: ★★★★★ **Webcasts/Videos**: Linked **Radio**: Linked **MP3 software**: ★★★★★

Music/MP3 news: ★★★★ **Chat/Msg. boards**: ★★★★★ **How-tos**: ★★★★★ **Links**: ★★★★ **Search engine**: ★★★★

Search:
This site
Web sites

Search by:
Artist
Album
Song
Genre
Software
Any Word
Buy music: Linked

This site is a great portal into the world of music on the Web with **excellent help** to get you on your way. If you're new to MP3, get started by reading MusicZDNet's MP3 beginner's guide and detailed **how-tos for using Gnutella and Napster**, and get even more help by using ZDNet's music/MP3 message boards to post any other questions you might have. These message boards are widely used so **you will most likely get a response**. To find music at MusicZDNet, type an artist's name in the search engine and it will pull up links to music downloads on the Web using Listen.com's search directory. You can also click Download Music to go right to the Listen.com genre page to begin your quest for music. To get radio, click Online Radio to find a link to RadioSpy.com and to find the Net Music Countdown with David Lawrence. NMC lists several different **Top 20 music charts** with links to BYAHO home pages, depending on who's on the charts at that moment. From here you also can go to the Station Locator and find links to radio stations that air the Net Music Countdown. You find links to some indie band sites from the

NMC section, too, by clicking Net Unknowns, and you get more new music by indies by clicking the **Ten Bands You Need To Hear** button—an Epitonic.com presentation—on MusicZDNet's home page. For MP3/music news, read the latest featured stories and click Articles to find lots of great MP3 special reports, interviews with artists (BYAHO), interviews with spotlighted online DJs, more how-to guides including **how-to Webcast music and videos legally,** plus many other great articles. At Music.ZDNet.com, you also find reviews of MP3/music hardware and other musical new gadgets; links to buy it; and great MP3 software downloads with written reviews, **star ratings,** the number of people who have downloaded it, version numbers, and link to lots of other related software downloads.

5. DimensionMusic.com ✶✶✶✶ **CATEGORY: Portal > Megasite**
   URL: dimensionmusic.com

Best reasons to surf this site: Participate in great general and specific topic MP3 message boards and listen to streamed MP3 online radio with more of an edgy ring.

Audio file formats: MP3 **Streaming formats:** MP3 **Free BYAHO songs:** ✶✶ **Indie songs:** ✶✶✶

Music variety: ✶✶✶ **Speed:** ✶✶✶✶✶ **Webcasts/Videos:** None **Radio:** ✶✶✶✶ **MP3 software:** Linked

Music/MP3 news: ✶✶✶✶ **Chat/Msg. boards:** ✶✶✶✶✶ **How-tos:** ✶✶✶✶ **Links:** ✶✶✶✶ **Search engine:** ✶✶✶✶

Search:	
This site	
FTP sites	
Web sites	

Search by:	
Artist	
Album	
Song	
Genre	
Format	
News	
Buy music: No	

Focusing more on hip hop, alternative, punk, and the electronic side of music, DimensionMusic is an MP3 site with an attitude. Most of this edgy music is found at DM by connecting to the DM and **Scour.com-**partnered MP3 radio broadcaster called MyCaster. You also use DM's search engine to look up all kinds of MP3s from FTP sites and HTTP sites. But DM's best dimension is its message boards. Post all sorts of MP3-related questions, including asking for URL addresses to find MP3s on the Web, to the site's great, **wide-ranging MP3 message board.** Read and post messages about a specific topic, such as Napster, in guided topic forums to get in-depth information and help about various topics. Unlike many other sites that have message boards that people rarely actually use, DM's message boards are used daily by many people, so the chances of your question getting a response is greatly increased. You can also post messages about software and music news. DM has tons of great links to music/MP3 software, utilities, and hardware, and **very good MP3 how-tos,** including in-depth explanations of how to use Napster, Music Match, Sonique Player, Winamp, and Windows Media Player. DimensionMusic is not the *most* multi-dimensional site out there, but what it has runs deep.

Other edgy sites include **www.epitonic.com,** which has lots of WMA and MP3 streams by mostly indie bands, MP3 downloads, and its own hip hop and indie rock radio. At **www.spinrecords.com** check out Spinner's artists and listen to their MP3, MOV, and ASF (Windows Media) streams. Get band info, buy their CDs, and download songs for 99 cents. At **www.snakenetmetalradio.com** listen to heavy metal radio broadcast in Shoutcast and Real Audio. Good metal charts and music scene news focus on what's hot.

6. Launch.com ★★★★★ CATEGORY: Portal > Megasite
URL: www.launch.com

Best reasons to surf this site: Watch lots of streamed music videos by BYAHO and set up a radio station tailored to your tastes. Easy look-ups for info on BYAHO, news, and reviews.

Audio file formats: MP3, WMA, LQT **Streaming audio formats:** RA, WMA, LQT **Free BYAHO songs:** ★★★ **Indie songs:** ★★★

Music variety: ★★★★ **Speed:** ★★★★★ **Webcasts/Videos:** ★★★★★ **Radio:** ★★★★ **MP3 software:** Linked: ★

Music/MP3 news: ★★★★ **Chat/Msg. boards:** ★★★★★ **How-tos:** ★★★ **Links:** ★★★★ **Search engine:** ★★★★

Search:	
This site	

Search by:	
Artist	Album
Song	Genre
Video	News
Reviews	Wizard

Buy music: Linked to CheckOut.com, where you may be able to find a used version of a CD for less money.

Launch.com is your good, basic, all-purpose, **has-a-little-of-everything site**—except for streaming videos, which it has a lot of. The best feature at Launch.com, though, is its **LaunchCast**. By asking questions about which artists and radio stations you like, Launch.com streams you the music and videos that you'll like. You share your radio station with other Launch members and listen to theirs. You also share music by email, or chat at "The Hang" to find other people with **similar musical interests**. Because this site is so well visited, there are a lot of people to share the musical wealth with. Use Launch's search engine to look up bands and get their bios, interviews, album reviews, and related news; watch streamed videos; buy their CDs; listen to song clips from the CDs; get concert info; and connect to LaunchCast stations by fans of the band. Launch has a **huge, free video section** with videos by BYAHO and indie artists, and **high-bandwidth users** can go to LaunchCity to get more videos and Webcasts. For lots of great links to music and MP3 sites, go to Launch's www.omg.com (Online Music Guide).

Having a program that nabs video comes in handy when you're on a site like this. Download a free version of a video catcher called "**HyperCam**" at www.hyperionics.com. HyperCam captures anything moving in a window, along with its sound, and automatically **converts it to an AVI file**. Because it's an AVI, you can use a program such as the Real Producer G2—a free download from www.real.com that allows you to stream AVI files—so you can stream your own video program over the Internet.

7. Listen.com ★★★★★ CATEGORY: Portal > Megasite
URL: www.listen.com

Best reasons to surf this site: Find music and video downloads on the Web by BYAHO that Listen.com has verified to be legal.

Audio file formats: MP3, WMA, LQT **Streaming formats:** MP3, RA, WMA, LQT **Free BYAHO songs:** Linked **Indie songs:** Linked

Music variety: ★★★★★ **Speed:** ★★★★★ **Webcasts/Videos:** Linked **Radio:** None **MP3 software:** Linked

Music/MP3 news: ★★★ **Chat/Msg. boards:** ★★★ **How-tos:** ★★★★★ **Links:** ★★★★★ **Search engine:** ★★★★★

Search:	
Web sites	

Search by:
Artist
Wizard
Buy music: Linked

This excellent directory site links you to other Web sites that Listen.com has verified as having **legal music downloads**. Just pick the music category you want to hear, or type a specific artist's name in the search engine, and Listen.com hunts the Web for songs available for free, song downloads for sale, music clips, and music videos. It categorizes the results by Web site. With Listen's extended partnership with Launch.com, **you'll find more videos than ever**. A good way to search for music by BYAHO is to click the Big Shots tab. The drawback when looking for BYAHO is that the majority of the search results turn out to be **30-second song previews or downloads you have to pay for**. If it comes up with at least a few complete and free downloadable songs, that's pretty good. But hey, Listen.com is doing its job as a directory site, and getting even a few songs for free by an artist you really like can be pretty exciting. When looking for songs, Listen.com also provides reviews of the song and band histories, pulls up links to similar artists you might like, and, if you become a member of Listen.com, you can vote on artists and send in your own comments. By becoming a member you can also use the **"My Page" feature**. This allows you to have your own page where you can keep up to 12 links to your favorite genres and keep a list of your favorite artists so that Listen.com can notify you if any new—and legal—downloads become available. Look in Listen.com's Help section to find a lot of good how-tos and an easy-to-use **Beginners Guide**. You'll find links to MP3/music player–related software in this section, too, and get music-related news by subscribing to Listen.com's free newsletter. For pure legal listening pleasure of music by bands you've actually heard of, this is the site.

8. MP3-City.com ✭✭✭✭ CATEGORY: Portal > Beginners
URL: www.mp3-city.com

Best reasons to surf this site: People just starting out can get basic MP3 how-tos, link to software and MP3 search engines, and use the www.mamma.com searcher to hunt the Web for any kind of site they want.

Audio file formats: N/A **Streaming audio formats:** N/A **Free BYAHO songs:** None **Indie songs:** None **Music variety:** N/A **Speed:** N/A **Webcasts/Videos:** None **Radio:** None **MP3 software:** Linked **Music/MP3 news:** None **Chat/Msg. boards:** None **How-tos:** ✭✭✭✭ **Links:** ✭✭✭✭ **Search engine:** ✭✭✭✭

Search:
Web sites

Search by:
All Words
Any Word
Buy music: No

This site has or links to **all your basic needs** to get started with MP3s. Get good MP3 help and how-tos, link to sites for tried and true MP3 software and hardware, jump to some popular MP3 search engines, and even link to some lyrics sites on the Web. MP3-City's onsite portal search engine is powered by **www.mamma.com**—"The Mother of All Search Engines." This is a very easy site to use **for those just getting familiar with MP3s**. Another similarly easy site to use with good MP3 guides and how-tos, but with a few more links to MP3 news, other MP3 sites, and a link to MP3 radio, is **www.dailymp3.com**.

9. MP3Meta.com ★★★★★ **CATEGORY: Portal > Megasite > Beginners**
URL: www.mp3meta.com

Best reasons to surf this site: Use its metacrawling MP3 search engine to learn about all MP3 has to offer. Find loads of links to all sorts of MP3-related resources, including newsgroups, karaoke, DJ, tape trading, and song writing sites.

Audio file formats: NA **Streaming audio formats:** N/A **Free BYAHO songs:** Linked **Indie songs:** Linked

Music variety: ★★★★★ **Speed:** N/A **Webcasts/Videos:** Linked **Radio:** Linked **MP3 software:** Linked

Music/MP3 news: ★★★★ **Chat/Msg. boards:** Linked **How-tos:** ★★★★★ **Links:** ★★★★★ **Search engine:** ★★★★

Search:
This site
FTP sites
Web sites
Multiple search engines

Search by:
Artist
Song
Genre
Lyrics
CD Covers
Buy music: Linked

This is a great site to find the music you're looking for through links or by search. Its **metacrawling search engine** finds MP3s from FTP sites and MP3.com, an HTTP site. It also looks for other music/band sites, CD covers, and lyric/song writing sites. MP3Meta **links by genres**. For example, if you look under "Psychedelic Rock", you'll find a link to the Syd Barrett Homepage. But the links don't stop there. No siree. It links to **MP3 newsgroups**; MP3 hardware; other MP3 search engines; musical instrument sites; music magazines; **DJ sites**; karaoke; **vocal training**; **tape trading**; music history and educational sites; sites that specifically support or relate to MP3, WAV, MIDI, RA, or MOD files; **Music That Sucks**—the list goes on. If you're new to the whole MP3 thing, MP3Meta is a good place to go because just looking through all the links gives you an idea of what MP3 can do. Don't miss the incredible "How To" section.

10. MP3Yes.com ★★★★★ **CATEGORY: Portal > Megasite**
URL: www.mp3yes.com

Best reasons to surf this site: Download MP3s by BYAHO and thousands of skins and link to MP3 software, MP3 hardware, music industry news, lyrics sites, MP3 search engines, and MP3 newsgroups.

Audio file formats: MP3 **Streaming audio formats:** N/A **Free BYAHO songs:** ★★★★ **Indie songs:** ★★★

Music variety: ★★★★ **Speed:** ★★★★★ **Webcasts/Videos:** Linked **Radio:** None **MP3 software:** Linked

Music/MP3 news: Linked **Chat/Msg. boards:** Linked **How-tos:** ★★★★ **Links:** ★★★★★ **Search engine:** ★★★★

Search:
Web sites
Multiple search engines

Search by:		
Artist		
Album		
Song		
Genre		
Video		
Buy music: No		

Unlike many other MP3 sites that offer you a lot of everything related to MP3, but fall short on giving you actual MP3 music downloads, MP3Yes remembers to include **quite a few MP3s by BYAHO**. MP3Yes is one of the best Web sites in the **Change Music Network**, and you can find or link to just about anything MP3 here. From MP3Yes, download lots of MP3 tracks, **thousands of skins**, and link to music news, MP3 software, MP3 hardware, MP3 search engines, MP3 newsgroups, general MP3 sites, and lyrics. Also, look for more MP3s and videos on the Web with **various searchers found throughout the site**. Artists can have their songs posted in the Top Downloads section for a month, and for five months in a prominent position in their archives for a flat rate of $150. If you're willing to pay that, it might be good exposure for your song because MP3Yes is visited by more than **9,000 people a day**. The only thing this site doesn't have is radio, but what it lacks in that department it makes up for with its MP3 downloads.

11. MPEG.org (AskMP3.com) ✭✭✭✭✭ CATEGORY: Portal > Technical

URL: www.mpeg.org (or, more specifically: www.askmp3.com)

Best reasons to surf this site: Find links to everything related to MP3 and the MPEG standard.

Audio file formats: N/A **Streaming formats:** N/A **Free BYAHO songs:** Linked **Indie songs:** Linked

Music variety: N/A **Speed:** N/A **Webcasts/Videos:** Linked **Radio:** Linked **MP3 software:** Linked

Music/MP3 news: Linked **Chat/Msg. boards:** Linked **How-tos:** Linked **Links:** ✭✭✭✭✭ **Search engine:**✭✭✭

Search:		
This site		
Web sites		
Multiple search engines		

Search by:		
All Words		
Any Word		
News		
Buy music: Linked		

You won't find any music downloads at MPEG.org, but you will find **great links in just about every MP3 category** you can think of. If it relates to MPEG, there's a link for it here. This award-winning site is an incredible source of information about the **MPEG standard** itself. Access the MP3 section by clicking "MP3" on MPEG.org's home page or by typing www.askmp3.com when you first get on the Internet to go directly there. The MP3 section is **simply organized**, too, and the links are often accompanied by a brief synopsis. If you want to conveniently and comprehensively branch out into the MP3 world online, consider making MPEG.org (or, AskMP3.com) **your home page**.

Other good MP3 technical sites are www.id3.org and www.iis.fhg.de (the site of the German Fraunhofer IIS-A, the original **developers of MPEG technology**). To find information right on the cutting edge of developing multimedia technology, go to MIT's www.media.mit.edu, and also check out their wild **Brain Opera**—"an interactive musical journey into your mind, that is to be presented simultaneously in physical and cyber space!"—at www.brainop.media.mit.edu.

12. MTV.com ✭✭✭✭ CATEGORY: Portal > megasite
URL: www.mtv.com

Best reasons to surf this site: Great for looking up recent and archived music news, interviews, reviews, and video.

Audio file formats: MP3, WMA, QT **Streaming audio formats**: RA **Free BYAHO songs**: ✭✭✭ **Indie songs**: ✭

Music variety: ✭✭✭✭ **Speed**: ✭✭✭✭✭ **Webcasts/Videos**: ✭✭✭✭ **Radio**: None **MP3 software**: Linked

Music/MP3 news: ✭✭✭✭✭ **Chat/Msg. boards**: ✭✭✭ **How-tos**: ✭✭✭ **Links**: ✭✭✭✭ **Search engine**: ✭✭✭✭

Search:
This site

Search by:
Artist
Song
Genre
Alphabet
News
Buy music: Linked

MTV.com focuses on more than music. It aims to be the one-stop popular culture shop for today's angst-ridden youth. (Those of you who feel a little out of touch with the times—those of us who were watching MTV 10 years ago—can go to MTV's sister site, VH1.com.) At MTV.com you can look up hundreds of popular bands and get video clips and an **amazing amount of recent and archived news**; read bios, reviews, and interviews; and visit the MTV Store to stock up on your favorite artist's paraphernalia. Also look for **local events** in your town, check music charts, chat, download some featured **MP3s and WMAs by BYAHO**, and find video/Webcasts and more MP3s sprinkled throughout the site from all the MTV shows. Find out how "Tom Green's Nuts" are doing, contribute to his charity, and, of course, don't forget to check out how the cast of the artificial *Real World* are coping.

Go to **www.mtvdd.com** for lots of **MP3** direct downloads by popular artists, but **beware of pop-ups**.

13. Music.com ✭✭✭✭✭ CATEGORY: Portal > Minimega
URL: www.music.com

Best reasons to surf this site: Buy custom CDs, download lots of indie tracks (indies can create their own band page for free), get a name for your band with the Band-O-Tron 2000, watch videos, and more.

Audio file formats: MP3, WMA, LQT **Streaming audio formats**: RA, WMA **Free BYAHO songs**: ✭✭✭ **Indie songs**: ✭✭✭✭✭

Music variety: ✭✭✭✭✭ **Speed**: ✭✭✭✭✭ **Webcasts/Videos**: ✭✭✭✭ **Radio**: ✭✭✭ **MP3 software**: Linked

Music/MP3 news: ✭✭✭✭✭ **Chat/Msg. boards**: ✭✭✭✭ **How-tos**: ✭✭✭ **Links**: ✭✭✭ **Search engine**: ✭✭✭

Search:
This site

Search by:	
Artist	Song
Genre	Alphabet
Wizard	

Buy music: Yes

Ships CDs: Yes

Avg. Price: $12.99

Custom CDs: Yes

Pay per track: Yes

Price per track: 99 cents a song plus a 5-cent burn charge

Immediate Download: No

Some site had to have the all-encompassing title of Music.com. Not only is this site the one to get it, but with its treasure-trove of music-related features, Music.com is **worthy of the title**. First of all, you can listen to **30-second Real Audio samples** of all the songs available at Music.com by indie bands and lots of BYAHO. Then, you can **buy the tracks for 99 cents** each and compile them on a customized CD that Music.com burns and mails to you. Also download free MP3s, WMAs, and Liquid Audio tracks (some by BYAHO); download the **Music.com tuner** to listen to its radio station; check concert listings and music charts; and read music news, reviews, and band interviews. Or listen to short, talking news clips and stream artist and soundtrack music videos. Subscribe to Music.com's free e-zine to get advanced notice on promotions and upcoming releases. There are links to indie artist and indie labels and a **music auction** site, **www.fleamarket.music.com**. You can also check out your horoscope to see if it's your lucky day—whatever that has to do with music—or go to Music.com's grim R.I.P. section to find **music by deceased artists**. Unsigned bands can post their music and create their own band page at The Garage for free, and, if your band doesn't have a name, get one with the Band-O-Tron 2000 **random band name generator**. There's even more good stuff to do at this site, but you get the idea…it's all about the music, man, at Music.com.

14. Pages.com ★★★★ CATEGORY: Portal > Links
URL: www.pages.com

Best reasons to surf this site: This is an easy-to-use directory site that lists more than 50,000 links to music-related sites. It's a useful resource for musicians, song writers, and fans alike.

Audio file formats: N/A **Streaming audio formats:** N/A **Free BYAHO songs:** Linked **Indie songs:** Linked

Music variety: ★★★★★ **Speed:** N/A **Webcasts/Videos:** Linked **Radio:** Linked **MP3 software:** Linked

Music/MP3 news: Linked **Chat/Msg. boards:** Linked **How-tos:** None **Links:** ★★★★★ **Search engine:** ★★★★

Search:	
This site	
Web sites	

Search by:	
Artist	
Song	
Any Word	
Buy music: Linked	

Pages.com is an **all-purpose directory** site that takes a somewhat **minimalist approach**. In all, the Music section at Pages.com comprises more than **50,000 links** to music-related sites. The sites are divided into various music categories and when you choose one, Pages.com very simply pulls up a page with a list of links to available sites in that category. Surprisingly, there's no MP3 category, but, whether you're looking for band sites, lyric sites, song writing sites, radio sites, Webcasts, karaoke, musical theater, composition sites—there are **too many categories to mention them all**—you'll find a link here. If you don't want to look by category, use the search engine—which is particularly good for looking up individual artists and songs—to browse Page's entire database of links. This is an **easy site to use**, and its bare bones interface makes for **quick-loading pages**. Of note, Pages.com is home to the popular **Lyrics.com**.

15. Real.com ★★★★★ CATEGORY: Portal > Megasite > Streaming
URL: www.real.com

Best reasons to surf this site: The home of the RealJukebox and Player on this book's CD, Real is loaded with streaming Webcasts tailored to the speed of your Internet connections and links to more audio and video.

Audio file formats: RA, MP3, LQT **Streaming audio formats**: RA, MP3, LQT **Free BYAHO songs**: ★★★ **Indie songs** ★★★★

Music variety: ★★★★ **Speed**: ★★★★ **Webcasts/Video**: ★★★★★ **Radio**: ★★★★★ **MP3 software**: ★★★

Music/MP3 news: ★★★ **Chat/Msg. boards**: None **How-tos**: ★★★★★ **Links**: ★★★★★ **Search engine**: ★★★★★

Search:		
This site		
Web sites		

Search by:		
Artist		
Album		
Song		
Genre		
Any Word		
News		
Buy music: Linked		

Even though the free version of the Real Entertainment Center—RealJukebox, RealPlayer, and RealDownload—is on the book's CD-ROM, surf to the home base to check out all the things you can do with your new player. Real.com is a terrific source for, you guessed it, finding Real Audio and Real Video. Get **streamed music/audio, music videos, video clips, television, radio, short movies, and movie trailers** from many channels available right at Real.com, or use its search engine to find the streams you need. Because RealPlayer can play **MP3 and Liquid Audio**, the search often turns up streams and downloads in these formats as well as its own Real Audio/Video formats. You can also download a **decent number of free tunes** by BYAHO. **Look for live events**, which you can capture as waves or MP3s, and check out the Webcast section—they call it Broadband—to watch featured music videos and interviews. There are **loads of skins** for the Real products and some other enhancements that may have cropped up since this book was published. And, of course, Real's **tutorials and FAQs** are the place to go if you can't figure out something from our instructions in the book.

16. RollingStone.com ★★★★★ CATEGORY: Portal > Megasite
URL: www.rollingstone.com

Best reasons to surf this site: Get music news, lots of free music downloads by indie bands and BYAHO, and tons of great audio Webcasts and videos.

Audio file formats: MP3, WMA, RA **Streaming**: MP3, WMA, RA **Free BYAHO songs**: ★★★★ **Indie songs**: ★★★★★

Music variety: ★★★★★ **Speed**: ★★★★★ **Webcasts/Videos**: ★★★★★ **Radio stations**: None **MP3 software**: ★★★

Music/MP3 news: ★★★★★ **Chat/Msg. boards**: ★★★★ **How-tos**: ★★★★ **Links**: ★★★★★ **Search engine**: ★★★★

Search:	
This site	

Search by:	
Artist	Album
Song	Genre
Format	News
Reviews	Wizard

Buy music: Linked to CDNow, EMusic

There are some things online magazines can do that paper magazines can't. RollingStone.com is a faithful extension of the magazine that **segues smoothly into online interactivity**. Of course, you get many of the articles, reviews, interviews, and charts in the print magazine, augmented by video, audio, and great links. As you'd expect, the **really hot artists** are in RollingStone.com's Webcasts and Videos sections. Download featured MP3s by BYAHO in the MP3 and More section, click Browse All Songs to find more than **12,750 MP3s** ranging from stars to lesser known bands. For radio, download the **Rolling Stone Radio tuner** at **www.rsradio.com**, where you'll also find the **David Bowie Radio Network** playing his favorite music. Indie musicians upload their MP3s to RollingStone.com, and every two weeks **editors listen to them**, pick their top 10 favorites, and feature them on the front page of the MP3 and More section. Look up a band with the Rolling Stone search engine and the results provide links to Emusic or CDNow, where you can buy the track or CD, and to other sites on the Web—such as band paraphernalia auctioned at **eBay**. For fans of *Rolling Stone Magazine* itself, find photos of all the *RS* covers from 1967 to today, order back issues of *RS* from 1993, and buy *RS* T-shirts or hundreds of band T-shirts at the Rolling Stone store. The site is part of the **E-Music** and **Tunes** networks.

17. SearchByMedia.com ★★★★★ **CATEGORY: Portal > Software**
  URL: **www.searchbymedia.com**

Best reasons to surf this site: Download the Media Hub, which allows you to search for MP3s, images, and video files on the Web; manages your files; and integrates them with external hardware.

Audio file formats: MP3 **Streaming audio formats:** RA **Free BYAHO songs:** Linked **Indie songs:** Linked

Music variety: ★★★★ **Speed:** ★★★★ **Webcasts/Videos:** Linked **Radio stations:** Linked **MP3 software:** Linked

Music/MP3 news: Linked **Chat/Msg. boards:** ★★★★ **How-tos:** ★★★★ **Links:** ★★★★★ **Search engine:** ★★★★

Search:	
Web sites	

Search by:	
Artist	Album
Song	Genre
Video	Images
All Words	Any Word

Buy music: Linked

Search By Media is a multimedia searcher and file manager that "acts as a personal multimedia portal [for] users to interface between the Internet, PC, and external hardware." If that sounds like a good idea to you, download Search By Media's tool, Media Hub. Media Hub's search screen lets you hunt the Web for **MP3s, images, and videos.** You then **flip to another interface** to manage your audio and video downloads; play them; and store images that can be used as album covers, wallpapers, and screensavers. It lets you import from MP3 players, scanners, and digital cameras. SearchByMedia.com also has an **Album Builder** tool you download that imports all your MP3s from your hard drive and stores them with artist information, album covers, or other images. At the site itself, listen to streamed music clips by popular BYAHO from several different genres, link to buy the artists' CDs, read music/MP3 and other media topic headlines, link to read the full news story, participate in multimedia forums, and go to the Site Map to find links to many great MP3 and multimedia sites. And, if you have any questions about how to use this site or its great tools, an **animated guided tour** will walk you through it.

18. MP3.Box.Sk ★★★★★ CATEGORY: Portal
URL: www.mp3.box.sk

Best reasons to surf this site: Get loads of MP3 software, link to indie music sites offering MP3 downloads, and listen to music based on the Top 40 charts from 9 different countries.

Audio file formats: MP3 **Streaming:** MP3 **Free BYAHO songs:** Linked **Indie songs:** Linked

Music variety: ★★★★★ **Speed:** ★★★★★ **Webcasts/Videos:** Linked. **Radio stations:** Linked **MP3 software:** ★★★★★

Music/MP3 news: ★★★★ **Chat/Msg. boards:** None **How-tos:** ★★ **Links:** ★★★★★ **Search engine:** ★★★★

Search:
FTP sites

Search by:
Artist
Album
Song

Buy music: No

The idea of this site is to give you your "MP3 world in a box," by providing **links to an amazing number** of MP3-related resources. At MP3.BOX.SK (SK stands for the Slavic Republic) read the latest MP3 news; download tons of MP3 software; and link to hundreds of indie band sites, MP3 sites, Shoutcast and other MP3 online radio stations, MP3 search engines, MP3 hardware, **Winamp Stuff**, lyric sites—and my personal favorite—the **Top 40 Charts** from **9 different countries**. You can stream and download many unusual MP3s in this section. If you want to find MP3s by BYAHO, use MP3.BOX.SK's search engine to check a database of more than **130,000 MP3s from FTP sites**. Its search engine does not contain sites that haven't been working for more than four hours, so the chances of finding **successful downloads** is increased. Be sure to check out the other **BOX.SK** projects while you're here, too. For example, you can find anything related to the **visual arts at eye.box.sk**, game cheats and reviews at **gameguru.box.sk**, and links to **hacking text and utilities at neworder.box.sk**.

19. Shockwave.com ★★★★ CATEGORY: Portal > Shockwave media
URL: www.shockwave.com

Best reasons to surf this site: Find sites on the Web that use Shockwave audio and movie file formats.

Audio file formats: SWA (an MP3 file) **Streaming formats:** SWA **Free BYAHO songs:** Linked **Indie songs:** Linked

Music variety: N/A **Speed:** N/A **Webcasts/Videos:** Linked **Radio:** Linked **MP3 software:** ★★

Music/MP3 news: Linked **Chat/Msg. boards:** Linked **How-tos:** ★★★ **Links:** ★★★★ **Search engine:** ★★★★

Search:
Web sites
Multiple search engines

Search by:		
Artist		
Song		
Format		
Any Word		
Buy music: No		

Shockwave is a multimedia technology and player, similar to QuickTime, developed by Macromedia to view and listen to Shockwave **animation and audio files**, which can be impressive. This site's a great starting point to search the Web for music and multimedia sites that use the Shockwave format. Have the search engine look up artists and it will pull up, let's say, an **Alice in Chains site** where you can do a 360-**degree pan of their recording studio** or watch an interview with the band. It's like finding sites with Webcasts, but with all these animated flashes (SWF files) and **blinking lights**. The search engine looks up MP3s on the Web via **Listen.com's** directory site. Shockwave is a particularly popular format used in **interactive games and cartoons**, but music fans use this site to search for music news, video, radio, chat rooms, and soundtrack sites that use Shockwave. Shockwave.com is a pretty happenin' and popular interactive site in and of itself. While you're there, be sure to **download the Shockmachine** to save Shockwave files and play them offline.

20. SonicNet.com ★★★★★ CATEGORY: Portal > Bands
URL: www.sonicnet.com

Best reasons to surf this site: Find news and reviews on practically every BYAHO in every genre and link to other sites relating to that band. SonicNet is also great for getting radio and video Webcasts.

Audio file formats: MP3, WMA **Streaming formats:** RA, WMA, SWA **Free BYAHO songs:** ★★★ **Indie songs:** ★★

Music variety: ★★★★★ **Speed:** ★★★★★ **Webcasts/Video:** ★★★★★ **Radio:** ★★★★★ **MP3 software:** Linked

Music/MP3 news: ★★★★★ **Chat/Msg. boards:** ★★★★ **How-tos:** ★★★ **Links:** ★★★★ **Search engine:** ★★★★

Search:		
This site		

Search by:		
Artist		
Album		
Song		
Genre		
Alphabet		
Radio		
News		
Reviews		
Buy music: Linked		

SonicNet, part of the MTVigroup, is geared toward looking up **bands by genre**. When you select a genre, it pulls up related music news and links to related artists, magazines, labels, radio, concert info, and subgenres. They have **practically every BYAHO** and many you may not have heard of. You'll get lots of band info and bios. Listen to 30-second clips from their albums, post a message on the bulletin board, read chat transcriptions, and link to **Tower Records** to buy CDs. Check out SonicNet's All Downloads section to find a decent amount of free MP3s and WMAs by BYAHO. Click Radio SonicNet to listen to more than 40 of SonicNet's own **radio stations in more than 10 genres** and find links to more radio. Enter the All

Videos section to watch a huge amount of streamed **music videos and interviews** with BYAHO. There's quite a lot to do at SonicNet.com, whose mission is to "ignite, inspire, and nurture the passion for music that fans of all genres share."

21. Team-MP3.com ★★★★ CATEGORY: Portal > Megasite
URL: www.team-mp3.com

Best reasons to surf this site: Download tons of skins and software and get detailed descriptions and how-tos on products. Also, link to lots of recent and archived MP3 news and more MP3 resources.

Audio file formats: N/A **Streaming formats**: N/A **Free BYAHO songs**: Linked **Indie songs**: Linked

Music variety: N/A **Speed**: ★★★★★ **Webcasts/Videos**: Linked **Radio**: Linked **MP3 software**: ★★★★★

Music/MP3 news: ★★★★★ **Chat/Msg. boards**: None **How-tos**: ★★★★★ **Links**: ★★★★★ **Search engine**: None

Buy music: No

Search:	
This site	

Search by:	
Artist	

This is a refreshingly **intuitive** site to navigate, with no jumbled messes of offerings being thrown at you from every direction in an attempt to have a little of everything. You go here, you see what you can get, and you get it. As Team-MP3 says, you get **"Less Noise, More Toys!"** Download tons of MP3-related software, with each download coming with **great, and I mean great, explanations**, descriptions, and how-tos of the product. But if Team-MP3 doesn't answer your questions to your apparently hard-to-please satisfaction, there are links to **good FAQ sites** that you can try, too. Second, find loads of recent and archived MP3 news headlines and then link to the full story from Team-MP3. And third, link to lots of MP3 music sites and handy MP3 resources such as search engines, lyrics databases, and MP3 hardware. This is simple and as cool as ice tea on a hot summer day.

22. Tunes.com ★★★★★ CATEGORY: Portal > Megasite
URL: www.tunes.com

Best reasons to surf this site: Preview and buy music; listen to Tunes' own radio; post messages; and watch many long Webcasts of concerts, music videos, and interviews with bands. Also find good cover art.

Audio file formats: MP3, WMA **Streaming formats**: MP3, WMA, RA **Free BYAHO songs**: ★★★★ **Indie songs**: ★★★★★

Music variety: ★★★★★ **Speed**: ★★★★★ **Webcasts/Videos**: ★★★★ **Radio**: ★★★★ **MP3 software**: ★★

Music/MP3 news: ★★★★ **Chat/Msg. boards**: ★★★★ **How-tos**: ★★★★ **Links**: ★★★ **Search engine**: ★★★★

Search:	
This site	

Search by:	
Artist	Album
Song	Genre
Label	Reviews

Buy Music: Yes

Ships CDs: Yes

Price Avg.: $ 9.99 – $14.49

Custom CDs: No

Pay per track: No

When I first visited Tunes.com, besides being captured by its ethereal, fluorescent glow, I was immediately struck by the multitude of things you can do here. Besides the normal fun stuff, such as music news, Tunes has a good collection of free copy-and-pastable band photos, lots of free streaming music videos, its own radio station, message boards, contests where you can win anything from an **autographed guitar by Machinehead** to a Yak Pack filled with Beck CDs, its own online store with BYAHO paraphernalia, a great Webcast section, and a feature called My Tunes. My Tunes gives you access to the message boards and allows you to keep a list of the CDs and songs you own, or wish to own, so that **Tunes can recommend other bands** you might like. Choose from more than **150,000 CDs** to buy, and preview most of the songs before you buy them. In all, there are more than 8,000 free, fully downloadable songs, mostly from indie bands—but still a good amount are by BYAHO. To check out the complete list of free downloads, click Downloads and Browse All Songs. Check out **Hot Downloads** to find a more concentrated list of tracks available by BYAHO. Tunes' radio has good sound quality, and there are **five stations** from which to choose: alternative, jazz, electronic, hip hop, and country. As the radio is playing, a window displays the name of the song, artist, album, and other albums by that artist, and suggests similar artists you might like. If you like the song you're listening to, there is also a link to the CD so you can check it out and buy it—pretty handy stuff to be able to get from a radio station. This is, overall, an awesome site, and it is part of the **E-Music Network**, so registering here applies to the rest of the sites in the network, too.

23. UBL.com ★★★★★ CATEGORY: Portal > Band resources
URL: www.ubl.com

Best reasons to surf this site: Get band information; musicians can find tons of music-related resources and post their music at UBL.com.

Audio formats: MP3, WMA, RA **Streaming**: MP3, WMA, RA, Shoutcast **Free BYAHO songs**: ★★★★
Indie songs: ★★★★★

Music variety: ★★★★★ **Speed**: ★★★★★ **Webcasts/Videos**: ★★★★ **Radio**: Linked **MP3 software**: ★★

Music/MP3 news: Linked **Chat/Msg. boards**: ★★★★★ **How-tos**: ★★ **Links**: ★★★★★ **Search engine**: ★★★★

Search:	
This site	

Search by:	
Artist	Album
Genre	Alphabet
ResourceLabel	Promoter
Tickets	Venue
Retail	Tour dates
Magazines	Meta site
Festival	

Buy music: Yes

Ships CDs: Yes

Avg. Price $9.99 – $14.99

Custom CDs: No

Price per track: N/A

Pay per track: No

The Ultimate Band List could also be called the **Ultimate Band Resource**. Find just about any BYAHO or indie band and get the band's tour dates, reviews, interviews, CDs, videos, tablature, lyrics, mailing lists, newsgroups, and links to the band's home page or fan sites. You also can find the occasional free download. UBL broadcasts long music video streams and live Webcasts at UBL TV. You even find links to **political protest** events and activism in the Who Cares! section. UBL.com is part of the **Artist Direct Network** (**ArtistDirect.com**)—a network of sites that combines to give you direct access to much more BYAHO merchandise, CDs, downloads, Webcasts, chat rooms, and so on, found throughout the other sites on the network. The Downloads (**DownloadsDirect.com**) section of the Artist Direct Network is the main place on the Internet where you'll find songs you can download by BYAHO in the **MJuice** format. MJuice can't easily be converted to MP3 the way other audio formats can, but remember you can always use programs such as **Total Recorder** to capture the MJuice track as a WAV file. Between UBL and the rest of the A.D.N., you'll find comprehensive results to practically anything that's related to music. This site is heavily geared toward **rock, pop, alternative, and hip hop** categories, but if it has to do with any kind of band or music, it's most likely on this popular site.

24. VH1.com ★★★★ CATEGORY: Portal > megaportal
URL: www.vh1.com

Best reasons to surf this site: Listen to streams of music, full-length concerts, and long interviews with bands; watch streamed videos; and get tons of recent and archived music news.

Audio formats: MP3, WMA **Streaming formats**: RA, WMA, QT **Free BYAHO songs**: ★★★★ **Indie songs**: ★★

Music variety: ★★★★ **Speed**: ★★★★★ **Webcasts/Videos**: ★★★★ **Radio**: ★★★ **MP3 software**: ★★

Music/MP3 news: ★★★★★ **Chat/Msg. boards**: None **How-tos**: ★★ **Links**: ★★★ **Search engine**: ★★★

Search:
This site

Search by:
Artist
Song
Genre
Alphabet
News
Reviews
Wizard
Buy music: Linked

VH1.com, a division of MTV Networks, is a more user-friendly site than MTV.com, with its all-over-the-place layout. I guess it's because VH1 is the mellower, preppier, old-fogy cousin of MTV (like, for people who were watching MTV when it first aired way back in the '80s). Whatever. VH1.com turns out to be a great site. At VH1, look up over **7,000 artists** and get their bios, link to the bands' related Web sites, read album reviews, listen to short music clips off their albums, look up concert information in your town, and check out a list of similar artists to explore. There are also over **101 BYAHO fan clubs** you can join where you'll find TV info, tours and tickets, photos, memorabilia, message boards, Web links, CD reviews, and more about your favorite bands. VH1.com's crowning jewels, however, are its Webcasts and videos sections. At **VH1 @ Work Radio** you can check for upcoming Webcasts, tune in to VH1's own radio station, and listen to archives of long interviews and full-length concerts. Also, get more streamed videos in the Videos and VH1.0 sections and find even more archived Webcasts under Events. Between the music videos, Webcasts, and radio, **you end up getting a lot of free music**, even if it is all streamed, but don't forget, you can capture it with **TotalRecorder on this book's CD-ROM**. VH1 also has a few MP3 and WMA downloads, mostly by indie artists, and lots of recent and archived music news at The Wire. Go to

VH1's Store to **bid in auctions** for collector's items and to link to an online store to buy CDs. Finally, check out the Help section to find out how you can **be an audience member** on one of VH1's shows or be a participant on *Rock & Roll Jeopardy*.

25. WindowsMedia.com ★★★★ CATEGORY: Portal > Windows media
URL: www.windowsmedia.com

Best reasons to surf this site: Download the latest version of the Windows Media Player and find or link to WMA audio and video downloads, Webcasts, and radio.

Audio formats: WMA **Streaming formats:** WMA **Free BYAHO songs:** Linked **Indie songs:** Linked

Music variety: ★★★★ **Speed:** N/A **Webcasts/Videos:** ★★★★★ **Radio:** ★★★★★ **MP3 software:** ★★★

Music/MP3 news: Linked **Chat/Msg. boards:** ★★★ **How-tos:** ★★★★ **Links:** ★★★★ **Search engine:** ★★★★

Search:	
This site	
Web sites	
Search by:	
Artist	
Song	
Genre	
Site	
Webcast	
Radio	
News	
Buy music: No	

This Microsoft-owned site is home to the rapidly improving **Windows Media Player** and the **Windows Media Audio** (WMA) formats. Like MP3, WMA uses an audio compression technology and, although this is certainly arguable, it has been reported in a few studies that WMA **sounds better than MP3**. But, that is for you to decide. At WindowsMedia.com you can link to a pretty good selection of free audio and video WMAs by BYAHO and link to hundreds of radio stations around the world that are compatible with the Windows Media Player. There's also a **Broadbands** section that links to featured music Webcasts and a search engine that finds links to more Webcasts, music, and videos available on the Web. While the songs are downloading, prop up your feet, grab a pipe, and watch the **latest news from MSNBC** in Broadband's Today's Highlights window. Then, when the songs are finished downloading, listen to your new WMAs and **see how** *you* **think it compares** to its rival formats.

Outlaw Sites

26. 2000MP3.com ★★★★★ CATEGORY: Outlaw
URL: www.2000mp3.com

Best reasons to surf this site: Download a huge number of free MP3s by BYAHO or use the 11 MP3 search engines on the home page to find the song you want.

Audio formats: MP3 **Streaming formats:** N/A **Free BYAHO songs:** ★★★★★ **Indie songs:** ★★

Music variety: ★★★ **Speed:** ★★★★ **Webcasts/Videos:** None **Radio:** None **MP3 software:** None

Music/MP3 news: None **Chat/Msg. boards:** ★★ **How-tos:** None **Links:** ★★★★ **Search engine:** ★★★★★

Search:	
This site	
FTP sites	
Web sites	
Multiple search engines	

Search by:	
Artist	
Song	
Alphabet	
Country	
Year	

Buy Music: No

Find more than **6,000 free MP3s by BYAHO** on this great and very easy-to-use site. If it doesn't have the song you're looking for, try finding it with one of the **11 MP3 search engines** conveniently included on their home page. Also, get free MP3s based on **Billboard's charts** from '83 to the present, and from other music charts around the world. Many downloads from 2000MP3 may not be successful, it's a sort of **hit and miss kind of thing**, but most of them download just fine. **Right-clicking the song** and then clicking Save Target As is highly recommended, and you may have to **rename file extensions to .MP3** every now and then. Still, this site is a great stop for simply hunkering down and looking up MP3s by BYAHO. If you need a diversion, link to some popular artists' home pages, **full album download sites**, or a lyrics search site, or check out some Korean tourist information.

27. EvilErnie.net/MP3 (FinalMP3.com) ★★★★★ CATEGORY: Outlaw
URL: www.evilernie.net/mp3 (AKA: www.finalmp3.com)

Best reasons to surf this site: Download hundreds of free MP3s by BYAHO and some good MP3 utilities, too.

Audio formats: MP3 **Streaming formats:** N/A **Free BYAHO songs:** ★★★★★ **Indie songs:** ★★
Music variety: ★★★★ **Speed:** ★★★★★ **Webcasts/Videos:** None **Radio:** None **MP3 software:** ★★★★
Music/MP3 news: None **Chat/Msg. boards:** None **How-tos:** ★★★★ **Links:** ★★★ **Search engine:** None

Search:	
This site only	

Search by:	
Artist	
Song	
Label	

Buy music: No

Welcome to Evil Ernie's MP3s, where music and the terrifying converge. Actually, there's nothing about this site that seems evil. Similar to **2000MP3.com**, Evil Ernie's a place where one can just simply sit down and easily download **many MP3s by BYAHO**. Evil Ernie's doesn't have as many as it used to because it **was forced to stop** giving MP3s by *Brein*—the Dutch RIAA—but, it has managed to provide some other pages with hundreds of links (which seem more like direct downloads to me, but maybe I'm wrong). So for all practical purposes, **they're in business**. To get the MP3s at Evil Ernie's you simply click the songs you want, which are listed in alphabetical order according to artist, and let Go!Zilla do the work. Sometimes you may have to rename the file extension to .MP3 after you've downloaded it, and other times it just won't download at all—probably because of a broken link. But, overall, the MP3s download fine. You can also nab some **good MP3 utilities**, get MP3 how-tos and tips on downloading, and link to some MP3 sites and non-MP3 sites, including "Bert is Evil!" I knew it was an Ernie and Bert thing. Note: You also can get to Evil Ernie's MP3s by going to **www.finalmp3.com**.

28. GoodMP3.dhs.org ★★★★★ CATEGORY: Outlaw
URL: www.goodmp3.ghs.org

Best reasons to surf this site: Find thousands of free, reliable MP3 downloads by BYAHO.

Audio formats: MP3 **Streaming formats**: MP3 **Free BYAHO songs**: ★★★★★ **Indie songs**: ★★★★★

Music variety: ★★★ **Speed**: ★★★★★ **Webcasts/Videos**: None **Radio stations**: None **MP3 software**: None **Music/MP3 news**: None **Chat/Msg. boards**: None **How-tos**: None **Links**: ★★ **Search engine**: None

Search:
This site

Search by:
Artist
Song
Alphabet
Other

Buy music: No

Wow! You've hit the jackpot at Good MP3 if what you're looking for is simply to download MP3s. Choose from more **50,000 MP3s**—over 30,000 of which are by BYAHO. And most amazingly, over 95 percent of the downloads work! This site lists the MP3s alphabetically according to either song title or artist name, so what you end up with are **massive lists of MP3s**. But, the good thing about scrolling through such huge lists (as opposed to looking for specific MP3s on a search engine) is that you may come across **songs that you always liked, but had forgotten,** such as "Ahab the Arab" or Monty Python's "Penis Song." **Go!Zilla works very well** with the site. Sometimes, usually not, the downloads are **.ZIP files**. If this is the case, go ahead and download it as a .ZIP and then unzip it with your Zip! Zilla program. This site doesn't offer much more, but who cares? It's a true treat to so easily, quickly, and reliably download so many songs.

29. MP3BR.net ★★★★★ CATEGORY: Outlaw
URL: www.mp3br.net

Best reasons to surf this site: Find thousands of free MP3 downloads by BYAHO.

Audio formats: MP3 **Streaming formats**: MP3 **Free BYAHO songs**: ★★★★★ **Indie songs**: ★

Music variety: ★★★ **Speed**: ★★★★ **Webcasts/Videos**: None **Radio**: None **MP3 software**: None

Music/MP3 news: None **Chat/Msg. boards**: None **How-tos**: None **Links**: ★ **Search engine**: None

Search:
This site

Search by:
Alphabet

Buy music: No

Here's another site that's good for the simple enjoyment of just downloading MP3s. When you first get there, forget about the banner that comes up asking whether you want to vote for this or that—just click Cancel—scroll down past **the porn ad,** and head straight down some more until you see the **big, brazen yellow letters** of the alphabet. It may look like just an ordinary alphabet, but behind these letters lie your keys to happiness. Click a letter and poof! a page quickly appears displaying the names of bands you've actually heard of that begin with that letter. Then, take your **magic mouse,** lay it over a song you want, and right-click. When the shortcut menu comes up, click Save Target As and the song will be yours. Or, if you want, use your friend Go!Zilla, with its extra nimbleness and strength, to download the song. Sadly, some of the downloads are dead links, but otherwise it's just that easy, and you can try to summon more than 14,000 songs on this **Brazilian** MP3 site.

30. MP3MP4.com ★★★★ **CATEGORY: Outlaw**
URL: www.mp3mp4.com

Best reasons to surf this site: Get lots of free MP3s by BYAHO.

Audio formats: MP3 **Streaming formats:** MP3 **Free BYAHO songs:** ★★★★★ **Indie songs:** ★

Music variety: ★★★ **Speed:** ★★★★ **Webcasts/Videos:** None **Radio:** None **MP3 software:** ★

Music/MP3 news: None **Chat/Msg. boards:** None **How-tos:** ★★★ **Links:** ★★★ **Search engine:** None

Search:
This site

Search by:
Artist
Album
Song
Alphabet
Buy music: No

Grow some hair on your neck and get used to pop-ups at MP3MP4.com because **this site is worth it** for all the MP3s you can get. The pop-ups are fairly manageable, and the ones you have to put up with occur mainly when you veer off the site's path and into unknown realms. So stay onboard and follow my directions and maybe, just maybe, you'll **avoid the pop-up minefields**. The clickable buttons on this site that lead to the dormant pop-ups are **deceiving**, often disguising themselves with the same lettering as the legitimate buttons. When you first enter the site, look to your left, look to your right, and look in the middle. Notice that you have three windows. The middle one's your main compadre and door to the MP3s. When you click a button in the left or right window, and it *doesn't* open up in the middle window, you've hit a link that'll most likely take you off to a pop-up land, and you'll have to make your way back through the pop-up madhouse. If you click a button to the left or right and it *does* open up in the middle window, you're in business. This is basically what you want. This means that in the middle window you can start scrolling through lists of MP3s to download by BYAHO. Here's a rundown of the good buttons to click to get great MP3s: The **MP3 Archive New** button is the main button and the best one. Here, you'll find a section of 3,500 reliable, quality MP3 downloads, and a section of 35,000 less reliable, but still worth checking out, MP3s from the rest of the archives. The next few buttons are self-explanatory and are good for more MP3s: The **U.S. Top 20 button** (in the left window), the **U.K. Top 20** button, the **Euro Top 20** button, the **Full MP3 Albums** button, and the **Billboard 50 MP3** button. Of note, when you click an MP3 to download from the middle window, another window opens up, but don't mistake this for a pop-up. In this new window you will see the song title again. **Go!Zilla does not work very well with this site** because many of the songs have been blocked, so, from here you should **right-click the song** and click Save Target As to perform a direct download. **Good luck out there**, and some of you dangerous fools may want to check out the intriguing **Live Ftpz** and **Zip Passwords** buttons for a little **hacker-ish** and **Warez**-related stuff.

31. Free-MP3s.net ★★★★ **CATEGORY: Outlaw**
URL: www.free-mp3s.net

Best reason to surf this site: Find links to a lot of sites that have a curiously large number of free MP3s by BYAHO.

Audio formats: MP3 **Streaming audio formats:** N/A **Free BYAHO songs:** Linked **Free indie songs:** Linked

Music variety: N/A **Speed:** N/A **Webcasts/Videos:** None **Radio stations:** None **MP3 Software:** Linked **Music/MP3 News:** None **Chat/Msg. Boards:** None **How-tos:** None **Links:** ★★★★ **Search Engine:** Linked

Search:	
This site	
Web sites	

Search by:	
Link	

Buy music: No

This nicely interfaced site has done an excellent job putting together **a host** of MP3 sites that have a "curiously" large number of free MP3s. You'll find most of these MP3-filled sites in Free-MP3s' Files section. Here, in the "file collection," they have even gone so far as to include accurately written summaries of each site, star ratings (actually, they use tiny pictures of files instead of stars), and a statement telling you the "Downside" of each site it links to. From Free-MP3s' home page, you can go to their **Links** section to find more sites with free MP3s. As in the Files section, the links in the Links section come with good descriptions letting you know, for example, if the site is good for getting individual MP3s, full album downloads, "freebies," or other "stuff" before you go there. But take note: While the Files section has some manageable pop-ups, the Links section often leads you to sites filled with pop-ups. The descriptions in the Links section tell you if a link contains *no* pop-ups, but not if it *does*. So, **if it** *doesn't* **mention pop-ups, the link will** most likely lead to ferocious, infinitely replicating sites. Between these two sections, though, you can find **a lot** of free MP3s by BYAHO. Free-MP3s.net also links to very basic MP3 software, hardware, and skins, and has conveniently placed links to their MP3 Favorites, including a couple to MP3 search engines, and Top 10 Referers on their home page. If you can stand **the array of pop-ups**, you can also—eventually—find a lot of free MP3s by famous artists at sites like `www.top25mp3.com`, `www.top-mp3-music.com`, `www.t100.to/`, `www.mp3sound.com`, and `www.mp3downloads.org`. You're on your own there, but you should come out okay, matey, if you just keep forging ahead, and plow your way through. Oh yeah, did I mention that you could download free programs such as **PopUp Killer** and **Close Popup** at `www.davecentral.com`? Those might help, too. Enter the word "popup" in Dave's keyword window to find those programs, and note: DaveCentral.com is a terrific place for both Windows and **Linux** users to download **gobs of free software** in many categories, including MP3 and Audio.

32. PureMP3.org ★★★★★ CATEGORY: Outlaw
URL: `www.puremp3.org`

Best reasons to surf this site: Find many good links to reliable sites that are guaranteed to contain no porn and have free MP3s by BYAHO. Bonus: links to sites with free, full-album downloads.

Audio formats: MP3 **Streaming formats:** MP3 **Free BYAHO songs:** Linked **Indie songs:** Linked

Music variety: ★★★★ **Speed:** N/A **Webcasts/Videos:** None **Radio stations:** None **MP3 software:** Linked **Music/MP3 news:** Linked **Chat/Msg. boards:** Linked **How-tos:** None **Links:** ★★★★★ **Search engine:** None

Search:	
This site	

Search by:	
Genre	

Buy music: No

One thing's for sure: You will not find any MP3 sites that contain porn at PureMP3.org. In fact, they promise that "the members of PURE MP3 not only do not have pornographic banners or pictures on their sites, but they will not link to sites which have anything pornographic on them." It's sort of their mantra (although **some foul language is okay**). A lot of the sites they link to are from **fans** who've decided to put music by their favorite artists on their Web pages, and others are the more traditional MP3 sites. Either way, PureMP3, founded by Dimension Music, has links to over **1,760 sites** that may have the songs, or even the complete album downloads, you're looking for by BYAHO. Look under the Music tab to check out many of the MP3 links divided into genre, and look under the All-Purpose, Software, **Trade**, and Search tabs to find more related sites, including a section with links to **Non-English MP3 sites**. PureMP3 does a good job of keeping the bullshit sites out, so even clicking around on all its interesting sites in **idle curiosity** is enjoyable and frustration-free. You'll find more complete album downloads by popular BYAHO and much more at **www.mp3fever.net**, although this site does have pop-ups.

Big Five Record Labels

33. BMG.com ★★★★★ CATEGORY: The Big Five
URL: www.bmg.com

Best reasons to surf this site: Visit all the famous BMG artists' Web sites to get audio clips and video streams. Purchase their music at BMG's popular music club: BMGMusicService.com.

Audio formats: N/A **Streaming formats**: RA, WMA **Free BYAHO songs**: ★★★★★ **Indie songs**: ★★★★

Music variety: ★★★★ **Speed**: N/A **Webcasts/Videos**: ★★★★★ **Radio**: None **MP3 software**: Linked

Music/MP3 news: ★★★★ **Chat/Msg. boards**: None **How-tos**: ★★ **Links**: ★★★ **Search engine**: None

Search:	
This site	

Search by:	
Artist	
Composer	
Album	
Genre	
Catalog #	
Buy music: Yes	
Ships CDs: Yes	
Avg. Price: $16.98	
Custom CDs: No	

Check out **www.musicstation.com** to get a complete list of CDs and catalog numbers available at **www.bmgmusicservice.com**.

BMG is an entertainment company that publishes, distributes, markets, and sells music by all sorts of BYAHO and is owner of over **200 record labels** around the world, including Arista and RCA Records. It is also home to the largest online music club, **BMGMusicService.com**, where you can buy all the BMG artists' music. Not surprisingly, you can visit all these artists' Web sites right from BMG.com to get their bios, listen to featured audio clips, watch music video streams, and more. And, this ain't sayin' nothin' because BMG owns some of the **biggest names around**. Just a partial list of their megastars include: **2Pac, Britney Spears, Christina Aguilera, Backstreet Boys, 'N Sync, TLC, Monica, Toni Braxton, Whitney Houston, Sarah McLachlan, Foo Fighters, Creed, Bush, Tool, Anthrax, Motorhead, Judas Priest, Dokken, Motley Crue, Lynyrd Skynyrd, Joe Cocker, Grateful Dead, Yes, Jefferson Starship, Carlos Santana, Dave Matthews Band, Clint Black, Alabama, Waylon Jennings, ZZ Top, Elvis Presley, Aretha Franklin, Eurythmics, Blondie, Mercury Rev, Fats Waller, Keith Lochhart, Enrico Caruso,** and **Michael Tilson Thomas**. You'll also find BMG's influence at its online partners, including: **Get Music,**

Album Direct, Artist Direct, Bugjuice, Connect2Music, Egreetings, Eritmo, Intervu, Liquid Audio, Listen.com, Peeps Republic, Real.com, Riffage, Rock Universe, Twang This, Ultimate Band List, Windows Media, and **Yam.com.** And, you can read lots of recent and archived news about BMG itself, and because BMG is such a huge company in the music world, you find out what's going on with some of your favorite artists before most of the public does.

34. SonyMusic.com ✶✶✶✶ **CATEGORY: The Big Five**
URL: **www.sonymusic.com**

Best reasons to surf this site: Find every artist from Sony Music's record labels, link to the artists' Web sites, and buy their music. Labels include Columbia, Epic, Relativity Entertainment Group, and Sony Classical.

Audio formats: N/A **Streaming formats:** RA, Audio Base **Free BYAHO songs:** ✶✶ **Indie songs:** ✶

Music variety: ✶✶✶✶✶ **Speed:** N/A **Webcasts/Videos:** ✶✶✶ **Radio stations:** None **MP3 software:** Linked

Music/MP3 news: ✶✶✶ **Chat/Msg. boards:** None **How-tos:** ✶✶✶ **Links:** ✶✶✶✶✶ **Search engine:** ✶✶✶✶

Search:	
This site	

Search by:	
Artist	Genre
Lyrics	Alphabet
Label	Format
Wizard	

Buy music: Yes

Ships CDs: Yes

Price: $9.98 – $15.98

Custom CDs: No

Pay per track: No

SonyMusic.com (the same Sony that, along with the help of CBS Records, **invented the compact disc** in 1982) includes record label giants such as Columbia and Epic Records Group. At SonyMusic.com, you'll find tons of big-time artists, and you can either link to their official Web pages or stream lots of 30-second Real audio and QuickTime video clips. **An interesting frivolity** is to browse through all the Sony Music artists alphabetically just to see how many there are and who they are. The list is quite impressive: **Mariah Carey, Oasis, Savage Garden, Will Smith, Jennifer Lopez, Barbra Streisand, Macy Gray, Mandy Moore, Ricky Martin, Celine Dion, Fiona Apple, Dixie Chicks, Pink Floyd, Rage Against the Machine, Korn, Slayer, Cyprus Hill, Bruce Springsteen, Kansas, Blue Oyster Cult, Mahavishnu Orchestra, Thelonius Monk, Charles Mingus, Louis Armstrong, Joe Satriani, Yo-Yo Ma, Benny Goodman, Duke Ellington, Bill Evans, Zubin Mehta, Glenn Gould, Bob Dylan, Marvin Gaye, Pearl Jam, Alice in Chains,** and many, many more. Using the search engine to look up artists will take you to the artists' home pages only if they are signed with Sony Music. If you look up an artist who is *not* with Sony, it will pull up artists similar to the one you're looking for who are signed with Sony. For example, if you look up The Backstreet Boys, SonyMusic's search engine will pull up C-Note and Joey McIntyre. Also check out the Live button for **upcoming tour dates,** television appearances, and live Webcasts with Sony Music artists. Search **The Vault** to buy CDs, cassettes, vinyls, and VHS and DVD videos from the Sony Music Store. Go to Globe Trotter to buy hard-to-find music from around the world. It's kind of eye-opening to see what a wide reach Sony has on the world of musical entertainment when you explore this site.

35. TimeWarner.com ★★★★★ CATEGORY: The Big Five
URL: www.timewarner.com

Best reasons to surf this site: Link to the record labels that make up the Warner Music Group to find tons of BYAHO official sites with music, bios, news, videos, and more.

Audio formats: N/A **Streaming formats**: N/A **Free BYAHO songs**: Linked **Indie songs**: Linked

Music variety: ★★★★★ **Speed**: N/A **Webcasts/Videos**: Linked **Radio**: Linked **MP3 software**: Linked

Music/MP3 news: Linked **Chat/Msg. boards**: Linked **How-tos**: ★★★★ **Links**: ★★★★★ **Search engine**: None

Search:	
This site	

Search by:	
Label	

Buy music: Linked
Buy CDs from the individual record labels' sites that make up the Warner Music Group.

Time Warner Inc., is the parent company to giants in publishing (such as *Time, People, Fortune,* and *Sports Illustrated*), cable (CNN, HBO, and Turner Entertainment), and film (Warner Bros. and New Line Cinema), and it is also parent to many record labels that make up the Big Five record companies known as the "**Warner Music Group.**" Some of its more famous labels are **Atlantic Records, Rhino, Reprise, Sire, Elektra**, and, of course, **Warner Bros. Records**. Yes, Time Warner is a **huge-ass company**. And, it will be getting even bigger, as Time Warner Inc. and EMI Group have announced that they are going to combine their music recording and music publishing businesses into a single company called Warner EMI Music. Time Warner and AOL are also planning a merger, but this is more to enable **AOL** to have a better claim to the cable modem industry, and it shouldn't affect the music recording industry too much. Until then, to start exploring the world of music in the Warner Music Group, click the Music button on Time Warner's home page, then click Warner Music Group, and then click Web Sites to find links to the record labels. **Go to the record labels** mentioned previously to find tons of BYAHO Web sites where you can download music, stream audio/video, get bios, check tour dates, read music news, and buy music or band paraphernalia—it all depends on which label's site and which artist's site you visit. Warner Bros. Records' site is particularly happenin' and you can see all your favorite Warner Brothers **cartoon characters** and check out some more animation in the DC Comics section while you're downloading music. Just some of the artists ultimately owned by Time Warner are **Madonna, Red Hot Chili Peppers, Seal, Talking Heads, Phil Collins, The Cure, Steve Winwood, Tom Petty, Joni Mitchell, Jimi Hendrix, Black Sabbath, Led Zepplin, Rush, Jethro Tull, ELP, Neil Young, Eric Clapton, The Who, Van Halen, Prince, The Scorpions, Queensryche, Alice Cooper, The Mothers of Invention, Rod Stewart, Green Day, Jane's Addiction, The Sex Pistols, Faith Hill, Steve Martin, Richard Pryor, George Carlin, Adam Sandler, Hank Williams Jr., R.E.M., Björk, Wilco, Phish, Stone Temple Pilots, Filter, Metallica, Pantera, AC/DC, Third Eye Blind, Kid Rock, Bad Company, Genesis, Fleetwood Mac, Stevie Nicks, Jewel, Philip Glass, Steve Reich**, and **Kronos Quartet**.

36. UniversalRecords.com (part of Universal Music Group) ★★ CATEGORY: The Big Five
URL: www.universalrecords.com

Best reasons to surf this site: Link to UR artists' Web sites and partner record labels. And check if Universal Records' artists will be appearing on TV or at a concert hall near you.

Audio formats: N/A **Streaming formats**: RA **Free BYAHO songs**: ★★ **Indie songs**: ★

Music variety: ★★★ **Speed**: ★★ **Webcasts/Videos**: ★★ **Radio**: None **MP3 software**: Linked

Music/MP3 news: ★★ **Chat/Msg. boards**: None **How-tos**: None **Links**: ★★★★ **Search engine**: ★★★

Search:	
This site	

Search by:	
Artist	
Genre	
Label	
State	

Buy music: Linked

From here, you can buy CDs at the artists' Web sites.

The best thing to do on this **painfully slow site** is just to click the names of its artists or partnered labels so it will link you to their respective home pages, where you can breathe a sigh of relief. This site does not really offer that much more, although you can check to see if any of Universal's artists are going to be **appearing live** or on TV in your state, listen to a few Real Audio music streams, link to Real.com to get the RealPlayer (**UR's one and only software link**), and watch a few featured **behind-the-scene videos** of UR artists in The Studio. Universal Records' partner labels include **Mojo Records, Republic Records, Cherry Entertainment, Cash Money Records, Biv 10 Records, and ZTT Records**, and you can look up UR's artists alphabetically, or from a **whopping** number of six genres. Universal Records' artists include **98 Degrees, Tonic, Bee Gees, Art of Noise, Boyz II Men, Moody Blues, Spin Doctors**, and **Goldfinger**, to name but a few. If this site were not so slow, it probably wouldn't seem so bad, buuutt...fooorrrr...noowww....

37. EMIGroup.com ★★ CATEGORY: The Big Five
URL: www.emigroup.com

Best reason to surf this site: Doubtful, but if you can find it up, check out EMIGroup's artists. If the Our Artists section is down, link to EMI's individual record labels' home page to find artist. Also, check out the Abbey Road Studios from the Links section.

Audio formats: N/A **Streaming audio formats:** N/A **Free BYAHO songs:** N/A **Free indie songs:** N/A
Music variety: N/A **Speed:** N/A **Webcasts/Videos:** N/A **Radio stations:** N/A **MP3 Software:** Linked
Music/MP3 News: ★★★ **Chat/Msg. Boards:** None **How-tos:** None **Links:** ★★★ **Search Engine:** None

Search:	
This site	

Search by:	
Label	
Link	

Buy music: Go to EMIGroup's individual record labels to buy music from artists.

In the Fall of 2000, as this book goes to print, EMI Group is joining with Warner Music Group. Now, and for the longest while, whenever I'd go to EMI Group's site, basically, all I could do was read about EMI's company history, **get a quick lesson is what music publishing is**, and check out their **Environmental Report**. I'll give them that, **they do seem to be concerned with reducing polluting emissions from their manufacturing plants.** But, the Our Artists button at their site (where undoubtedly all the potential music downloads and/or video streams—something good—would have been) never worked. Maybe next year we'll be able to give you something more substantial. Once EMI Group has joined with Warner Music Group you should be able to look up and buy EMI artists' music from the newly formed conglomerate to be called: **Warner EMI Music.** For now, just go right to EMI Groups' individual record label sites, which include, **Capitol Records, Virgin Records, Blue Note, Angel, Priority**, and naturally, **EMI Records**, to check out their artists. Some of The EMI Groups' giant acts are: **Garth Brooks, The Rolling Stones, David Bowie, Bob Marley, Lenny Kravitz, Smashing Pumpkins, Ice-T, Meat Loaf, Queen, George Michael**, and **Tina Turner**, and EMI discovered **Miles Davis, The Beatles, Pink Floyd**, and **The Spice Girls.**

Search Engines

38. AudioFind.com ★★★★★ **CATEGORY: Searcher > HTTP**
URL: www.audiofind.com

Best reasons to surf this site: Get thousands of free, easy, and reliable audio downloads (mainly MP3s) by BYAHO and indie bands.

Audio formats: MP3, WMA **Streaming formats:** MP3, ,WMA **Free BYAHO songs:** ★★★★★ **Indie songs:** ★★★★★ **Music variety:** ★★★★ **Speed:** ★★★★★ **Webcasts/Videos:** None **Radio:** None **MP3 software:** None

Music/MP3 news: None **Chat/Msg. boards:** None **How-tos:** None **Links:** ★ **Search engine:** ★★★★★

Search:
This site
Web sites

Search by:
Artist
Album
Song
Alphabet
Year
Filename
Buy music: No

Aaahhh. Here's a searcher that simply looks on the *Web* for audio files. No FTPs, no SMBs, **no hassle, no aggravation**. Just use its search engine to type in exactly what you want, or search for the songs alphabetically in different, nicely laid out categories. **Go!Zilla** works well at this site, too, or you can do the **right click, "Save Target As"** thing to download the songs. As with all the music search sites, not every download attempt is successful, but most of them seem to work just fine on this site. You can find thousands of songs here by BYAHO and by indie bands, so sit back, relax, and enjoy surfing the Web for the **universal language** of happiness: laughter…I mean, music.

39. AudioGalaxy.com ★★★★★ **CATEGORY: Searcher > FTP**
URL: www.audiogalaxy.com

Best reasons to surf this site: Search engine is one of the best for finding MP3s on FTP sites. Also, get good FTP how-tos and download lots of indie MP3s right from this site.

Audio formats: MP3 **Streaming formats:** N/A **Free BYAHO songs:** ★★ **Indie songs:** ★★★★★

Music variety: ★★★★★ **Speed:** ★★★★★ **Webcasts/Videos:** None **Radio:** None **MP3 software:** ★★★★★

Music/MP3 news: ★★ **Chat/Msg. boards:** ★★★★ **How-tos:** ★★★★★ **Links:** ★★★ **Search engine:** ★★★★★

Search:
This site
FTP sites
Web sites

Search by:	
Artist	
Album	
Song	
Genre	
Wizard	
Buy music: No	

The most immediately obvious good reason to go to Audiogalaxy.com is to use its **famed search engine**, discussed in Chapter 3, "Where Can I Find MP3 Music?" to find **MP3s on FTP sites**. Choose whether you want the search to include **ratio sites**, type in the name of any band or song, and then the search engine not only finds the FTP sites with the song/band you're looking for, but **ranks the sites' speeds**, gives their upload/download ratio info, tells you your **chances of the sites being open**, and suggests other bands you might like. When the search result comes up, start trying to download from the infamous FTP sites. (At press time for this book, Audiogalaxy was testing a beta program to look for songs in a database of more than 350,000 files on HTTP Web sites.) Strangely enough, another one of the best reasons to go to AudioGalaxy.com comes from its help section. **If you're confused**, like most people, about how to download MP3s from FTP sites—well, first read Chapter 4, "How Do I Download MP3s Once I Find Them?"—but then click the site's Info/Help tab, and click Using FTP to Download Files. Still another good reason to peruse Audiogalaxy.com is its more than **12,000 free MP3 downloads** from indie bands. These songs are easy downloads from the Web (as opposed to being from FTP sites that come from *outside* the Web), and look for them among a *huge* list of musical genres under the Music tab. You may not have heard of these bands, but if you want songs by BYAHO, get the FTP thing down and use the search engine. And, for you musicians out there, click the Backstage tab to sign up with Audiogalaxy.com and they'll give you **25MB of free Web space** to host your band's Web site and show off your music. Nifty.

40. Jugalug.com ★★★★★ CATEGORY: Searcher > FTP, HTTP
URL: www.jugalug.com

Best reasons to surf this site: This metacrawling MP3 search engine looks in several different databases and protocols at the same time, and then suggests the best way to download the MP3.

Audio formats: MP3 **Streaming formats:** MP3 **Free BYAHO songs:** ★★★★★ **Indie songs:** ★★★★★

Music variety: ★★★★★ **Speed:** ★★★★ **Webcasts/Videos:** None **Radio:** None **MP3 software:** Linked

Music/MP3 news: Linked **Chat/Msg. boards:** None **How-tos:** ★★★★ **Links:** ★★★★★ **Search engine:** ★★★★★

Search:	
FTP sites	
Web sites	
Shared sites	
Multiple search engines	

Search by:	
Artist	Song
Genre	Alphabet
Buy music: No	

This site is home to a **fantastic** metacrawling search engine that not only uses several searchers at once to find your MP3, but can simultaneously or individually look for them on **three different protocols**: FTP, SMB shares, and HTTP. The search results turn up reliable MP3s—especially if you just have it search for HTTPs on the Web—and **suggests the best way to download** them. If a download doesn't work, Jugalug offers a friendly explanation of why and suggests another method you can try. Also, set the search engine to look for sites that have been open during the **past 24 hours** to ensure download reliability, and check out its great links to other MP3 sites, MP3 software, music news, and **JugaSpy** (as they like to call it), which spies on the last 10 searches that were done by others at Jugalug on a page that reloads itself every 10 seconds. Jugaspying is actually pretty dull and pointless, but maybe the voyeur in you will like it.

41. Look4MP3.com ★★★★ CATEGORY: Searchers > FTP, HTTP
URL: www.look4mp3.com

Best reasons to surf this site: Find free MP3 downloads from HTTP sites and FTP sites. This site also has very good help and information about FTPs.

Audio formats: MP3 **Streaming formats:** MP3 **Free BYAHO songs:** ★★★★★ **Indie songs:** ★★★★★

Music variety: ★★★★★ **Speed:** ★★★★★ **Webcasts/Videos:** None **Radio:** None **MP3 software:** None

Music/MP3 news: Linked **Chat/Msg. boards:** ★★ **How-tos:** ★★★★★ **Links:** ★★ **Search engine:** ★★★★★

Search:		
FTP sites		
Web sites		
Search by:		
Artist		
Song		
All Words		
Any Word		
Buy music: No		

Although you'll find a few other features here, this site is basically an MP3 search engine. But it's a good one, and it has a huge database of songs from which to search. But this site can seem kind of confusing when trying to download songs from it, so **here's a walk-through**: When you first go to Look4MP3.com, you have a choice of searching for MP3s in two windows: the FTP or the HTTP window. You can search using only one of these paths at a time. HTTPs live on Web servers, as opposed to FTPs, which dwell outside the Web—but still on the Internet. HTTP is generally **better and much easier** for conducting any MP3 search. To download a song using the HTTP search, type in the name of a song or band, and when it comes up, click the song you want. Another page will open that has an Analyze button. Click Analyze and you'll go to another window where you'll see the Click Here to Download button. Click it and **let Go!Zilla download the MP3 for you**. If you want to be **wild and crazy** and launch into searching for music on FTPs, this is a good place to try it. Look4MP3.com provides a lot of help for downloading from FTP sites. Its **FTP Daemon** analyzes the source of the FTPs and determines whether the server is accepting logins at the moment. A **green light** means that the site was up as of 30 seconds ago, and **a red light** means the site was down as of 30 seconds ago, but check back later. If it's a go, grab that FTP info you need and use it with CuteFTP. Or, investigate the file further by clicking the song you want to download. This will present you with a choice of selections that are good for finding out all sorts of information about the MP3 and the FTP site it's from. Select Login to find information such as **how long the site has been running**, how many times the song has been downloaded since it has been up, how long you should wait until you try to download again, and to get a suggested HTTP address to try if the download doesn't work. Click Analyze to find out whether it's a ratio site or not; click FTP Data to view the remote site's instructions on how to download; and check Activate Help to get detailed instructions on how to FTP to the site in general. Look4MP3.com also has a tool called WWW Status that lets you check the status of any site or server around the world, and, for some reason, there's **a checkers game**. I guess the idea here is to play a game of checkers while your MP3 downloads. Or, to give you something to beat so you can reclaim some dignity after being defeated by the FTP protocol. At any rate, it's nice of them to have put it there. To use another similar and pretty reliable search engine to get MP3s, go to **www.mp3board.com** and **www.21look4.com**, which also searches with **Gnutella**.

42. MP3Bee.com ★★★★★ CATEGORY: Searchers
URL: www.mp3bee.com

Best reasons to surf this site: This friendly, guaranteed-to-have-no-porn Web site lets you conveniently choose from 14 popular MP3 search engines to find your song.

Audio formats: N/A **Streaming formats:** N/A **Free BYAHO songs:** Linked **Indie songs:** Linked
Music variety: N/A **Speed:** N/A **Webcasts/Videos:** None **Radio stations:** None **MP3 software:** ★★★★★
Music/MP3 news: ★★★ **Chat/Msg. boards:** None **How-tos:** ★★ **Links:** ★★★★ **Search engine:** ★★★★★

Search:
FTP sites
Web sites
Shared sites
Multiple search engines

Search by:
Artist
Song
News

Buy music: No

This friendly Web site offers many basic and useful MP3 services with a guarantee of no pop-ups or "mature" advertisements. The best reason to go to MP3 Bee, however, is for its search engines. Type in a band and/or song title in one window and then choose one of **14 popular MP3 search engines** to find the song. If one searcher does not find the MP3, simply try another. This searching convenience is reason enough to go to MP3 Bee, but at this site, you can also get lots of MP3 software, news about MP3 software, and links to many other MP3 sites that have passed the **no porn and pop-ups test**. These other MP3 sites are mostly lesser known, but are usually reliable and worth checking out. Also visit MP3 Bee's WWW Portal section to access the same 14 MP3 search engines, plus **12 popular portal searchers**, and link directly to popular online stores that support the purchase of music and music software.

43. Lycos MP3 search ★★★★★ CATEGORY: Searcher > FTP
URL: www.mp3.lycos.com

Best reasons to surf this site: Use all its search windows to find music, *except* for its main MP3 Search, and use its mammoth message board/chat area to discuss, find, and trade music.

Audio formats: MP3, WMA, RA, LQT **Streaming formats:** MP3, RA, WMA, LQT, Shoutcast **BYAHO songs:** Linked **Indie songs:** Linked

Musical variety: ★★★★★ **Speed:** ★★★★★ **Webcasts/Videos:** Linked **Radio stations:** Linked **MP3 software:** ★★★★

Music/MP3 news: ★★★★★ **Chat/Msg. boards:** ★★★★★ **How-tos:** ★★★ **Links:** ★★★★★ **Search engine:** ★★★★

Search:
This site
FTP sites
Web sites
Multiple search engines

Search by:
Artist
Album
Song
Genre
Alphabet
Label
Country
Wizard
Buy music: Linked

The well-known MP3 search engine at this site boasts having the **largest and most up-to-date database** of MP3s on the Internet, with over 1 million available to download. The only thing is, they're mainly from those frustrating, usually **unreliable FTP sites**. MP3.Lycos.com does make it better, however, by arranging the search results according to their star-rated reliability guide. The **most reliable sites** are listed first, and the results include whether or not it is a ratio site—a red star next to the site means it's a ratio site. When trying to download MP3s from these FTP servers, I was, *way* more often than not, denied access even though the reliability was rated very high. But still, if you want to try to get MP3s from FTPs, this site is worth checking out, if for nothing else because of the sheer number of potentially downloadable MP3s. The real, and less frustrating, power of MP3.Lycos.com lies in its capability to **link to the other search windows in Lycos' music network**, which are good for finding music and other multimedia files on the Web. From MP3.Lycos.com click Lycos Rich Media Search to search for streams, pictures, movies, and sounds. Go to Music Home to use Lycos as a music directory site (like Listen.com) to link to downloads by BYAHO and read lots of music news. In the Music Listening Room, search for indie bands and link to radio. Visit the Music Message Boards to check for music events in your town, chat, trade music, and link to free game downloads. And finally, download MP3 software in the MP3 Tools section, and go to the Entertainment Web Guide to link to everything else related to entertainment. There is a **lot of good stuff to find** or link to at MP3.Lycos.com, and this site would be phenomenal if its main MP3 search engine searched the HTTP protocol instead of those hard-to-reach FTPs.

44. Scour.net (aka Scour.com) ★★★★★ CATEGORY: Searcher
URL: www.scour.net (AKA: www.scour.com)

Best reasons to surf this site: Scour.net has the *best* search engine for finding free MP3 downloads on the Web by BYAHO. It is also an excellent searcher for finding multimedia downloads in general.

Audio formats: MP3, RA, LQT, WAV, MIDI, AU, VQF, WindowsMedia **Streaming formats:** MP3, RA, LQT, QT, Windows Media **Free BYAHO songs:** ★★★★★ **Indie songs:** ★★★★★

Music variety: ★★★★★ **Speed:** ★★★★★ **Webcasts/Videos:** ★★★★★ **Radio stations:** ★★★★★ **MP3 software:** ★★★

Music/MP3 news: ★★ **Chat/Msg. boards:** ★★★ **How-tos:** ★★★ **Links:** ★★★ **Search engine:** ★★★★★

Search:
This site
Web sites
Shared sites

Search by:
Artist
Song
Genre
Radio stations
Format
Any Word
Buy music: No

With Scour.com you can **bathe in the music love-fest** because Scour has the **best search engine known to man**. Scour.com is a "broadband entertainment portal" that searches six different protocols to find your audio or video file, and claims, "If you can hear it, see it or both, we'll find it for you [and] no Web site remains unturned." This sure seems to be true. Use Scour's **Advanced Search** to have the search engine look for MP3 files—although you can search for other audio formats, such as Liquid Audio, RA, MIDI, and WAV files, with the advanced search, too—then, type in the name of the song or artist, click Go, and chances are very good that you will find the song you're looking for—maybe even from several sources. Whether or not it is a successful download usually depends on whether or not the MP3 provider is online, and they usually are. If you don't find the song, try searching for it later, or under a different format. For many people, **this may be the only Web site they have to visit** to get their music, and now with Scour's new **Napster-like** program **Scour Exchange (SX)**, Scour.com is more incredible than ever. To download a song from Scour, you can click the MP3 Play button to download it as you normally would to your hard drive, or you can download it with your SX program. In addition, you can even sideload the song to an I-drive account, if you're running out of room on your local hard drives. With all Scour's audio file search capability, it is easy to forget that its comprehensive multimedia Web crawling search engine can also look up music videos; movie trailers; movie clips; full-length, streamed B movies; images; sites with Shockwave animation; and Internet radio. You can also broadcast your own MP3 radio station from Scour.com with its easy-to-use **My Caster** tool. This is just an excellent site and perhaps the best one, too. **Here's a tip:** If you can't remember the name of a song, but you know who performs it and how the tune goes, type the band's name in Scour's search engine and have it look for *MIDI* files. MIDIs usually take only seconds to download but sound good enough to tell whether it's the one you wanted. After you know the name of the song, you can look for it as an MP3, a WAV, or an LQT to get the good sounding version of it.

Music Genre-Specific

45. AlternateMusicPress.com ★★★★ CATEGORY: Genre > Alternative
URL: www.alternatemusicpress.com

Best reasons to surf this site: Read news and reviews in the alternative music scene and find great links to music resources and musicians' home pages.

Audio formats: N/A **Streaming formats:** N/A **Free BYAHO songs:** Linked **Indie songs:** Linked

Music variety: ★★★★ **Speed:** N/A **Webcasts/Videos:** None **Radio stations:** None **MP3 software:** Linked **Music/MP3 news:** ★★★★★ **Chat/Msg. boards:** None **How-tos:** ★★ **Links:** ★★★★★ **Search engine:** None

Search:
This site

Search by:
Artist
Genre
News
Reviews
Buy music: Linked

Extra! Extra! Get your Celtic news here! Get your **ambient, electronic, and fusion** reviews here, too! But that's not all. Get lots of news and reviews about **jazz, classical, blues, acoustic, folk, world, new age, progressive,** and "new" music, as well. You'll find all these categories under the Reviews section. Browse through the rest of the site to find great links to a wide variety of alternative music resources and musicians' home pages, and also get some CD-ROM and book reviews, place ads in the AMP classifieds, and discover new tunings for your Bazantar.

46. House Of Blues ★★★★★ CATEGORY: Genre > Blues
URL: www.hob.com

Best reasons to surf this site: Get lots of Webcasts of full-length concerts performed at various HOB venues, get Webcasts of artist interviews, and download free, live WMA tracks from HOB shows.

Audio formats: WMA **Streaming formats:** WMA, RA **Free BYAHO songs:** ★★★★ **Indie songs:** ★★

Music variety: ★★ **Speed:** ★★★★★ **Webcasts/Videos:** ★★★★★ **Radio:** ★★★★ **MP3 software:** ★★
Music/MP3 news: ★★★★ **Chat/Msg. boards:** None **How-tos:** ★★★★ **Links:** ★★★ **Search engine:** ★★

Search:	
This site	

Search by:	
All Words	
Any Word	
Buy music: Linked	

This is a surprisingly **upbeat site** considering it's the House of *Blues.* Although its overall look is dark, don't let that fool you; there are plenty of cheery things to do at HOB.com. There aren't a whole lot of music genres to explore—mainly rock and blues—but that's to be expected. By far, its best feature is that you can get **many, many streams** of **full-length audio and videotaped concerts** that have been performed at the various House of Blues theaters. You can also get long, streamed interviews with lots of popular artists. HOB really takes advantage of the fact that they can provide this, and between the archived concerts and the archived interviews, the Webcast—they call it cybercast—section at HOB.com is incredible! Look for upcoming **live cybercasts,** too. It's worth going to this site just for that, but at HOB.com you can also preview and download more than **200 free, live tracks** from HOB shows, download featured videos (for $2.99 each), listen to its own HOB radio stations, read lots of music news, check for emerging artists, get artists' bios, get CD reviews, **play with interactive musical programs** and games, look for ticket giveaways in your region, participate in contests, take a HOB virtual reality tour, and send HOB happy birthday and get well postcards. It's almost as if they're trying to go out of their way to keep us from getting depressed! Do you think maybe they're overcompensating?

47. Country.com ★★★★★ CATEGORY: Genre > Country-Western
URL: www.country.com

Best reasons to surf this site: Get country music stars' bios, tour dates, song/video clips, articles, and album reviews. Also, get historic audio/video clips, country music history, and information about dance contests.

Audio formats: RA, MOV **Streaming formats:** RA, QT, AU **Free BYAHO songs:** ★★★ **Indie songs:** ★★

Music variety: ★★ **Speed:** ★★★★★ **Webcasts/Videos:** ★★★★ **Radio:** None **MP3 software:** Linked
Music/MP3 news: ★★★★ **Chat/Msg. boards:** ★★★ **How-tos:** ★★★ **Links:** ★★★ **Search engine:** ★★★

Search:	
This site	

Search by:	
Artist	Album
Song	Genre
Alphabet	All Words
Any Word	News
Buy music: Linked	

If you're a little bit country, then barrel on down the information highway and mosey into Country.com. Go to the music section to look up **hundreds of country music stars** and read their bios, get their pictures, read related articles, view their discographies, read album reviews, check out awards they've won, listen to audio clips, and in many cases, view some of their videos. Enter the Jukebox for some featured song clips and videos from CMT (Country Music Television). Chat in the Green Room, look up country western **dance competitions** around the world, get lots of country music news, check which artists are on tour, visit the Country Music Hall Of Fame and Museum, and check out some downright interesting information on the **history of country music** with explanations of country music sub-genres and sound clips from various backwoods musical instruments. You'll even find historic audio and video clips! Yes ma'am or sir, you can do a little bit of everything here if your heart so desires. To wrestle with some other good country-type music sites, take **a gander** at `www.nashvillemusiclink.com`, `www.twangthis.com`, `www.roughstock.com`, `www.zydeco.crazygator.com` (Louisiana Cajun swamp music), `www.S-W-B-A.com` (bluegrass site), `www.opry.com`, `www.acmcountry.com` (Academy of Country Music), and `www.hobcountry.com` (House Of Blues live concerts). But, don't forget to come on back, now, ya' hear!? Now 'git!

48. Jtronic.com ✷✷✷✷ **CATEGORY: Genre > Electronic/Dance**
URL: `www.jtronic.com`

Best reasons to surf this site: Download free, electronic music MP3s, get a primer on the differences between the sub-genres of electronic music, and find good links to other MP3 and electro/dance sites.

Audio formats: MP3 **Streaming formats:** MP3, RA **Free BYAHO songs:** ✷✷ **Indie songs:** ✷✷✷

Music variety: ✷✷ **Speed:** ✷✷✷✷✷ **Webcasts/Video:** None **Radio stations:** ✷✷✷ **MP3 software:** ✷✷✷✷

Music/MP3 news: ✷✷ **Chat/Msg. boards:** None **How-tos:** ✷✷✷✷ **Links:** ✷✷✷✷✷ **Search engine:** None

Search:
This site

Search by:
Artist
Song
Alphabet
Buy music: No

At Jtronic.com, download a good amount of hand-selected electronic music and **feel like you're at a rave**—or in outer space. Listen to its own Web radio station; find lots of good MP3 links, including other electro/dance music sites; and, if you have some good electronic music, send it in and maybe it will show up on their site. The overall variety of music available at this site is **not wide-ranging**, but within the electronic category, you can find several sub-genres. If you're not sure about what the difference is between house, breakbeat, techno, and other sub-genres of electronic music, go to the **Elecronica Primer** to read explanations and hear music samples. Then download free MP3s, grab your **surgical masks, pacifiers, and glow sticks**, and dance like **the dancing fool you know you want to be**. Then, boogie your way to `www.raveworld.net` for another "Dance! Mother Sucker, Dance!" site with a good amount of free remix digital downloads, Webcasts, and more. `www.dotmusic.com` is a U.K. site that is your insider's guide to popular music, dance, and artists, with chat rooms, forums, and music news and reviews. Check `www.anthems.com` for more rave, house, garage, disco, DJ mixes, plus lots of good links to other dance-related sites. Then check `www.danceland2000.co.uk` and `www.house2k.co.uk` for more maniacal dancing sites.

49. HipHopSite.com ★★★★ CATEGORY: Genre > Hip hop/DJ
URL: www.hiphopsite.com

Best reasons to surf this site: Get news about the hip hop industry; check out the latest and upcoming 12"-inch singles; read interviews and album reviews; listen to sound clips; and buy CDs, mix tapes, and vinyls.

Audio formats: N/A **Streaming formats:** RA **Free BYAHO songs:** ★★ **Indie songs:** ★★★

Music variety: ★★ **Speed:** N/A **Webcasts/Videos:** ★★★ **Radio:** None **MP3 software:** Linked

Music/MP3 news: ★★★★★ **Chat/Msg. boards:** None **How-tos:** ★★★ **Links:** ★★★ **Search engine:** ★★★

Search:
This site

Search by:
Artist
Album
Song
Producer
Buy music: Yes
Ships CDs: Yes
Price: $9.99 – 14.99
Custom CDs: No

Whether it be about the artists, the mix masters, or the underground hip hop scene in general, this is the place to go for the latest **news and rumors** in the hip hop industry. Catch up on what's going on and then check out interviews, album reviews, and featured videos in the spotlight section. Listen to **long sound clips** found throughout the site; go to the store to **browse through vinyls**, CDs, mix tapes, and gear for sale from HipHopSite's catalogs; and also check out the latest 12"-singles. You'll find more reviews on forthcoming 12"-singles in the new joints section. From HipHopSite, also link to the hip hop section of the **www.AKA.com network** (a network of good multi-genre sites), and find more links to hip hop industries and recording studios in the affiliate department. Other good hip hop, rap, and music mix/DJ sites out there are **www.blaze.com, www.thesource.com, www.publicenemy.com, www.rebirthmag.com, www.mixmag.com, www.rapstation.com, www.hiphop.tunes.com/ sections/dds, www.platform.net, www.djmag.com, www.turntablism.com, www.wicked-styles.com, www.scratch.dk** (*dk* for Denmark), and **www.ss7x7.com** (a particularly cool, interactive site that allows you to mix your own tracks online in Shockwave). Also download some good **DJ software** at **www.pcdj.com** to get DJ/MP3 mixing software. At **www.carrot.prohosting.com**, get **Virtual Turntables**, which allows you to perform CD-quality MP3 decoding, and real-time mixing with volume swells, pitch bends, crossfades, and more. So, get hoppin' if you wanna start boppin'.

50. Peeps.com ★★★★ CATEGORY: Genre > Hip hop, R&B, Pop
URL: www.peeps.com

Best reasons to surf this site: Get audio and video streams of famous hip hop, R&B, and pop artists; buy music from Peeps' host site GetMusic.com; and post messages in a wide range of music forums.

Audio formats: MP3, LQT **Streaming formats:** RA **Free BYAHO songs:** ★★★★ **Indie songs:** ★

Music variety: ★★ **Speed:** ★★★★★ **Webcasts/videos:** ★★★★ **Radio:** None **MP3 software:** None

Music/MP3 news: ★★★★ **Chat/Msg. boards:** ★★★★ **How-tos:** None **Links:** ★★★ **Search engine:** N/A

Search:	
This site	

Search by:	
Artist	
Song	
Forums	
Buy music: Yes	

Ships CDs: Yes

Price: $9.97 – $13.97

Buy music from Peeps' parent site: **www.getmusic.com**.

Peeps is the much-traveled hip hop, R&B, and pop music section of GetMusic.com, and it is a particularly good site for getting music and video streams by **big name artists**. Get the streams in the archives of the **Audio + Video** section, and on the home page link directly to more than 140 artists to get some of their free music, videos, news, and bios. At **Ya Heard?** you'll find the latest music news and featured Webcast concerts and interviews with hip hop acts from **www.88hiphop.com**, and you can look up your favorite Peeps artists' tour dates. Post your thoughts and messages in a wide range of forums, and for even more free music, click Downloads to get featured MP3s and LQTs.

51. GMN.com ★★★★★ CATEGORY: Genre > Jazz, Classical
URL: **www.gmn.com** (Global Music Network)

Best reasons to surf this site: Get classical and jazz radio, get Webcasts, read about performances, and buy music at GMN's own online store, where you can also buy music in all genres.

Audio formats: MP3, WMA **Streaming formats:** RA, WMA **Free BYAHO** songs: ★★★★ **Indie songs:** ★★ **Music variety:** ★★ **Speed:** ★★★★★ **Webcasts/Videos:** ★★★★ **Radio:** ★★★★ **MP3 software:** Linked **Music/MP3 news:** ★★★ **Chat/Msg. boards:** None **How-tos:** ★★★★ **Links:** ★★★ **Search engine:** N/A

Search:	
This site	

Search by:	
Artist	Album
Song	Composer
Conductor	Ensemble
Surname	Genre
Venue	Event
Alphabet	Radio
Any Word	Phrase
Buy music: Yes	

Ships CDs: Yes

Price: $11.97 - $16.12

Custom CDs: No

The **Global Music Network** has just about anything you could want related to classical, jazz, and opera. Listen to full-length, streamed classical and jazz performances, download featured MP3s and WMAs, and get your Webcast of the day. Plus, check for upcoming Webcasts for the next month, listen to classical and jazz radio, and read about all the performances and artists. GMN even has its own music store where you can buy music in any genre. GMN **doesn't have a whole lot of MP3s to download**, but between the ones it does have, the Webcasts, the featured streams, and the radio, the site ends up dripping with **lots of succulently juicy, free music** highlighted with tasty solos by cool jazz musicians and powerful, **semi-chaotic, grande lento onslaughts** by somber classical composers. But, if you like classical or jazz music, this site should leave you yelling **"Bravo!"** or clapping appreciatively. Other good jazz and classical sites are `www.downbeatjazz.com`, `www.bluenote.com`, `www.jazz-clubs-worldwide.com`, `www.classical.net`, `www.eclassical.com`, `www.classicaliscool.com`, `www.newyorkphilharmonic.org`, `www.lso.co.uk` (London Symphony Orchestra Web site), and `www.culturekiosque.com/opera`.

52. Progressive Rock Ring ★★★★★ **CATEGORY: Genre > Progressive Rock**
URL: `members.home.net/jr27/prog.htm`

Best reasons to surf this site: Download lots of progressive music from the more than 300 indie bands' Web sites within the ring and find lots of good links to progressive music–related sites and progressive BYAHO.

Audio formats: MP3, RA **Streaming formats:** RA **Free BYAHO songs:** Linked **Indie songs:** ★★★★★

Music variety: ★★ **Speed:** ★★★★★ **Webcasts/Videos:** Linked **Radio:** Linked **MP3 software:** Linked

Music/MP3 news: Linked **Chat/Msg. boards:** Linked **How-tos:** ★★★ **Links:** ★★★★★ **Search engine:** ★★★★

Search:		
This site		
Web sites		
Search by:		
Artist		
Ring		
Web Ring		
All Words		
Any Word		
Phrase		
Wizard		
Buy music: Linked		

A *ring* on the Web is a giant collection of independent sites on the same topic that are linked together in a gigantic loop. You can start anywhere on the loop, but a good launching point for this one is `members.home.net/jr27/prog.htm`—home page of "The Progessive Rock Ring." With all the complaints about **rock being dead**, uninspired, unoriginal, and in the doldrums of a restless generation fueled only by boredom, I don't know why progressive music isn't looked to more often to regain that sense of inspiration and hope that **there *is* something exciting out there.** Call it progressive rock, prog, art rock, symphonic rock, eclectic, esoteric, or even fusion, there's a whole history of it—well, from about 1965 on—just waiting to be discovered, or rediscovered, and oftentimes the music even combines the rarely seen together: **talent *and* attitude.** Such better-known bands are **Frank Zappa, King Crimson, Rush, Nektar, Yes, Jethro Tull, John Zorn's Naked City,** and **Slipknot.** Sure it's usually difficult to dance to, but real rock-n-rollers don't care about that, do they? Well then, **throw away your dancing shoes** and wobble on over to The Progressive Rock Ring and you'll find loads of sufficiently **atonal, rhythmically skewed,** and/or just plain beautifully intricate music in more than 300 indie bands' Web sites within the ring. If you're in a band, you can submit your Web site with your music, and if it fits the bill, you can be on the inside of the ring, as well. Find music to download by reading the descriptions of the artists and their influences and link directly to their sites to check them out, or use the search engine to type in a name of a progressive BYAHO and it will pull up links to similar bands' sites within the ring. Akin to jazz and even classical, this music is, by its nature, often **mind-boggling and difficult**. Considering some of the amazing feats and innovations that have already been reached in progressive music, I wonder what the future of progressive rock will be? To check out many more Web rings in all categories—not just music—go to **www.webring.org**.

53. WOMAD.org ★★★★ CATEGORY: Genre > World Music
URL: **www.womad.org**

Best reasons to surf this site: Find music and video clips of great international musicians on Peter Gabriel's Real World Records label and buy their music, check tour info, and download a few free MP3s.

Audio formats: MP3 **Streaming formats:** QT, SWA, RA **Free BYAHO songs:** ★★ **Indie songs:** ★★

Music variety: ★★ **Speed:** ★★★★ **Webcasts/Videos:** ★★★★ **Radio:** None **MP3 software:** Linked

Music/MP3 news: ★★★ **Chat/Msg. boards:** None **How-tos:** ★★★ **Links:** ★★★ **Search engine:** ★★★

Search:	
This site	
Search engines	

Search by:	
Artist	Album
Song	Country
Continent	
Buy music: Yes	
Ships CDs: Yes	
Price: $8.99	
Custom CDs: No	

WOMAD, the World of Music, Arts and Dance, is the international festival organization that was started by the one-and-only **Peter Gabriel** in 1980, who went on to found the Real World Records label in 1989. WOMAD's purpose has always been to bring people together to expose them to music, art, and dance from talented artists around the world. Now you can be exposed to many of these great musicians, too, by going to www.WOMAD.org and entering the Radio Real World section. This section is your central point for going off and exploring the rest of WOMAD and Real World Records' **flash animation-enhanced** network. Along the various paths, you'll discover music and video streams, some free MP3s, and lots of music for sale by the Real World musicians. Also, learn more about the WOMAD festival and its educational workshops, masterclasses, and charities; look up artists' touring information; and take a tour yourself of the **Real World Studios**. The Real World label has become one of the most popular labels for international music; however, there is a collection of more exclusive WOMAD Select recordings that you can only get from the Real World Trading store, at the festivals, and at discerning record stores around the world. For other good or related world music Web sites, fly away to **www.petergabriel.com**, **www.realworld.co.UK**, **www.realmusic.co.uk**, **www.ancient-future.com**, **www.rootsworld.com**, **www.dirtynelson.com/linen**, **www.wpcworld.com**, **titan.spaceports.com/~asianMP3/**, **www.AsiaMix.com**, MP3import.homepage.com/ (The Premier All Asian MP3 Site), **i.am/djmimmie** (Chinese music site), **www.klezmershack.com**, **www.reggaesource.com**, **www.niceup.com** (reggae site), **www.latinworld.com**, **www.alllatinomusic.8k.com**, **www.fronteramag.com** (Latino site), **www.narada.com** (part of Virgin Music Group), and **www.nfak.com** (the official site of Nusrat Fateh Ali Khan).

Online Music Stores

54. MusicMaker.com ★★★★ **CATEGORY: > Buy Music > Custom CDs**
URL: **www.musicmaker.com**
Best reasons to surf this site: Purchase your own customized CD.
Audio formats: MP3, WMA **Streaming formats:** RA **Free BYAHO songs:** ★★★ **Indie songs:** ★
Music variety: ★★★★★ **Speed:** ★★★★★ **Webcasts/Videos:** None **Radio:** None **MP3 software:** Linked
Music/MP3 news: None **Chat/Msg. boards:** None **How-tos:** ★★★★ **Links:** ★★★ **Search engine:** ★★★★

Search:	
This site	

Search by:	
Artist	Song
Genre	Composer
Release date	All Words
Any Word	
Buy music: Yes	
Ships CDs: Yes	
Custom CDs: Yes	
Price per track: 99 cents	

Here's a good site for feeling like a **kid in a candy store**, only you get to pick and choose tracks to put on a CD that Music Maker will then burn and mail to you, instead of candy. "Let's see... on my CD I want the Beastie Boys to go with Charles Ives and Thelonius Monk should come after Floyd...." You get the idea. As I was looking through the songs available at MusicMaker to put on a CD, I saw that I had to choose **at least five tracks** before they would accept my order. Okay, I really only wanted one song, but at the same time, I would feel a little silly waiting 1–2 weeks—the non-rushed delivery time for this site—for a whole CD with one 3-minute song on it. So, I searched the recesses of my brain and came up with four more tracks. While adding the songs to my shopping cart, I noticed an indicator that told me I still had 59 minutes of space available on my CD, even though I had already chosen my five songs (four of which I didn't really want). So, I ditched the four tracks and replaced them with four 18-minute long tracks that I didn't really want, but that filled the CD. The tracks were still only $0.99 each. The CD was therefore **$4.95** ($7.90 after shipping and handling). Three days later, after pacing around the house anticipating the arrival of my creation, I decided to check the mail to see if some other CDs I had ordered had come. As I opened the mailbox I felt like Charlie in *Willie Wonka and the Chocolate Factory* when he was about to open his candy bar. When I looked inside, I suddenly felt like Steve Martin in *The Jerk* yelling, "The new phonebook's here! The new phonebook's here!" That's right, I'd gotten the CD from MusicMaker. I don't know why it came in three days, but I'm not gonna argue with it. The CD cover was a lovely lavender with semi-effluvial "MusicMaker.com" logos on the front, and had the song titles, artists' names, and track times on the back. The CD itself was white and had "MusicMaker.com" and the song titles printed on it. **It sounded good, too.** MusicMaker.com is a very easy site to use. You can also listen to 30-second clips of all MusicMaker's songs, download a decent selection of free MP3s and WMAs by BYAHO, and check out and buy music from lists of the Top 101 Artists, Top 101 Tracks Featured Artists, New Artists, and New Labels. There's even a list of songs appropriate for upcoming holidays. Join the Insiders Club to get a free track every time you mix your own CD and to get gift certificates, gift ideas, and suggestions of songs it thinks you might like based on your shopping history there. Also, look for **exclusive releases** by famous artists who have cut deals with MusicMaker. For example, they had "Jimmy

Page and The Black Crows Live at the Greek" that you could only get at MusicMaker.com. MusicMaker.com could stand to have more artists and songs available, however. A lot of times they'll have an artist but only one of their CDs, and in many cases **I didn't find the artists I was looking** for at all, even though they were big names—it depends on which record labels MusicMatch has signed deals with. I also wish the tracks were available for immediate download. They should be able to do this. MusicMaker is striking deals with record labels all the time, though, and at present they have more than **200,000 tracks from over 101 labels.** You can't beat having only the songs you want on a CD, and this model is bound to be the wave of the future, even if you have to burn the CDs yourself. Other good sites that can burn a custom CD for you are `www.customdisk.com`, `www.cductive.com`, `www.cdj.co.uk`, `www.towerrecords.com`, and `www.riffage.com` (for indie music).

55. Amazon.com ★★★★★ **CATEGORY: Buy Music > All Formats**
URL: `www.amazon.com`

Best reasons to surf this site: Buy CDs, cassettes, vinyls, DVDs, music videos, and music software. Plus, copy and save album cover art, and indie bands should check out the Amazon.com Advantage program.

Audio formats: MP3, LQT **Streaming formats:** RA **Free BYAHO songs:** ★★★ **Indie songs:** ★★★
Music variety: ★★★★★ **Speed:** ★★★★★ **Webcasts/Videos:** None **Radio:** None **MP3 software:** ★★★★
Music/MP3 news: ★★★ **Chat/Msg. boards:** None **How-tos:** ★★★ **Links:** ★★ **Search engine:** ★★★★

Search:	
This site	

Search by:	
Artist	Album
Song	Genre
Composer	Label
Reviews	
Buy music: Yes	
Ships CDs: Yes	
Price: $9.99 - $13.99	
Custom CDs: No	

As most people agree, this is a great online store for music, books, movies, games, software, and so on. As far as music goes, what makes this site worth visiting is the fact that they sell practically **every CD and cassette available** in the world! They also have a huge selection of **vinyls, DVDs,** and **music videos** that, let's not forget, can be converted to **MP3,** as well. When checking out various CDs, tapes, and so on, Amazon provides a star rating of the album and written reviews by its editorial staff and customers, and has a "Customers Who Bought This Title Also Bought…" feature that lets you get an idea of similar artists you might like. Amazon also shows the picture of the album, making this a **great place to get album cover art** that you can tag to your MP3s so the album cover displays on your Jukebox every time you play that MP3, a feature supported by both RealJukebox and MusicMatch Jukebox. **Pre-order music** at Amazon in the New and Future Releases section or use the Amazon.com Alerts feature to automatically be notified if any new albums come out by your favorite artists. Check out Essentials to find **classic albums,** look under **10 Under $10** to find a list of 10 CDs in different genres available for under $10, and find more than 120 Liquid Audio and/or MP3 (usually LQT) downloads, many by BYAHO, under Free Downloads. This is all great stuff for online buyers, and for you independent labels and artists out there who want to reach a larger audience and sell your CDs, Amazon.com has the **Amazon.com Advantage** program that you can join for free. By joining, Amazon will order copies of your CDs; put them in their distribution center; and list the CDs in their online catalog with cover art, track samples, and liner notes. They'll also email you your online sales and inventory reports and pay you automatically the month after they sell the CDs. From the Electronics and Software section, type **MP3** in the search engine to get a huge list of **MP3 related software** and **hardware** available for sale at Amazon, or, if you know what you want, just type in the name of the product. When it pulls up what you're looking for, you get a description of the product, editorial and customer reviews, a list of other related items, and it might even tell you in which cities the product is most popular. The only thing I wish you could do is link to the products' home pages to see whether a free version is available. At Amazon, the software is all for sale. Still, it's a good way to check out what's on the market, and, oh yeah, you *could* even buy something. Similar sites are **www.barnesandnoble.com** and **www.bordersbooks.com**.

56. Amuz.net ★★★★ CATEGORY: Buy Music > Discounted
URL: **www.amuz.net**

Best reasons to surf this site: Buy CDs, cassettes, DVDs, and VHS tapes at discounted prices; read music news; chat; and link to music art sites.

Audio formats: LQT **Streaming formats:** WMA, LQT **Free BYAHO songs:** ★★ **Indie songs:** ★★

Music variety: ★★★★★ **Speed:** ★★★★★ **Webcasts/Video:** ★★★ **Radio stations:** None **MP3 software:** Linked

Music/MP3 news: ★★★★ **Chat/Msg. boards:** ★★★★ **How-tos:** ★★★ **Links:** ★★★ **Search engine:** ★★★

Search:	
This site	
Search by:	
Artist	
Album	
Song	
Genre	
Buy music: Yes	
Ships CDs: Yes	
Price: $8.95 – $14.55	
Custom CDs: No	

Although the main function of this site is to sell music and videos—and they do have **good prices** on practically every CD and tape out there—you can also **amuse yourself**—make that "amuz"—by chatting in chat rooms; viewing Webcasts; checking out the U.K. charts; reading lots of music news, album reviews, and interviews; and downloading up-and-coming artists' LQTs. While you're here, check out the Movies department to buy **DVDs and VHS tapes** and link to **music-related art sites** in the Art section to get some great pictures and artwork that can be used on your MP3 players or as wallpaper. If any of these extra features do not amuse you, you weiner, remember that this site never fails in its main goal of offering its customers "over **260,000 titles** of pre-recorded music on CD, Cassette and video from all major record labels and studios and over **4,000 independent music labels**" to purchase. I didn't know there *were* over 4,000 independent record labels! Go to **www.gemm.com** for a similar and comprehensive site that carries lots of **used CDs** and **LPs** from **importers, collectors,** and **discounters** around the world, and go to **www.secondspin.com** to buy and **sell CDs**.

57. EMusic.com ★★★★ CATEGORY: Buy Music > Immediate Download
URL: **www.emusic.com**

Best reasons to surf this site: Purchase MP3 tracks available for immediate download by BYAHO.

Audio formats: MP3, RA **Streaming formats:** MP3, RA **Free BYAHO songs:** ★★ **Indie songs:** ★★

Music variety: ★★★★★ Speed: ★★★★★ Webcasts/Videos: None Radio: None MP3 software: Linked Music/MP3 news: ★★★★ Chat/Msg. boards: None How-tos: ★★★★ Links: ★★★ Search engine: ★★★

Search:	
This site	

Search by:	
Artist	
Genre	
Alphabet	
Label	
Buy music: Yes	
Ships CDs: No	
Price: $8.99 (album)	
Price per track: 99 cents	

Emusic.com—an Internet music distributor with license agreements with some of the biggest record labels—specializes in letting you purchase MP3 tracks by BYAHO. More significantly, it's one of the few places where you can buy MP3s, **download them right then and there**, and start listening. **This could be the new business model for buying music.** If people can legally get **a song for a dollar**, many of them would do it. But, if the choice is between having to pay $15 or $17 for a CD to get that one song or getting it for free off the Internet—even though it may not be legal—they're going to opt for the latter. We already know that. At any rate, EMusic does not mail you a CD, but if you have a CD-R burner, you can always convert the MP3s to WAVs and **burn them to a CD** if you want that music for your car or home stereo. Actually, it's more fun to burn a CD than have one mailed to you. And, the MP3s you get have been encoded at 128kbps, so they have CD-quality sound and convert to WAVs nicely. Emusic has more than **75,000 tracks** for sale. Individual tracks are 99 cents, and unlike other sites, Emusic actually lets you put **as little as 99 cents on your credit card**. You can **download the entire album, on average, for $8.99**. Also, listen to free 30-second MP3 and Real Audio streamed samples of the tracks before you buy them—RealPlayer works well for both. Not a bad deal, but I do wish they had an even larger list of artists and tracks to buy. Even though they have a lot of music, it's not an every-track-in-the-world site. But they add **5,000+ new downloads every month,** so they may soon get there. At Emusic, you also can read headlines and stories about what's hot in music, and don't forget its Free Tracks section, where you can get a few MP3s by BYAHO for free. All-in-all, this is a very good site, and one of the only sites, for those who have a credit card and want to pay to start downloading and listening to music now!

58. LiquidAudio.com ★★★★ **CATEGORY: Buy Music > Liquid Audio Format > Immediate download** URL: www.liquidaudio.com

Best reasons to surf this site: Purchase, and download immediately, Liquid Audio (LQT) tracks by BYAHO and link to other sites that have LQTs in the Liquid Music Network.

Audio formats: LQT **Streaming formats:** LQT, RA **Free BYAHO songs:** ★★★ **Indie songs:** ★★

Music variety: ★★★★★ Speed: ★★★★★ Webcasts/Videos: ★★★ Radio: Linked MP3 software: ★★ Music/MP3 news: ★★★★ Chat/Msg. boards: None How-tos: ★★★★ Links: ★★★★★ Search engine: ★★★★

Search:	
This site	

Search by:

Artist

Album

Song

Genre

Alphabet

Label

Buy music: Yes

Payper download: Yes

Price per track: $0.99[en]$2.49 (usually $1.49 or $1.62)

Sort of like Emusic, LiquidAudio.com sells many individual tracks by BYAHO that are available for immediate download, except the tracks are compressed in **Liquid Audio format (LQT)** instead of MP3. Liquid Audio uses **AAC** (Advanced Audio Coding), which is part of MPEG-2 technology, but is often thought of as **MP4** because it has better compression rates. Though **LQTs generally sound better** than MP3s, most people probably could not really tell the difference if the MP3 has been encoded at a higher bit rate (128kbps or higher). Because the AAC software is expensive to license, LQTs generally cost more when you find them on the Net. However, some free ones are out there (try **www.amazon.com, www.billboard.com, www.nordicdms.com, www.planetofmusic.com, www.audiocandy.com**, and **www.atomicpop.com**). You can preview and buy loads of LQTs right at LiquidAudio.com or go to its Liquid Music Network to get an extensive list of links to Liquid Audio affiliates and even links to online radio stations. However, you should be aware of the many restrictions that come with using the Liquid Audio format. Liquid Audio is a proprietary and secure format that **cannot be directly converted to MP3 or WAV** files (although the Liquid Player does play MP3s). This means that you can burn tracks to a CD only as an LQT, which means you can listen to the CD only on your computer. Liquid Audio also has code embedded on its LQTs that **let you burn the track to a CD only one time.** You can listen to the tracks from your hard drive all you want, though. **Gee, thanks,** after all I bought the track, didn't I? They also make it **a pain** to transfer LQTs to other computers. First, you have to get a Liquid Audio Passport and then, when you decide to play Liquid Tracks on another computer, copy passport.lqp into the root directory of the Liquid Player installed on the computer. What!? Seems kind of stingy to me. **You can get around a lot of this** by capturing the LQT with an audio catcher, such as **Total Recorder** on the book's CD. It captures and converts the LQT to a WAV file as it's playing. But, when you can find so many MP3s on the Internet for free that can also easily be moved onto other computers, converted to WAVs, and recorded as many times as you like onto CDs that can be played in a car or home stereo, the question is, "Why even bother with Liquid Audio format?" It's a good question. And its answer is that Liquid Audio files generally sound better and can be downloaded immediately after being purchased. Liquid Audio may also be an answer for a business model that's needed to help deal with the whole industry.

59. TowerRecords.com ★★★★★ CATEGORY: Buy Music > Retail on-line
URL: www.towerrecords.com

Best reasons to surf this site: Buy music and create your own customized CDs, including songs from *Billboard's* charts from the 1940s to 1980s, look for upcoming releases, and buy out-of-print CDs and imports.

Audio formats: MP3, WMA, **LQT Streaming formats:** RA **Free BYAHO songs:** ★★ **Indie songs:** ★★
Music variety: ★★★★★ **Speed:** ★★★★★ **Webcasts:** None **Radio:** None **MP3 software:** ★★
Music/MP3 news: ★★★ **Chat/Msg. boards:** None **How-tos:** ★★★ **Links:** ★★ **Search engine:** ★★★★

Search:
This site

Search by:	
Artist	
Album	
Song	
Genre	
Label	
Release date	
Year	
Reviews	
Buy music: Yes	
Ships CDs: Yes	
Avg. Price: $8.99 – $12.99	
Custom CDs: Yes	
Price per track: 99 cents	
Immediate download: No.	

The first thing that struck me about this site was that I could buy **used CDs**, and, as expected, they were at a very discounted price. TowerRecords.com has good prices on non-used CDs, too. Then, as I browsed through album after album, band after band, I realized that this site has **practically every album out there!** The question is: "*What* should I buy?" Well, buy any CD you dag-blam want, or pick individual tracks and **create your own CD**. Although the choices of songs available to make a custom CD are limited, there are still many to choose from, including songs on *Billboard's* top hits charts from the '40s to the '80s. Before buying a CD, listen to 30-second previews with your Real Player and read reviews of the album, too. It's really your **one-stop shopping** for CDs like Amazon.com is, but here you can create your own CDs! Yee-haw, ride 'em cowboy. This site is **not the place to go** to download much music software or find many links, but that's made up for by the fact that you can check out the latest releases from every genre of music, check for any upcoming releases (which you can pre-order), check out the **top 1,000 selling albums** (updated daily), look for every CD under $7, look for **out-of-print CDs**, pick from a huge selection of **imports**, order gift certificates, get good gift ideas, and play a semi-fun music **trivia game for money**. TowerRecords.com also has its listening station (like you find in the real stores) where you can listen to streamed sound clips from 84 of the latest releases, and let's not forget that the site is good for buying cassettes, videos, DVDs, and music-related books, too.

Independent (Indie) Bands

60. ChangeMusic.com ★★★★★ CATEGORY: Indie Band > Musicians
URL: www.changemusic.com

Best reasons to surf this site: Get lots of good indie MP3s, and indie artists can get their own free band page where they can post their MP3s and promote themselves. Also find good MP3 resources throughout the CM Network.

Audio formats: MP3 **Streaming formats:** N/A **Free BYAHO songs:** Linked **Indie songs:** ★★★★★

Music variety: ★★★★★ **Speed:** ★★★★★ **Webcasts/Videos:** Linked **Radio:** Linked **MP3 software:** Linked

Music/MP3 news: Linked **Chat/Msg. boards:** ★★★★ **How-tos:** ★★★★ **Links:** ★★★★ **Search engine:** ★★★★★

Search:		
This site		
FTP sites		
Multiple search engines		

Search by:	
Artist	
Song	
Genre	
Wizard	
Buy music: Linked	

If you're an indie artist, get hooked into the Change Music Network. Although this site is great for getting or linking to a little of everything related to MP3 music, it's specialty is in **helping you promote your music**. Create your own band page and upload your MP3s with your band's bios, comments, photos, histories, tour dates, and influences, and have fans rate and email your MP3 to other people. With Change Music's merger with Rare Medium's **www.CMJ.com**, Change Music also provides a free, non-exclusive service for its artist that makes your CD available for order in all major record stores and online retailers so you can get even more exposure! Also, all artists will be listened to by Change Music's A&R staff, and you can benefit from their contacts by accessing their music industry directory, thus making Change Music your **backstage pass** to the music industry. All this is free, too. Check out Artist Signup for more details. A good way to find the indie bands you might like is to type a name of a BYAHO in Change Music's search engine. This not only finds links to available MP3s by the BYAHO (from FTP sites only), but it also pulls up Related Artists in Change Music's network that you might like (MP3s at Change Music **download easily**, unlike the ones from the FTP sites). Checking the music news headlines at ChangeMusic.com takes you to CMJ's site, where you'll also find links to all sorts of BYAHO official Web sites, record labels, Internet broadcasters, and Webcasts. While you're here, check out some of the other well-known sites that are part of the Change Music Network, too, including **www.mp3park.com** (good for MP3 software and utilities), **www.mp3place.com** (has a little of everything), **www.mp3now.com** (little of everything, but especially good for software and great how-tos), **www.customize.org** (good links and *tons* of skins), and **www.palavista.com** (home to the MP3 metacrawling search engine).

61. Garageband.com ★★★★★ CATEGORY: Indie > Musicians
URL: www.garageband.com

Best reasons to surf this site: Indie bands can submit their music and participate in contests to win a $250,000 recording contract every time a new review period comes up. Visitors get to help decide who wins.

Audio formats: N/A **Streaming formats:** MP3, RA **Free BYAHO songs:** None **Indie songs:** ★★★★★

Music variety: ★★★★ **Speed:** N/A **Webcasts/Videos:** Linked **Radio:** None **MP3 software:** None

Music/MP3 news: ★★ **Chat/Msg. boards:** ★★★★ **How-tos:** ★★★ **Links:** ★★ **Search engine:** ★★★

Search:	
This site	

Search by:	
Artist	
Song	
Genre	
Hometown	
Buy music: Link to bands' Web sites to see if they have music for sale.	

At GarageBands.com, bands can send in their music, which visitors and fans can listen to in RA or MP3 streams (remember, if you like a song, catch it with your Total Recorder). But the main thing that makes this site stick out is a contest that gives a **$250,000 recording contract** to the winning band. Every few months a winner is picked by visitors and by Garageband.com's Advisory Board, which includes such big names as **Sir George Martin** (signer and producer of **The Beatles**, and Chairman of Garageband's Advisory Board), **Brian Eno** (musician and producer who has worked with **David Bowie** and **Robert Fripp**, to name a few), **Steve Lillywhite** (producer of **U2, The Dave Matthews Band**, and **Siouxsie and the Banshees**), and **Ed Stasium** (producer of **The Ramones**). One of the cofounders of Garageband.com is ex-**Talking Head**, and now much sought-out producer, **Jerry Harrison**. One of this site's main goals is to "check out new talent [and to make] garageband.com into the ultimate online music community; a place for new talent and established pros to meet as equals and help each other make better music." Visitors can listen to "tens of thousands of songs," and find music based on Best Vocalist, Best Guitars, Best Drums, Best Bass, Best Keyboard, and Most Original Track, Best Lyrics, and so on, handpicked by Garageband reviewers. Every song has its own profile page where you can review the song, get band info, and maybe even read the lyrics. In addition, at Garageband.com, you can link to the bands' Web sites to check them out further and see whether they have a CD for sell, send messages to the bands, and also "go backstage" to participate in many different music forums. May the best band win.

62. HarmonyCentral.com ★★★★★ **CATEGORY: Indie > Band & Musician**
URL: www.harmonycentral.com

Best reasons to surf this site: Mainly for musicians and other music professionals to find an extraordinary amount of music resources, including tablature, lyrics, industry news, audio software, forums…the list goes on and on.

Audio formats: N/A Streaming formats: N/A Free BYAHO songs: N/A Indie songs: N/A

Music variety: ★★★★★ **Speed:** ★★★★★ **Webcasts/Videos:** None **Radio:** None **MP3/Audio software:** ★★★★★

Music/MP3 news: ★★★★★ **Chat/Msg. boards:** ★★★★★ **How-tos:** ★★★★★ **Links:** ★★★★★ **Search engine:** ★★★★★

Search:	
This site	
Multiple search engines	

Search by:	
Artist	Song
Lyrics	Tablature
Alphabet	Site
Instruments	All Words
Any Word	Phrase
Sentence	Paragraph
Line	
Buy music: No	

This is a **musician's paradise**. You may not find music to download or post here, but that's not what this site is about. Rather, this is an *extremely* useful site for musicians and music professionals to find everything else music resource–related, and you might even get a sense that you can get a real music education here, too. At Harmony Central, you can find or link to practically **anything that you could possibly imagine** having to do with guitars, bass, drums, keyboards, recording, music computing, and help for bands, including resources for getting exposure. Also, find tons of music industry news, music/musician classified ads, used and rare gear auctions, buyer's guides; download sound editing effects and other audio software; join chat rooms, discussion groups, guitar forums, MIDI forums; find out what's hot in music technology; link to online music magazines, instrument makers, music educational services, theory/composition sites, tablature, lyrics, written music lessons by, say, Steve Vai or other famous musicians, and so on—there are too many more resources to mention (all good). And now you can use the Harmony Central Studios, in conjunction with technology by Rocket Network and sponsored by EMagic, to "make music online with anybody on Earth" by sharing your music projects with others to create collaborative recordings. Just phenomenal. For more music tablature, go to www.1-2-3-tabs.com, www.freshtabs.com, www.guitartabs.com, www.guitarsite.com (great guitar site), and www.nutz.org; to find sheet music, try www.encoremusic.com, www.sheetmusicplus.com, www.sheetmusicdirect.com, and www.jumpmusic.com.

63. IMNTV.com ★★★★★ CATEGORY: Indie > Band & Musician
URL: www.imntv.com

Best reasons to surf this site: Send in your self-produced music video, no matter what format, and IMNTV will show it on their national TV station. The top artist every month gets a 30-minute special and record contract.

Audio formats: N/A Streaming formats: RA, WMA Free BYAHO songs: ★★★★ Indie songs: None
Music variety: ★★★★★ Speed: N/A Webcasts/Videos: ★★★★★ Radio: None MP3 software: None
Music/MP3 news: None Chat/Msg. boards: ★★★★ How-tos: ★★★ Links: ★★ Search engine: ★★★

Search:	
This site	
Search by:	
Artist	
Genre	

Buy music: Link to the artists' homepages to see if they have CDs for sell.

This is the Web site for the new television channel Independent Music Network Television, which may become the MTV for indie bands. Send in your videos, whether they are on VHS, 8 MusicMatch, DV cam, or Betacam SP. It doesn't matter. "All artists and bands that submit music videos will be broadcast on national TV - Free." The IMN Advisory Board will also pick the top 10 artists every month and give them a 30-minute featured segment that will be shown on their national TV network and Webcast simultaneously at the Web site during the next month. The top artist will also be given the opportunity to sign a deal with IMN's record label, Ecity Records. According to founder and president of IMNTV James Fallacaro, "For the first time amateur musicians who dream of achieving star status will have the opportunity to showcase their talent to an international audience…IMNTV will significantly increase the chances for a band to find success at a time when corporate consolidation in the entertainment industry is stifling creativity." Artists can also buy and sell equipment in IMN's classifieds, post messages, build home pages, and check the status of their videos. Visitors can watch IMNTV programs, including streamed videos by the Top Ten artists every month, and give viewer feedback. If you want to make a video, don't forget to consider using your local public access television centers to help you out. That's what they're there for, they're free, and look where it got Wayne and Garth! Some good indie film/TV and short movie/animation sites, where you may be able to learn some tricks of the trade and get ideas, are www.alwaysif.com, www.kkrs.net (Kanakaris), www.farmclub.com (check out FCTV), www.sputnik7.com, and www.ifctv.com (Independent Film Channel). You also can find more with Scour.com's search engine.

64. IUMA.com ★★★★★ CATEGORY: Indie > Band & Musician
URL: www.iuma.com

Best reasons to surf this site: Get lots of indie music, and indie musicians have a free place to promote themselves by setting up a Web page, posting their MP3s, and offering their CDs for sale.

Audio formats: MP3 **Streaming formats:** RA **Free BYAHO songs:** ★ **Indie songs:** ★★★★★
Music variety: ★★★★★ **Speed:** ★★★★★ **Webcasts/Videos:** None **Radio:** ★★★★ **MP3 software:** Linked

Music/MP3 news: ★★ **Chat/Msg. boards:** ★★★★ **How-tos:** ★★★★ **Links:** ★★★ **Search engine:** ★★★★

Search:	
This site	

Search by:	
Artist	
Song	
Genre	
Alphabet	
Country	
State	
Year	
Buy music: Linked	

IUMA, short for **Internet Underground Music Archive**, is part of the EMusic Network and was created by the same guys who brought you the song "Cold Turd on a Paper Plate." But you'll find no cold turds here. Rather just the hottest, steamiest indie bands around on a huge platter of musical genres. At IUMA, "post your music where actual musicians are watching out for you - **not weasels watching the numbers**. You have your own URL with your band name first, and a custom Web page where you can post all your band info and MP3s, sell CDs, create message boards, fan lists, and of course, get e-mail from your fans - all Free." Sounds good, and it is. IUMA also has its own IUMA Radio stations, and for industry tips, tricks, and advice, check out the **Sue Few's Sound Check** newsletters. IUMA is a great place to discover new acts and a chance for indie musicians to gain worldwide exposure and sell their music.

65. MusicGlobalNetwork.com ★★★★ CATEGORY: Indie > Battle of the Bands
URL: www.musicglobalnetwork.com

Best reasons to surf this site: Indie Bands can participate in the Battle of the Web Bands contests to win cash, software, and other prizes. Visitors can download lots of Indie MP3 and get great MP3 how-tos.

Audio formats: MP3 **Streaming formats:** N/A **Free BYAHO songs:** None **Indie songs:** ★★★★
Music variety: ★★★★ **Speed:** ★★★★★ **Webcasts/Videos:** None **Radio:** None **MP3 software:** ★★★★

Music/MP3 news: ★★ **Chat/Msg. boards:** ★★★★★ **How-tos:** ★★★★★ **Links:** ★ **Search engine:** ★★★

Search:	
This site	

Search by:	
Artist	
Song	
Genre	
All Words	
Any Word	
Buy music: Yes	
Ships CDs: Yes	
Avg. price: $11.28	

Not to be confused with GlobalMusicNetwork.com, the jazz and classical site (see review earlier in this section), the Music Global Network is a terrific site to **discover new indie bands**, a great place for indies to submit their music, and the place to participate in MGN's centerpiece: their *Battle of the Web Bands!* Winners are based on who gets the most downloads, and to the victors go hard cold cash, software, and other prizes. This is the largest battle of the bands on the Web, and it's also free to enter. For people just getting started with downloading and recording MP3s, this site has great MP3 how-tos with relevant MP3 software to download, and you can get more help in the forums, including a **forum on tips and tricks for home recording**. For people with short-term memory loss, there's even a handy calendar you can use at MGN so you can keep track of important concerts you think other people should know about, or so you won't forget about it while you daydream of winning The Battle of the Web Bands contest or just having one of your songs be among the more than 101 available on The Battle of the Web Bands CD.

66. PlanetPromo.net ★★★★ CATEGORY: Indie > Promotion
URL: www.planetpromo.net

Best reasons to surf this site: Find out how to promote your music, link to sites that support promoting indie bands, and enter contests to win merchandise to help market your band.

Audio formats: N/A **Streaming formats:** N/A **Free BYAHO songs:** N/A **Indie songs:** N/A
Music variety: N/A **Speed:** N/A **Webcasts/Videos:** None **Radio:** None **MP3 software:** None
Music/MP3 news: None **Chat/Msg. boards:** None **How-tos:** ★★★★★ **Links:** ★★★★ **Search engine:** None

Search:
This site

Search by:
State
Province

Buy music: No

Here's the site your band needs to visit if you want to find out about **promoting your music**. PlanetPromo has gathered great links and information so you can **get heard by music critics and record labels**, sell your CDs and merchandise, and extend your fan base. Learn the **10 steps to promoting your music**, how to get signed, how to write a press release and about press relations, how to replicate CDs, the dos and don'ts for CD replication, how to insert CD graphics; link to Web sites that support band promotion and let you sell your CDs; contact one of PlanetPromo's brokers to ask them about making copies of your CDs, DVDs, or videos; ask them any other questions you may have; and enter PlanetPromo's contests to win stuff you can use to promote your band, such as 500 copies of your MP3 CD and merchandise with your band's name and logo on it that you can sell at your next show. Between going to sites such as KohnMusic.com, where you can find out about your **legal rights** to broadcast your music over the Internet and about performing publicly, and going to sights such as PlanetPromo, you and your band will definitely **be ahead of the game** and, hopefully, be on your way to superstardom. Find more tips on promoting your band and sell your CDs, too, at www.cdbaby.com; go to www.taxi.com to have them help you promote your CD or tape, no matter how crappy it may sound (see review of Taxi.com); and, go to www.musiciansguide.com to order a *Billboard* publication with info on touring and promotion.

67. Riffage.com ★★★★★ CATEGORY: Indie > Band & Musician
URL: www.riffage.com

Best reasons to surf this site: Bands make 85 percent of the sales of their music and merchandise, and fans download lots of music from indie bands, chat, write reviews, and purchase customized indie CDs.

Audio formats: MP3 **Streaming formats:** MP3, RA **Free BYAHO songs:** ★ **Indie songs:** ★★★★★
Music variety: ★★★★ **Speed:** ★★★★ **Webcasts/Videos:** ★★★ **Radio:** None **MP3 software:** Linked
Music/MP3 news: ★★★★ **Chat/Msg. boards:** ★★★★ **How-tos:** ★★★★ **Links:** ★★★ **Search engine:** ★★★★

Search:	
This site	

Search by:	
Artist	Song
Genre	Alphabet
Country	State
City	Year
Date	Rating
Wizard	
Buy music: Yes	
Ships CDs: Yes	
Price: $7.99 – $9.99	
Custom CDs: Yes	
Avg Price: $8.99	

Opportunities abound here for the indie artist, for this is **one of the most visited sites** on the Web that provides a forum for musicians to post and sell their MP3s, CDs, and other merchandise. Set your own prices and keep **85 percent** of the sales from this site that "invests in radio, online, print, event, and TV advertising to drive traffic to the site." Also **keep in touch with your fans** and let them help promote you by setting up message boards, calendars, and email, all for free. Visitors and fans can listen to previews and download many free MP3s and set up a My Riffage account. This allows you to post your own reviews, receive recommendations, chat, use the message boards, and **create playlists of songs you like** that can also be **shared with other members** as if you were a DJ. Get music industry news under the not-so-noticeable Read This button, and order customized CDs with up to 10 indie songs for $8.99. Finally, look for Riffage to start presenting more Webcasts and check out the ones they have at **www.RiffageLive.com** to hear some hot guitar riffs.

68. Songfile.com ★★★★★ CATEGORY: Indie > Bands & Musicians
URL: **www.songfile.com**

Best reasons to surf this site: Find lyrics, sheet music, musical instrument classifieds, instrument manu-facturers, and concert tickets.

Audio formats: N/A **Streaming formats:** RA **Free BYAHO songs:** N/A **Indie songs:** N/A
Music variety: ★★★★ **Speed:** N/A **Webcasts/Videos:** None **Radio:** None **MP3 software:** None
Music/MP3 news: None **Chat/Msg. boards:** None **How-tos:** ★★ **Links:** ★★★★ **Search engine:** ★★★★

Search:	
This site	

Search by:	
Artist	
Album	
Song	

Writer

Lyrics

All Words

Any Word

Buy music: Linked

This site is a great stop for musicians, songwriters, and fans alike. From Songfile's database of more than 2 million songs, listen to audio clips; link to online stores to buy the CD the clips are on; get sheet music, **licensing information**, general band/song information; and find other recordings by that artist. At Songfile.com, you'll also find great links to music instrument classifieds, instrument manufacturers, music magazines, **music industry resources**, concert promoters, concert tickets, and lyrics from the widely used **Lyrics.ch** lyrics server, and you can get it all in **five different languages**—English, French, Spanish, Italian, and Dutch—if you can handle it.

69. Songs.com ★★★★★ **CATEGORY: Indie > Folk, jazz, blues**
URL: www.songs.com

Best reasons to surf this site: Check out hundreds of folk, blues, and jazz indie acts; download many of their MP3s; buy their CDs; participate in music/MP3 forums; and find links to music/musician resources.

Audio formats: MP3 **Streaming formats:** RA **Free BYAHO songs:** ★★ **Indie songs:** ★★★★

Music variety: ★★★★ **Speed:** ★★★★★ **Webcasts/Videos:** Linked **Radio:** Linked **MP3 software:** Linked

Music/MP3 news: ★★★★ **Chat/Msg. boards:** ★★★★ **How-tos:** ★★★★ **Links:** ★★★★ **Search engine:** ★★★

Search:
This site

Search by:
Artist
Song
Genre
Keyword
Buy music: Yes
Ships CDs: Yes
Avg. Price: $14.95
Custom CDs: No

This is kind of a peaceful, **more manure, or rather, more mature** site that—although all genres are welcome—is particularly good for the more folksy/bluesy/jazzy indie musician to create their own band page, which they can do for free, and post their music and sell their CDs. This, in turn, means that this is a particularly **good site for visitors to find folksy/jazzy/bluesy** artists emerging in the indie scene and download lots of their free MP3s. At Songs.com, you also can participate in good music/MP3 forums, get MP3 help, find occasional links to audio Webcasts, order **indie box sets**, and link to MP3 software and online radio. Musicians can place musician/instrument wanted-type **classifieds**, and link to some indie record label, song writing, and music agent sites. Hundreds of indie artists are here, so, join them or check them out, and support them by buying their CDs if you like the MP3s or RA song streams you hear. Of note, this site has nothing to do with **Tunes.com**, even though both may make you think of whistling.

70. Taxi.com ★★★★★ **CATEGORY: Indie > Band & Musician**
URL: www.taxi.com

Best reasons to surf this site: Taxi will listen to any submitted recording and determine whether or not it should be passed on to their connections at major recording studios. It also has good music resource links.

Audio formats: N/A **Streaming formats:** N/A **Free BYAHO songs:** None **Indie songs:** Linked

Music variety: N/A **Speed:** N/A **Webcasts/Videos:** N/A **Radio:** Linked **MP3 software:** Linked

Music/MP3 news: Linked **Chat/Msg. boards:** N/A **How-tos:** ★★★ **Links:** ★★★★★ **Search engine:** ★★★★

Search:	
This site	
Web sites	
Search by:	
Artist	
Album	
Song	
All Words	
Any Word	
Buy music: No	

It's a rough world in the recording industry—a cold, heartless, dog-eat-dog existence where **no one cares if you live or die** as long as you make them money. Lay a golden egg or you're yesterday's news. They'll tell you it's just business, but you know it's personal. And on top of it, you've probably got a hangover. So if you want to make it, you're gonna need all the help you can get. **So who ya gonna call?** Not me. Not your mother. Call a Taxi, Harry. No, not that taxi, I mean that one over there…Taxi.com. That's what they're there for! If you're getting frustrated sending in your recordings to college radios or other "connections," only to have nothing come of them, try Taxi.com. Taxi will not only listen to each and every one of your submissions, but send them on to bigwigs at major recording companies if they feel it's got the right stuff. Taxi will also send you a **list of the criteria** that the companies are looking for in an act or music so you can pick the best recordings to submit and increase your chances of getting them accepted. The recordings don't even have to be that great. They're "looking for hits, not great engineers!" If your songs do not get picked, Taxi's staff will send them back to you with suggestions and reviews of your work written by their credited and veteran A&R staff. It's **$299.95 for a one-year membership** that includes all of Taxi's benefits, $5.00 per song to submit, and "typically more than 40% of [their] members get something forwarded in any given year [and their] 'success ratio' for members who score deals usually runs about 5-6%." Go to Taxi.com to get the rest of the details. Who knows, maybe you could be the one. I doubt it, but you never know….

71. WorldWideBands.com ★★★★ **Category: Indie > Band & Musician**
URL: www.worldwidebands.com

Best reasons to surf this site: Musicians can find great links to music and industry resources. Fans can get lots of free MP3s by indie bands.

Audio formats: MP3 **Streaming formats:** Real, WMA **Free BYAHO songs:** Linked **Indie songs:** ★★★★

Music variety: ★★★★★ **Speed:** ★★★★ **Webcasts/Videos:** None **Radio:** Linked **MP3 software:** Linked

Music/MP3 news: Linked **Chat/Msg. boards:** ★★★★ **How-tos:** Linked **Links:** ★★★★★ **Search engine:** ★★★

Search:	
FTP sites	
Web sites	

Search By:	
Artist	Album
Song	Genre
All Words	Any Word
Country	Phrase
Buy music: No	

Find great links to music industry resources, indie record labels, **music lawyers,** and other MP3/music-related sites, and also post your music at WorldWideBands.com. This **easy-to-navigate** site's objective "is to help promote indie bands and artists who play **music of all different styles.**" When looking up bands, you'll find brief band write-ups that come in handy for the artists to promote themselves, and for you to determine whether or not you want to go to their sites. There is also a section that contains all the artists who specifically offer MP3 downloads (bands who don't offer MP3 downloads usually have Real or WMA streams, so still check them out). For indie artists, this is one of the **better known Web sites** of its kind, and it provides an organized platform for bands to get their music out to the public and learn about the music industry.

Resources

72. HiFiHeaven.com ★★★★★ CATEGORY: Resources > Music hardware
URL: www.hifiheaven.com

Best reasons to surf this site: Find links to all kinds of high-end home and car audio equipment, including portable MP3 players, outboard sound cards, recordable CD and DVD-ROM drives, and more.

Audio formats: N/A **Streaming formats:** N/A **Free BYAHO songs:** N/A **Indie songs:** N/A

Music variety: N/A **Speed:** N/A **Webcasts/Videos:** None **Radio:** None **MP3 software:** Linked

Music/MP3 news: Linked **Chat/Msg. boards:** ★★★★ **How-tos:** ★★ **Links:** ★★★★★ **Search engine:** ★★★

Search:	
Web sites	

Search by:	
All Words	
Any Word	
Buy music: No	

This is a fantastic audio directory site that links you to all kinds of **home and car audio equipment** available for sale on the Internet. Not only can you link to sites to find your regular ol' sound equipment, but you can also go to HiFiHeaven's Multimedia, MP3 section and find links to **handheld MP3 players, MP3 players for your car,** computer speakers, CD and DVD recorders, DVD-ROM drives, and soundcards, including sound cards with a digital-to-analog converter that sits outside your computer and plugs into the USB port so it doesn't pick up the **whirlwind of electronic hums and noises going on inside your computer** as you play your MP3s. Plus, HiFiHeaven also links to lots of good MP3 sites, MP3 software and utilities, MP3 news, other audio hardware sites, and audio magazines. It also has a great message boards area, classifieds, product reviews, and a search engine you can use to look up audio sites and audio-related topics on the Web. Other good car and home audio hardware sites are **www.audioweb.com** to buy high-end car/home audio equipment, check ads, and bid in auctions; **www.digibid.com**, an audio and video auction network; **www.fleamarket.music.com**, a music auction; **www.audioworld.com**; **www.music4free.com**; **www.connectsound.com**; **www.circuitcity.com**; and **www.bestbuy.com**. Did you know that you can build your own MP3 player for your car with spare computer parts? Find out how at **Impee3.hypermart.net**, and feel like Dr. Frankenstein, or should I say, Dr. Fraunhofer.

73. StartingPage.com ★★★★★ CATEGORY: Resources > Beginners
URL: www.startingpage.com

Best reasons to surf this site: Get basic links to MP3/music-related sites and resources.

Audio formats: N/A **Streaming formats:** N/A **Free BYAHO songs:** Linked **Indie songs:** Linked

Music variety: ★★★ **Speed:** N/A **Webcasts/Videos:** Linked **Radio:** Linked **MP3 software:** Linked

Music/MP3 news: Linked **Chat/Msg. boards:** Linked **How-tos:** ★★★ **Links:** ★★★★★ **Search engine:** ★★★

Search:	
Web sites	
Search by:	
Artist	
Album	
Song	
Phrase	
Buy music: No	

Jump into the exciting, swirling cyberworld and don't look back! It's not that Starting Page has so many resources itself, but it leads you to virtually **anything you'll need for anything**. I mean everything, from gardening to *South Park* to the stock market. Of course, what we're concerned about is mainly MP3 and music, and, wouldn't you know it, Starting Page covers these topics, too. When you first go to this site, you'll see an MP3 button and a Music button. Click either button to find the many sites that will be your starting points into **fascinating realms** of online music and MP3. Starting Page offers a convenient and highly selective **Best of the Web** guide to the best MP3 sites on the Web, which amounts to you getting very useful and very reliable links to such niceties as MP3 utility software, search engines, and quality MP3/music Web sites. Even get direct links to the **Daily Top 10** jazz, country, pop/rock, easy listening, and general music MP3 downloads at MP3.com—a lot of them by BYAHO. If you're new to MP3s, you may want to begin your adventure at StartingPage.com. And, like a similar site—**MPEG.org** (AskMP3.com)—you may also want to have Starting Page as your home page.

74. AllMusic.com ★★★★★ CATEGORY: Resources > Artist info
URL: www.allmusic.com

Best reasons to surf this site: Find loads of information about every artist in every genre from any era; link to related and similar artists; and find complete discographies, genre explanations, and music glossary.

Audio formats: N/A **Streaming formats:** N/A **Free BYAHO songs:** N/A **Indie songs:** N/A

Music variety: ★★★★★ **Speed:** N/A **Webcasts/Videos:** N/A **Radio:** N/A **MP3 software:** N/A

Music/MP3 news: N/A **Chat/Msg. boards:** N/A **How-tos:** None **Links:** ★★★★★ **Search engine:** ★★★★

Search:	
This site	

Search by:	
Artist	
Album	
Song	
Genre	
Label	
Year	
Wizard	
Buy music: Linked	

AllMusic.com is the music portion of **AMG**—the All Media Guide—and AllMusic provides a tremendous amount of information on practically **every artist in every genre ever in existence!** When you look up a band, you not only get a history of the band, but you get bios of each of its members with cross-links to every artist, album, label, or genre with which they have ever been associated. You also get complete discographies, album reviews, **explanations of what the genres and sub-genres are all about**, and links to the bands' influences and similar artists. It should be noted that all these links lead to other areas within AllMusic.com, not to other sites on the Web. But this is part of the greatness of AllMusic.com, because exploring in this cross-link fashion gives you a sense of how all these artists and bands are **connected to each other**. And it reveals how they fit in to the **giant Web of music** and music history. This is truly a great resource for researching music, and for finding new artists you may like based on ones you know you already do.

75. CDDatabase.com ★★★★★ CATEGORY: Resource > Album info
URL: www.cddb.com

Best reasons to surf this site: Get CD track information for your jukeboxes such as names of all the CDs by the artist, names of all the songs by the artist, and genre information, and link to all the CDDB-enhanced Jukebox sites.

Audio formats: N/A **Streaming formats:** N/A **Free BYAHO songs:** None **Indie songs:** None

Music variety: N/A **Speed:** N/A **Webcasts/Videos:** None **Radio:** None **MP3 software:** Linked

Music/MP3 news: None **Chat/Msg. boards:** None **How-tos:** ★★★ **Links:** ★★★ **Search engine:** ★★★

Search:	
This site	

Search by:	
Artist	
Album	
Song	
Wizard	
Buy music: No	

When RealJukebox, MusicMatch Jukebox, or any other MP3 player displays the artist, album, and track information for a song, **this is where they got it**. CDDB (compact disc database) is the world's largest CD information database, and it's all created from information volunteers all over the world have provided. When you look up an artist at CDDB.com, you can view the names of all the artist's CDs and songs, and when you click a song, CDDB searches its database for other similar artists and songs you can check out. All along the way, you can link to an online store to buy whatever CD you're looking at. And now, **CDDB2** is available. CDDB2 has all the information that comes with CDDB, plus it provides **more track-by-track credits**, including crediting musicians who are not the primary artist; relevant Web links; genre, era, and region information; and language support. If the CD you're listening to on your CDDB-enabled jukebox is in CDDB.com's database, and it probably is, then all this new information will be automatically sent and displayed on your player, if you're online. This information is really handy to have if you want to be a DJ, stream music over the Internet as radio, or if you are just plain ol' **anal-retentive** about having your music and playlists nicely organized and categorized. A new plug-in for many MP3 jukeboxes that you can try is available at **www.kick.com** and is called **The Music Companion**. It identifies the track you're playing and gives you information about the artist, album reviews, news, new releases, and local concert information.

76. TheMusiciansResource.com ★★★★★ CATEGORY: Resource > Musicians
URL: www.themusiciansresource.com

Best reasons to surf this site: Musicians can find tons of great links to all kinds of music and music pro-motion–related resources; read indie news; and listen to hundreds of Internet and college radio stations.

Audio formats: N/A **Streaming formats**: Shoutcast, RA **Free BYAHO songs**: N/A **Indie songs**: Linked

Music variety: N/A **Speed**: N/A **Webcasts/Videos**: Linked **Radio**: ★★★★★ **MP3 software**: Linked

Music/MP3 news: ★★★★ **Chat/Msg. boards**: ★★★★ **How-tos**: ★★★★ **Links**: ★★★★★ **Search engine**: None

Search:
This site

Search by:
Link

Buy music: No

Here's a site that delivers exactly what its title promises: resources for musicians—and **lots of them**, too. Find tons of information and tremendous links to indie music news, reviews, instrument and recording equipment manufacturers, CD manufacturers, **indie e-zines**, MP3 sites for indie bands, consignment sites where you can **sell your CDs**, T-shirt and sticker sites, festivals, indie-oriented search engines, indie record labels, and more music resource sites. Look under the Information button and you'll find even more **fan-tastic links** to songwriting, recording/home recording, copyright legalities, band promotion, and specific instrument sites (including tablature sites). At The Musician's Resource, you can also listen to hundreds of Internet and **college radio stations** and post all kinds of musician/instrument-wanted and other music-related messages, too. If you're a solo musician or in a band, this site is a reliable and comprehensive starting point for gathering the resources you need to make your music and spread it around the world. For another good and similar site, but replete with **music-musician jokes**, too, go to **www.musicandaudio.com**.

77. Download.com ★★★★★ CATEGORY: Resource > Software
URL: www.download.com

Best reasons to surf this site: Download a huge number of MP3/music software, find lots of good links to MP3 resources, and get loads of helps and how-tos.

Audio formats: MP3 **Streaming formats**: MP3 **Free BYAHO songs**: Linked **Indie songs**: Linked

Music variety: N/A **Speed**: ★★★★★ **Webcasts/Videos**: None **Radio**: Linked **MP3 software**: ★★★★★

Music/MP3 news: ★★★★★ **Chat/Msg. boards**: ★★★★ **How-tos**: ★★★★★ **Links**: ★★★★★ **Search engine**: ★★★★

Search:
This site only
Web sites
Multiple search engines

Search by:	
Artist	Album
Song	Software
Date	Format
All Words	Any Word
Phrase	
Buy music: No	

Buried among everything at Cnet is a great, not-so-little MP3 section that you can get to by going to Download.com. And, as you might have guessed, this is a good place to get downloads of **MP3 utilities**. You won't find any actual MP3 songs to download around here, but you will find a pretty good search engine that will hunt the Web for links to the MP3 or artist you're looking for. Once at Download.com, click the Find MP3 button to go to a page where you'll find **all sorts of MP3/music software** downloads; the latest MP3/music headlines; links to other reliable MP3 sites; the search engine mentioned earlier; downloads of popular MP3 search tools, such as **Napster** and **MP3 Fiend**; MP3 hardware reviews; and **seas of helps, how-tos, and FAQs**. The centerpiece of this site, however, is the software downloads. And, they come conveniently with information such as a description and review of the product, whether it's free or shareware, whether the product is popular, and links to related software. So, **download away** and get lots of good stuff from Download.com—and that's just in the music department.

78. Layer3.org ★★★★★ CATEGORY: Resource > Software & hardware
URL: `www.layer3.org`

Best reasons to surf this site: Download a truckload of great MP3 software and utilities. Check out the latest handheld, car, home, and other MP3 hardware with pictures, reviews, and links to buy the products.

Audio formats: MP3 **Streaming formats:** MP3 **Free BYAHO songs:** Linked **Indie songs:** None

Music variety: N/A **Speed:** ★★★★★ **Webcasts/Videos:** None **Radio:** None **MP3 software:** ★★★★★

Music/MP3 news: ★★★★ **Chat/Msg. boards:** None **How-tos:** ★★★ **Links:** ★★★ **Search engine:** ★★★★★

Search:
This site
FTP sites
Web sites
Multiple search engines

Search by:
Artist
Song
Genre
Skins
Plug-ins
Software
News
Buy music: No

Layer3.org specializes in audio software and hardware, and for those two areas, it is as comprehensive as you get. They seem to know what MP3 stuff is important for people to have, so they provide a lot of it, and then they throw in a little frivolity in the form of **skins and plug-ins**—maybe its penchant toward **Winamp** is why the site *looks* cool, too. At Layer3.org you very simply can download *tons* of MP3 software and utilities; check out all kinds of MP3 hardware with pictures, reviews, and links to buy the

product; check out **new and updated** MP3 software and hardware releases; read recent and archived MP3 news; link to some technical MP3 sites; link to a couple of free MP3 downloads by BYAHO; and use one of 15 MP3 search engines on the home page to look for MP3s on the Web or on FTP sites. This site seems to have been perfected by **ancient, wise men** who have managed to achieve a delicate balance between excess and simplicity. Either that, or it's the brainchild of a computer-savvy 13-year-old pube. Either way, I love it.

79. MPEGX.com ★★★★★ CATEGORY: Resource > Software and Hardware
URL: www.mpegx.com

Best reasons to surf this site: Download all sorts of MP3 and other audio and video software and utilities. Search for MP3s from 14 MP3 searchers.

Audio formats: MP3 **Streaming formats**: MP3 **Free BYAHO songs**: Linked **Indie songs**: None

Music variety: N/A **Speed**: ★★★★★ **Webcasts/Videos**: None **Radio**: Linked **MP3 software**: ★★★★★

Music/MP3 news: Linked **Chat/Msg. boards**: ★★★★ **How-tos**: ★★★★ **Links**: ★★★ **Search engine**: ★★★★★

Search:
This site
FTP sites
Web sites
Shared sites
Multiple search engines

Search by:
Artist
Song
Lyrics
CD Covers
Software
Hardware
Buy music: No

The software section of this site is **incredible!** Download every kind of MP3 software and utility you can imagine whether it be freeware, shareware, demoware, evaluation versions, or trial versions, and get **star ratings** of the products, too. Just some of the harder-to-find software found here is **AAC (MPEG 4) encoder-decoders, DJ mixing utilities, FTP server utilities, volume control front ends, lyrics utilities, and MP3 streaming and file-fixing software**. But, you'll find much more, plus, lots of video software, too. The software downloads are enough to keep you stopping by, but at MPEGX you also can search for MP3s on **14 different MP3 search engines** (in cooperation with **MP3Bee.com**); search a database of more than **12,000 CD covers**; search for lyrics; search the Web for MP3 hardware to buy; and link to MP3 news, other MP3 sites, and *Billboard's* Top 101 songs. Or, you can listen to music streams and participate in MPEG and CD-R discussion boards.

80. Music4Free.com ★★★★★ CATEGORY: Resource > Software, Hardware, Help
URL: www.music4free.com

Best reasons to surf this site: Great MP3 software/utility, hardware, and chat areas, with excellent MP3 help and how-tos, including help with downloading from FTP sites, and more.

Audio formats: MP3 **Streaming formats**: MP3 **Free BYAHO songs**: None **Indie songs**: ★★★★

Music variety: ★★★★ **Speed**: ★★★★★ **Webcasts/Videos**: None **Radio**: None **MP3 software**: ★★★★★

Music/MP3 news: ★★★★★ **Chat/Msg. boards:** ★★★★★ **How-tos:** ★★★★★ **Links:** ★★★★ **Search engine:** ★★★★

Search:
Web sites
Shared sites

Search by:
Artist
Song
All Words
Any Word
Other:
Buy music: No

This is an excellent site for finding all sorts of MP3-related resources. One of the best things this site offers for free—besides acres of MP3 news articles and loads of MP3 software and utilities—is **help and how-tos** for working with MP3s and **cranky FTP servers.** Music4Free also has extremely informative Ultimate guides and reviews of hardware, such as portable MP3 players, car MP3 players, and home stereo MP3 players, and a **phenomenal chat.** Download the mIRC (**Internet Relay Chat**) program at **www.mirc.com** so you can connect to various servers, chat in thousands of IRC channels, and **trade MP3s around the world.** And, sign up to use the **Free Drive,** equivalent to an **i-drive** or **x-drive,** to upload, store, and retrieve up to **50MB of data for free,** including MP3s, so you don't use up space on your own hard drive. Lastly, download hundreds of Indie MP3s from Music4Free and use its search engine, powered by **www.MusicGrab.com** (part of the Artist Direct Network), to find MP3s by BYAHO. When downloading MP3s from Music Grab's search results, it is often the case that you will have to click the song, **rename the file extension to .MP3,** change the **Save as type** setting to **All Files (*.*),** and then download it; or, if the file is zipped, download the file, **unzip** it with **Zip!Zilla** (included on the book's CD-ROM), and save it as an MP3.

81. MusicMatch.com ★★★ CATEGORY: Resource > Software
URL: www.musicmatch.com

Best reasons to surf this site: Check for updates to MusicMatch Jukebox, one of the two MP3 suites on the book's CD. Also good for finding skins and Indie tracks.

Audio formats: MP3, WMA **Streaming formats:** MP3, WMA, Shoutcast **Free BYAHO songs:** ★★ **Indie songs:** ★★★★

Music variety: ★★★★ **Speed:** ★★★★★ **Webcasts/Videos:** Linked **Radio:** Linked **MP3 software:** ★★★★★

Music/MP3 news: Linked **Chat/Msg. boards:** Linked **How-tos:** ★★★★★ **Links:** ★★ **Search engine:** ★★★★

Search:
This site
Web sites

Search by:
Artist
Song
Genre
Home town
Alphabet
Buy music: Linked

Music Match Jukebox is the **most powerful** all-in-one MP3, WMA, WAV, and CD player/recorder/convert-er available right now. It's on the book's CD-ROM, but use the Music Match automatic check feature to have it frequently update itself so you'll be sure you have the latest version and features, or go right to the home site yourself and get an overhaul. Although the player is incredible, its Web site is not so thrilling. MusicMatch.com does have a few featured tracks that you can download by BYAHO, and it has its own search engine that searches its database for tracks by indie artists who have submitted their music. It also uses **Listen.com's** searcher so you can look for music on the Web (See the Listen.com review), and you can check with MusicMatch.com to get the **latest skins and plug-ins**, but that's about it. A lot of what can't be done at the Web site, however, can be done **on the player itself**. For example, while you may not find any links to, say, radio stations or chat rooms at MusicMatch.com, you can link to hundreds of them from the player. You also can use the player to link to other music sites and **stream Windows Media video**. Check out Chapter 4 and click the Help button on the Music Match player to find great how-tos for using all its features.

82. Supershareware.com ★★★★★ CATEGORY: Resource > Software
URL: www.supershareware.com

Best reasons to surf this site: Easily and conveniently download all sorts of free software—MP3- and audio-related.

Audio formats: N/A **Streaming formats**: N/A **Free BYAHO songs**: N/A **Indie songs**: N/A

Music variety: N/A **Speed**: ★★★★★ **Webcasts/Videos**: N/A **Radio**: N/A **MP3 software**: ★★★★★

Music/MP3 news: N/A **Chat/Msg. boards**: ★★★ **How-tos**: N/A **Links**: ★★★ **Search engine**: ★★★

Search:	
This site	
Search by:	
Software	

Buy music: No

This is an excellent one-stop source for discovering and downloading all sorts of free software, including, of course, MP3 and music programs. To find **the MP3 goodies**, click the Multimedia Tools button on the home page. Then, scroll through the various types of music software available and read the products' descriptions, get star ratings, rate the products yourself, view screen shots, and maybe even read an **interview with a program's creator**. Have the site arrange the downloads in order of whether or not they're freeware or shareware, and then download them directly from Supershareware.com. Or, link to the software company's home page to make sure you get **the latest version**. This site is so easy to use it makes finding and downloading software **a breeze**. Also, for similar thrills, check out **www.audiosoftware.com** and **www.sharewaremusicmachine.com**, "The Worlds Biggest Music Software Site."

83. HomeRecording.com ★★★★★ CATEGORY: Resource > Technical & Legal
URL: www.homerecording.com

Best reasons to surf this site: Learn all about making, recording, and mixing music at home with your computer, mixing boards, and other equipment. Also, learn to record MP3s and make your own audio equipment and instruments.

Audio formats: N/A **Streaming formats**: N/A **Free BYAHO songs**: Linked **Indie songs**: Linked

Music variety: N/A **Speed**: N/A **Webcasts/Videos**: None **Radio**: None **MP3 software**: Linked

Music/MP3 news: Linked **Chat/Msg. boards**: ★★★★★ **How-tos**: ★★★★★ **Links**: ★★★★★ **Search engine**: ★★★

Search:
This site
Web sites

Search by:
Artist
Software
Books
Video
All Words
Any Word
Buy music: Linked

If you want to mix and make music on your PC, create your own CDs, record music as MP3s, or anything else having to do with recording at home, this site is an **invaluable resource**. Whether you're in a band, a DJ, or a music enthusiast, this site will give you all sorts of useful tips, tricks, how-tos, reviews, and articles for **turning your home into a recording studio**, and if it doesn't provide the information right here, it'll link you to where you can get it. It even has instructions on how to **make your own audio equipment** and instruments. Also, find out about **mixing fundamentals** and sound card basics; get help with popular music mixing programs, such as **Cakewalk**; get help and info about widely used mixing boards, such as ones made by **Tascam**; learn how to convert your MIDIs to MP3s; get answers to FAQ; get tutorials; and much, much more. HomeRecording.com guides you to the right software to download for the recording job at hand. For even more help, you can post messages, chat, search for topics in archived discussion forums, check out the **Home Recording WebRing**, and join mailing lists to get tips and trade music. As more and more people are turning to creating and downloading music at home on their computers, a site like HomeRecording.com is that much **more valuable everyday**. Also, go to **www.angrycoffee. com** to learn more technical information about how to start playing your recorded music over the Internet, and to find out about your rights to record music at home, go to **www.hrrc.org** (**Home Recording Rights Coalition**). HRRC is an advocacy group that helps protect your right to download MP3s and use home recording equipment as long as it's for non-commercial use. You also may be interested in the **Audio Home Recording Act of 1992**, the **No Electronic Theft Act**, and the **Digital Millennium Copyright Act**, which you can read at KohnMusic.com.

84. Webnoize.com ★★★★★ CATEGORY: Resources > News
URL: **www.webnoize.com**

Best reason to surf this site: Get comprehensive news coverage of music, TV, film, and gaming industries. This is a good source for MP3 versus record industry news, and offers a great newsletter, too.

Audio formats: N/A **Streaming formats**: RA **Free BYAHO songs**: N/A **Indie songs**: N/A

Music variety: N/A **Speed**: N/A **Webcasts/Videos**: ★★★★ **Radio**: N/A **MP3 Software**: None

Music/MP3 News: ★★★★★ **Chat/Msg. Boards**: None **How-tos**: ★★★ **Links**: ★★ **Search Engine**: ★★★

Search:
This site

Search by:
Date
Year
Any Word
Buy music: No

Webnoize has been a top news source for the digital music industry since 1994 and is recognized in the industry and press as the authority on the music scene. Think of them as *Billboard* meets *Wired* meets *The*

Wall Street Journal. Get up-to-the minute and archived news and expert analysis of industry and market trends in the News section; watch Real streams of original programming, including interviews with industry moguls, in the Live department; and look for live Webnoize events under Events. Webnoize.com is great for keeping up with MP3 versus recording industry news, and they have recently moved their reporting expertise into covering other areas of online entertainment, such as TV, film, and gaming. Subscribe to their newsletter, filled with the latest entertainment industry news, to stay on top of what's going on and to gain unlimited access to Webnoize's archives. Other good sources of media news are **MusicNewswire.com, MusicDish.com, Wired.com, TheStandard.com, ImpactMedia.com, StreamingMedia.com, NewsDirectory.com** (link to every magazine, newspaper, television, and news resource you can think of), **AudioWorld.com** (digital music news, plus music/audio message forums), **Upside.com** ("The Tech Insider"), **Slashdot.org** ("News for Nerds" and part of the private ISP TheBinary.com), **MP3Freedom.com**, and **MP3.com**.

85. TheMusicLover.com ★★★★ CATEGORY: Resource > Music Charts
URL: www.themusiclover.com

Best reasons to surf this site: Download free MP3s by BYAHO based on the latest music charts and trade songs in its music forum.

Audio formats: MP3 **Streaming formats:** MP3 **Free BYAHO songs:** ★★★★ **Indie songs:** ★★

Music variety: ★★★ **Speed:** ★★★★★ **Webcasts/Videos:** None **Radio:** Linked **MP3 software:** ★★★★

Music/MP3 news: None **Chat/Msg. boards:** ★★★★ **How-tos:** ★★★ **Links:** ★★★ **Search engine:** ★★

Search:
This site
FTP sites
Web sites
Shared sites
Multiple search engines

Search by:
Artist
Album
Song
Buy music: Linked

TheMusicLover.com has come up with a **pretty neat idea:** Get free MP3 downloads by the latest BYAHO based on various **music charts from around the world.** Check out the MP3s available on the **U.K. Top 20, MTV Top 20, Billboard Top 60, Australia Top 50, Country Top 20, Soundtrack Songs, Thai Songs, English Songs**—you get the idea. In total, about **1,000 song downloads** are available, although often you will need to download the song "as is" and then **rename it with an .MP3 file extension.** Also, get more music by trading songs and posting requests in its music forum, and go to the MusicLover Shopping Mall to find links to online stores where you can buy music items and CDs. Also, check out **www.mp3charts.com** for Top 40 downloads in many genres from countries around the world.

Webcasts/Online Radio

86. WWMusic.net ★★★★★ CATEGORY: Webcast/Radio
URL: www.wwmusic.net

Best reasons to surf this site: Find a huge number of archived and upcoming streaming Webcasts plus tons more broadcasts and radio.

Audio formats: N/A **Streaming formats:** WMA, RA, QT, MP3 **Free BYAHO songs:** ✮✮✮✮✮ **Indie songs:** ✮✮✮✮✮

Music variety: ✮✮✮✮✮ **Speed:** N/A **Webcasts/Videos:** ✮✮✮✮✮ **Radio:** ✮✮✮✮✮ **MP3 software:** Linked

Music/MP3 news: ✮✮✮✮✮ **Chat/Msg. boards:** None **How-tos:** ✮✮✮✮ **Links:** ✮✮ **Search engine:** ✮✮✮✮

Search:	
This site	
Web sites	

Search by:	
Artist	
Song	
Genre	
Label	
Radio	
Any Word	
News	
Buy music: No	

This is a **fantastic site** if you're into Webcasts! At WWMusic.net, part of the WorldWide Broadcast Network (**WWBC.net**), look up **hundreds of archived music and video Webcasts** in their directory, and check for upcoming livecasts, too. It's just Webcast after Webcast of indie and BYAHO concerts, interviews, radio programs, music shows, and more at this site. Find the broadcasts easily from the music category sections or with the search engine, which is **"filtered for music relevancy."** If you get tired of looking up only music broadcasts, you can also look through the other categories in the WWBC Network, including **movies, news, sports, business, comedy, fashion, games, drama, education, health, kids, family, and travel,** to find hundreds more archived broadcasts available. The site claims to be "the most comprehensive site on the Internet for streaming media content," and I can believe it. Plus, it's all free, including becoming a member. Becoming a member allows you to use the My WWBC feature to easily organize your favorite broadcasts, receive email reminders of upcoming events, and get the **correctly converted time** that the event will be happening in your area no matter which time zone the live broadcast is coming from. If you're really into Webcasts, **this is the site for you.** For another similar and excellent site, check out **www.musicbroadcast.com**—not to be confused with Broadcast Music, Inc. (BMI).

87. WWW.com ✮✮✮✮✮ CATEGORY: Webcasts/Radio
URL: www.www.com

Best reasons to surf this site: Listen to streamed online radio broadcasts in every genre. Indie artists and labels get paid royalties for their music played on the WWW network, and listeners can link to buy the CD.

Audio formats: N/A **Streaming formats:** RA, WMA **Free BYAHO songs:** ✮✮✮✮✮ **Indie songs:** ✮✮✮✮✮

Music variety: ✮✮✮✮✮ **Speed:** N/A **Webcasts/Videos:** ✮✮✮ **Radio:** ✮✮✮✮✮ **MP3 software:** Linked

Music/MP3 news: ✮✮✮ **Chat/Msg. boards:** None **How-tos:** ✮✮✮✮ **Links:** ✮✮ **Search engine:** None

Search:	
This site	

Search by:	
Genre	
Radio	
Buy music: Linked.	

I'm not sure why this site has the name WWW.com, but what a great name for a site on the Internet—it must be the most popular and all encompassing site out there! Well, maybe it's not, but it is a very popular site, ranking consistently **among the top 25** music sites and top 300 Internet sites overall. It's the largest true broadcaster of music on the Internet, encompassing more than **325,000 songs** and more than 200 music stations in every genre. By "true" I mean that WWW broadcasts music from their own stations that have been programmed by their own staff of "**battle-hardened music junkies**," as opposed to a site such as Yahoo's **Broadcast.com**—another very popular site—that is more of a streaming audio portal for rebroadcasts. At WWW.com, you can listen to streamed music by BYAHO and indie artists, listen to talk shows, and watch some streamed videos. As always, when streaming audio or video, if the stream does not come through, try refreshing the page, or **ask for help** in WWW's 24/7 Live Support section. (This does not pass for a "chat room" even though it uses the same format.) **Artists and labels get paid royalties** for their music if it's broadcast over WWW's network, and this site is also "commerce enabled," which means listeners can buy the artist's CD by clicking a link to an online store as the song is playing.

88. NetRadio.com ✶✶✶✶ CATEGORY: Webcast/Radio
URL: www.netradio.com

Best reasons to surf this site: Listen to radio from tons of genres and sub-genres and learn about different styles of music.

Audio formats: N/A **Streaming formats:** RA, WMA **Free BYAHO songs:** ✶✶✶✶✶ **Indie songs:** ✶✶✶
Music variety: ✶✶✶✶✶ **Speed:** N/A **Webcasts/Video:** N/A **Radio:** ✶✶✶✶✶ **MP3 software:** Linked
Music/MP3 news: ✶✶✶✶ **Chat/Msg. boards:** None **How-tos:** ✶✶✶✶✶ **Links:** ✶✶✶ **Search engine:** None

Search:	
This site	

Search by:	
Artist	
Genre	
Radio	
Format	
Buy music: Linked	

Here's a very easy-to-use, **nicely laid out** site to help you develop an **aural fixation**. NetRadio not only lets you listen to more than **120 channels** of radio in many genres that have been programmed by its own staff of award-winning music experts, it also provides links to similar stations and related artists you might like and links you to an online store to buy the CD if you like what you hear on the radio. It even has a section where you can learn about the different styles of music so you can "**impress your co-workers, friends, & neighbors**," (yeah, right). You can also check out some music news and new releases, but the best reason to go to this site is to simply get the music or talk radio show so you can have it playing in the background while you explore the Internet or do your work or your play.

89. Broadcast.com ✶✶✶✶ CATEGORY: Webcast/Radio
URL: www.broadcast.com

Best reasons to surf this site: Check for upcoming live musical broadcasts, listen to radio, and stream more than 3,000 complete CDs—a decent amount of them by BYAHO.

Audio formats: N/A Streaming formats: RA, WMA, MP3 Free BYAHO songs: ★★★★ Indie songs: ★★★★

Music variety: ★★★★★ Speed: ★★★★★ Webcasts/Videos: ★★★★ Radio: Linked MP3 software: Linked

Music/MP3 news: Linked Chat/Msg. boards: Linked How-tos: ★★★★ Links: ★★★★★ Search engine: ★★★★

Search:	
This site	
Web sites	

Search by:	
Artist	
Song	
Genre	
Alphabet	
Radio	
Buy music:	Linked

When you first go to Broadcast.com, you'll be confronted with all the different categories of broadcasts you can stream from Yahoo! (I'm not yelling; that's just how you spell "Yahoo!") And there are some good categories here! But for the purposes of this review, go to the Music section! Here, you can check out a **schedule of upcoming musical live broadcasts**, including concerts, and link to more than **400 radio stations!** Also, stream more than 3,000 complete CDs—many by BYAHO—at CD Jukebox, watch streamed music videos, and look up artists to find more broadcasts with them in it! Sometimes you may have to listen to a 30-second or so advertisement before the broadcast begins, but **deal with it!** If you have a high-speed Internet connection, check out the **Broadband** section to find even more audio and video broadcasts! The **radio and CD jukebox** sections are the highlights here, but don't forget that you have all the other categories of broadcasts at Yahoo! to explore, such as audio books, sports, news, and business/stock market stuff, if you don't find anything you want in the music department.

90. RadioSpy.com ★★★★★ CATEGORY: Radio and Webcasts
URL: www.radiospy.com

Best reasons to surf this site: Listen to thousands of radio stations—especially Shoutcast! radio—in every genre.

Audio formats: N/A Streaming formats: Shoutcast, RA, WMA Free BYAHO songs: ★★★★★ Indie songs: ★★★★★

Music variety: ★★★★★ Speed: ★★★★★ Webcasts/Videos: None Radio: ★★★★★ MP3 software: ★★

Music/MP3 news: ★★★★★ Chat/Msg. boards: ★★★★★ How-tos: ★★★ Links: ★★ Search engine: ★★★★

Search:	
This site	

Search by:	
Artist	
Song	
Genre	
Format	
Country	
Radio Stations	
Buy music:	Linked

Listen to thousands of online radio stations streaming in Shoutcast! (an MP3 stream similar to **Icecast**), WMA, and Real Audio at RadioSpy.com (formerly known as **MP3Spy**). First, download the free RadioSpy Tool, and like an antenna and receiver, this program lets you access and listen to the stations. From within this program, you also can get station information, music headlines, interviews, and reviews; chat with DJs and online listeners; participate in forums; and, maybe its best feature, **have it notify you when stations are playing your favorite artists or songs** so you can immediately tune to that channel. Search for music on the radio by genre, or type in an artist's name or song title to see whether it's playing somewhere out there. If at any point you hear a song you like, RadioSpy lets you link to their online partner **CheckOut.com** (a good CD store), where you can preview other songs by the artist and buy the CD. If you really get into the whole online radio thing, download **RadioSpyDJ Tools**. With this, you can become your own DJ and stream your music collection or **rant and rave** on your own radio show. RadioSpy.com finds every Shoutcast station out there, and, if you have a high-speed modem, set the stream buffer at 256KB and the streams will rarely break up. Other good sites for online radio and specialized tuners are **www.shoutcast.com** (uses Winamp for MP3 streams), **www.icast.com/radio** (uses Icecast—open source MP3 broadcasting software—and is now home to the popular, banner-free, online radio broadcaster **www.greenwitch.com**), **www.vtuner.com** (for radio, television, and Webcams), AOL's **www.spinner.com** (Real Audio radio), **www.live365.com** (MP3 radio with chat, message boards, and links to buy CDs), **www.tuneto.com** (download the TuneTo Receiver and listen to all kinds of BMI-, ASCAP-, and SESAC-licensed music), **www.wiredplanet.com** (streaming "Music Your Way," 24 hours a day, and more), **www.rsradio.com** (Rolling Stone Radio using Real Audio), **www.imagineradio.com** (WMA and Real Audio), **www.waveradio.com** (WMA), **www.pirate-radio.co.uk** (pirated radio from London), **www.scour.com** (MP3 radio with its My Caster program), **www.talkradionews.com** (daily White House/Congressional coverage and more in Real Audio), **www.npr.com** (National Public Radio news, programs, and talk shows from around the world), **www.audible.com** (get daily newspapers read to you—or try loading it on your portable MP3 player while you make coffee in the morning so you can listen to it on your way to work—and listen to lectures, jokes, and other narrations in MP3), **www.yesterdayusa.com** (actual radio shows from the '20s to the '50s), and rubber-neck it over to **www.policescanner.com** to listen to live police busts, fire, aviation, and railway streams in Real Audio. So, get your Total Recorder warmed up.

91. AudioHighway.com ★★★★ CATEGORY:Webcasts/Radio
URL: www.audiohighway.com

Best reasons to surf this site: Get free streams of music, comedy, news, audio books, and TV and movie clips, and get the occasional MP3 by BYAHO. Check out The Buzz section for more BYAHO downloads.

Audio formats: MP3 **Streaming formats:** RA, WMA **Free BYAHO songs:** ★★★ **Indie songs:** ★★★★

Music variety: ★★★★ **Speed:** ★★★★★ **Webcasts/Video:** ★★★★ **Radio:** ★★★★ **MP3 software:** Linked

Music/MP3 news: ★★ **Chat/Msg. boards:** ★★★★ **How-tos:** ★★★ **Links:** ★★★ **Search engine:** ★★★★

Search:
This site

Search by:
Artist
Song
Genre
Radio
Any Word
Buy music: Linked

Get streams of music, audio books, news, TV/movie entertainment, and comedy at this very popular site on the Web. When you find what you're looking for, whether it be music, news, **poems**, whatever, you have the option to stream it as a **Windows Media file or Real file**, and in many cases you can download it onto your hard drive as an MP3. If you find a stream you know you're going to want to hear a lot, add it to My Jukebox. This feature allows you to keep an organized list of your favorite streams and MP3s found at Audio Highway, so you can conveniently access them later. You'll find some audio streams and MP3s by BYAHO, plus some music by Unsigned bands in Audio Highway's Music section. You'll find more music by BYAHO and music videos in **The Buzz** department. The Buzz also has a better search engine for finding an artist, or at least finding a related link, and message boards for different forums. Although Audio Highway is great for getting **CNN-type news**, it is not so great for music news. Just go here to listen to the music from Audio Highway's radio stations. Then, if you want, merge onto the Highway and get 24MB of free disk space to use to create your own Web site and put your audio files on it!

92. MusicSalad.com ★★★★★ CATEGORY: Webcasts/Radio
URL: www.musicsalad.com

Best reasons to surf this site: Get lots of high-quality song/complete album streams by popular BYAHO with your audio catchers and use various searchers to find audio, video, and CD covers.

Audio formats: N/A **Streaming formats:** RA **Free BYAHO songs:** ★★★★ **Indie songs:** N/A

Music variety: ★★★ **Speed:** ★★★★ **Webcasts/Videos:** Linked **Radio:** None **MP3 software:** Linked

Music/MP3 news: ★★ **Chat/Msg. boards:** None **How-tos:** ★★ **Links:** ★★★ **Search engine:** ★★★★★

Search:
FTP sites
Web sites
Multiple search engines

Search by:
Artist
Album
Song
Format
CD Covers
Buy music: No

Get Total Recorder ready to go and sit down and enjoy a healthy bowl of streamed music by many popular BYAHO at Music Salad.com. This site offers song streams in **Real Audio** that don't break up because they are **pre-loaded** before they play, and **the streams sound great**, too. Besides being able to get many individual songs, though, you also can stream quite a few very popular and **complete albums** ranging from The Backstreet Boys' *Millennium* to the Beatles' *Abbey Road*. One of the other great ingredients at MusicSalad.com is its Music Search section. Here you'll find a search engine that looks on the Web for **audio CD covers, PC CD covers, psx CD covers,** and **video CD covers**. It also has search engines for finding MP3s on FTP sites and Web sites, plus a couple more for looking up specific audio, video, and image files on the Web. To top it off, this site adds a dash of rebellious spiciness to its music salad medley by providing links to **Anti-MTV sites**. "It's a good thing," Martha Stewart would say.

Miscellaneous Sites

93. InkBlotMagazine.com ★★★★★ CATEGORY: Misc. > Music reviews
URL: www.inkblotmagazine.com

Best reasons to surf this site: This site is a great way to discover new music by reading edgy album and band reviews, getting good suggestions of other bands you might like, and exploring its links.

Audio formats: MP3 **Streaming formats:** RA **Free BYAHO songs:** Linked **Indie songs:** ★★★

Music variety: ★★★ **Speed:** ★★★★★ **Webcasts/Videos:** None **Radio:** None **MP3 software:** None **Music/MP3 news:** ★★★★★ **Chat/Msg. boards:** None **How-tos:** None **Links:** ★★★★★ **Search engine:** None

Search:
This site

Search by:
Artist
Alphabet
Wizard

Buy Music: Linked

There's just something about this site that seems immediately hip. The title alone conjures up images of ruffled journalists working like Woodward and Bernstein—maybe just Bernstein—on the cutting edge of media in a generation of disillusionment. Either that, or it just sounds sort of cute, bubbly, and friendly: "Blop." Either way, what they do promise is, **"If we like it, we'll cover it."** Fair enough. The preponderance of music that they apparently like is rock and jazz, and what Ink Blot Magazine provides is **simple and effective**. Click the Archives button to look up bands, and when you find the one you're looking for, read album reviews with the occasional brutal commentary, find interviews with the artist, listen to sound clips from the band's albums, get band bios, save the picture of the album cover to put on your music player, and, maybe its best feature, click around on **cross-links** to related or similar artists Ink Blot Magazine has determined you might like. This is a **great way to discover new music** from a site that has writers who have put **real thought** into their suggestions, and its cross links gives a sense of the connectivity between the artists as you search almost circularly throughout the site this way. On Ink Blot's home page, find some featured MP3s submitted by indie artists, featured reviews, a Mothership Archive of BYAHO that Ink Blot has a particularly large number of links to, and check out the Links button. Here, Ink Blot Magazine has assembled a large collection of really good and sometimes funky links that mostly relate to music.

94. StarSeeker.com ★★★★★ **CATEGORY: Misc. > Fan links**
URL: www.starseeker.com

Best reasons to surf this site: Links to hundreds of BYAHO official Web pages and fan sites, plus many more *great* links to general music, genre, music newsgroups, music associations, and music awards sites.

Audio formats: N/A **Streaming formats:** N/A **Free BYAHO songs:** N/A **Indie songs:** N/A

Music variety: N/A **Speed:** N/A **Webcasts/Videos:** Linked **Radio:** Linked **MP3 software:** None

Music/MP3 news: Linked **Chat/Msg. boards:** Linked **How-tos:** ★★★ **Links:** ★★★★★ **Search engine:** ★★★

Search:
This site

Search by:
Artist

Buy music: No

This is the site for star-crazed fans. Go to the music section from the home page and then it's links, links, links, and more links to hundreds of **superstar musicians'** official home pages and fan sites, listed in alphabetical order. You'll also find more **great links** to general music sites; music genre sites; music associations, such as the Recording Musicians Association; music newsgroups; MTV video awards sites; Grammy Awards sites; and concert sites. If you don't find what you want here, there are also links to popular portal search engines. If you're really a star-crazed fanatic, check out the other sections at StarSeeker.com, such as **Actors, Television, Movies, Sports,** and **Entertainment News,** or use Star Seeker's own search engine to search its entire database for the star you'd most like to stalk.

95. FTPMusic.com ★★★★ CATEGORY: Misc. > FTP, Utilities
URL: www.ftpmusic.com

Best reasons to surf this site: Find helpful FTP software and utilities and download the top 101 MP3s by big name acts from FTPMusic.com's own FTP server.

Audio formats: MP3 **Streaming formats:** N/A **Free BYAHO songs:** ★★★★ **Indie songs:** None

Music variety: ★★★ **Speed:** ★★★★★ **Webcasts/Videos:** None **Radio:** None **MP3/Musicsoftware:** ★★★★★

Music/MP3 news: Linked **Chat/Msg. boards:** ★★★ **How-tos:** None **Links:** ★★★ **Search engine:** ★★★

Search:
FTP sites

Search by:
Artist
Song
Any Word
Buy music: No

FTPMusic.com—affiliated with **Beyond.com** ("The Software Superstore")—is, appropriately enough, a good place to find and download **useful FTP utilities** and software. This site doesn't offer as much help for using FTPs as you might think, but it does have a message board you can use to post questions about FTPs. One of the best features of this site is the Top 101 MP3 section. Here, you'll find **101 free MP3s from big-time BYAHO** that you can download from FTPMusic.com's **own FTP server**, which helps guarantee **no broken links.** It also has an MP3 search engine that looks for MP3s from other FTP servers on the Internet. This is a handy site for stopping by and checking out the latest FTP-related utilities, so you can restock your inventory and keep your **FTP arsenal** up to date. Sites with good help and how-tos for using FTP are **www.globalscape.com** (home of Cute FTP) and **www.wsftp.com**.

96. Karaoke.com ★★★★ CATEGORY: Misc. > Ways to Look Silly > Karaoke
URL: www.karaoke.com

Best reasons to surf this site: Order all sorts of karaoke hardware, CGD, DVD, and laser discs; discuss karaoke in chat rooms and forums; participate in karaoke auctions; and check out karaoke classifieds.

Audio formats: N/A **Streaming formats:** N/A **Free BYAHO songs:** N/A **Indie songs:** N/A

Music variety: N/A **Speed:** N/A **Webcasts/Videos:** N/A **Radio:** N/A **MP3 software:** ★★

Music/MP3 news: ★★ **Chat/Msg. boards:** ★★★★ **How-tos:** ★★★ **Links:** ★★ **Search engine:** ★★★

Search:
This site

Search by:
Artist
Song
Genre
Item #
Label
Year
Buy music: Yes

Ships CDs: Yes

Avg. Price: $21.97

Custom CDs: No

At Karaoke.com, check out all sorts of karaoke hardware and accessories for sale and guaranteed to make you the **embarrassment of the party**. Order graphics-enabled CGD disks, DVD, and 12-inch laser discs from a catalog containing more than **50,000 karaoke songs** in all. Also, post messages and chat about karaoke and participate in auctions to find and get more gear. **CGD disks** can be listened to on a regular CD player, but you need a **karaoke machine hooked up to your TV** to see the words scroll by. Go to **www.EatSleepMusic.com**, for another kool karaoke site and download its free karaoke player to start singing right away with song samples that come with the player. At this site, you can also order entire discs, plus download complete karaoke songs for $1–$3.95 each. Build your own recording studio at Eat Sleep Music and get some free **singing lessons**, too, so you can show off those pearly whites, and start crooning away in that heavy eyelidded, Viva Las Vegas way! If that's your shtick, baby, 'cause you gotta be you, you gotta be *you*…!

97. KohnMusic.com ★★★★★ Category: Misc. > Legal > Copyright, Licensing
URL: www.kohnmusic.com

Best reasons to surf this site: Find out about legal aspects of Webcasting and delivering digital music over the Internet, music licensing, music copyright laws, and link to other related resources.

Audio formats: N/A **Streaming formats:** N/A **Free BYAHO songs:** N/A **Indie songs:** N/A

Music variety: N/A **Speed:** N/A **Webcasts/Videos:** N/A **Radio:** N/A **MP3 software:** N/A

Music/MP3 news: N/A **Chat/Msg. boards:** N/A **How-tos:** N/A **Links:** ★★★★★ **Search engine:** None

Search:		
This site		

Search by:		
Link		
Buy music: No		

This is a terrific place to get lots of information about the **legalities of music on the Web**. Read about **music licensing, music copyright laws,** and the legal aspects of Webcasting and delivering digital music over the Internet right from Kohn's site. Find links to many other **copyright resources**, as well as to **music industry associations, broadcast associations, music publisher organizations, music rights clearance organizations, songwriter organizations, music mechanical rights societies, collection agencies, music performing rights societies, music industry conferences,** and other music industry resources around the world. To browse all this information more leisurely, you may want to order Bob Kohn's must-have and authoritative book on the subject, *Kohn On Music Licensing*.

Other important music licensing organizations and music associations that indie bands, song writers, and home recording aficionados may want to look into are the **American Society of Composers, Authors and Publishers (www.ascap.com)**—an organization that protects performers' rights by licensing its members for public performances and paying royalties for copyrighted music; **Broadcast Music, Inc. (www.bmi.com)**—a music licensing organization founded in 1940 that pays royalties and offers a simple licensing solution for its members to legally stream their music on the Internet and perform publicly; **www.licensemusic.com**—this site has recently collaborated with BMI and is the only site that licenses and delivers music online for audio visual production industries. Also download or listen to more than 50,000 "pre-cleared" tracks in every genre from this site and get access to more than one million tracks through its network of providers: www.**songwriters-guild.com**—the **Guild of International Songwriters and Composers** Web site that provides musicians, songwriters, lyricists, and publishers with copyrights, publishing, and recording demos; the **American Federation of Musicians** (www.**afm.org**)—a union for protecting professional musicians; **Association for Independent Music** (www.**afim.org**)—a music association created by independent labels and distributors that teaches its members how to make it in the music business without having to go to the giant record labels; **Home Recording Rights Coalition** (www.**hrrc.org**)—an advocacy group that helps protect your right to download MP3s and use home recording equipment, including VCRs, as long as you're not trying to make money off it; **Electronic Frontier Foundation** (www.**eff.org**)—helps advance the right to free speech on the Internet; **Recording Industry Association of America** (www.**riaa.com**)—a trade group that advocates fair legislation for copyright owners, and has information about piracy, Web licensing, and censorship; and **Secure Digital Music Initiative** (www.**sdmi.org**)—whose aim is to bring together recording industries and technology companies to develop technical specifications for securing music over digital delivery platforms.

98. Lyrics.ch ✮✮✮✮ CATEGORY: Misc. > Lyrics
URL: www.lyrics.ch

Best reasons to surf this site: Find lyrics and then link to an online store to preview the song clips and buy the CD.

Audio formats: N/A **Streaming formats**: N/A **Free BYAHO songs**: N/A **Indie songs**: N/A

Music variety: N/A **Speed**: N/A **Webcasts/Video**: N/A **Radio**: N/A **MP3 software**: N/A

Music/MP3 news: N/A **Chat/Msg. boards**: N/A **How-tos**: ✮✮✮ **Links**: ✮✮ **Search engine**: ✮✮✮✮✮

Search:	
This site	

Search by:	
Artist	Album
Song	Lyrics
Alphabet	All Words
Any Word	Phrase
Wizard	
Buy CDs: Linked	

The greatness of Lyrics.ch is in all the ways it can look up lyrics. As usual, you can type in the name of the song, artist, or album to get what you want, but that's assuming you know their names. What if you don't know, or can't remember, the name of the song, artist, or album? You know how the song goes. You can hum it…you can feel it…it's almost there…but alas, that flash of recognition **slips from your brain** and slides back to the tip of your tongue. Whether you're in a band or a bank, a regular Joe or a lassie from Tallahassee, it can drive you nuts! You know a couple of words in the song, or that recurring phrase, but…wait a minute, **you're in luck!** Because this is all you need to know to find the song lyrics at Lyrics.ch (ch, by the way, stands for Switzerland). To get them, click "Full Text Search" from the home page, and then you can type in the words you know are in the song (hopefully more than "the" or "you"), and have the search engine look for those words in a song, or as a phrase. Lyrics.ch has a database of more than 62,000, and growing, songs. (Although there are the **expected legal obstacles** to putting up just any song's lyrics.) Also, if you know the name of the song or artist, but don't know how to spell it, you can have Lyrics.ch perform a **"Similarity Search,"** where you type the names in as best you can and it pulls up similar matches. When you get the lyrics, you also can click the name of the album the song is from to link to an online store where you can listen to a clip of the song and buy the album. Not bad for a little ol' lyrics site. Also, go to the very popular www.**lyrics.com** to look up lyrics from thousands of artists listed in alphabetical order, send in requests for lyrics via email, chat, and find links to many more lyrics and artist sites.

99. FestivalFinder.com ✭✭✭✭ **CATEGORY: Misc. > Music Festivals**
URL: `www.festivalfinder.com`

Best reasons to surf this site: Find music festivals in all kinds of genres happening all over North America. This site also has very good links to other music sites on the Web based on different genres.

Audio file formats: N/A **Streaming formats**: N/A **Free BYAHO songs**: Linked **Indie songs**: Linked

Music variety: ✭✭✭✭✭ **Speed**: N/A **Webcasts/Videos**: Linked **Radio**: Linked **MP3 software**: None

Music/MP3 news: Linked **Chat/Msg. boards**: None **How-tos**: ✭✭ **Links**: ✭✭✭✭✭ **Search engine**: ✭✭✭✭

Search:
This site

Search by:	
Artist	Festival
Genre	Country
State	Province
Date	
Buy music: No	

Okay, so you sought out the stars at **StarSeeker.com**. Well, now try finding them at FestivalFinder.com, so you can see them live in festivals and concerts **all over North America**. Find out when and where the event is happenin' and then strap on a helmet and head out on the highway, even if you don't own a motorcycle, 'cause you know you were **born to be wild**, you party maniac. FestivalFinder.com also has many great links to visual and sound music resources and to sites based on various genres. If you don't find the event or occasion you're looking for here, try these other good sites: `www.festivals.com` to look up events around the world (not necessarily music-related), `www.ticketmaster.com`, `www.localmusic.com` (for major U.S. cities), and `www.musi-cal.com` to find concerts around the world.

100. ArtRock.com ✭✭✭✭✭ **CATEGORY: Misc. > Posters, memorabilia**
URL: `www.artrock.com`

Best reasons to surf this site: Copy and save pictures of all the funky posters and memorabilia for sale to be used with your MP3 player in place of the usual album cover art.

Audio formats: N/A **Streaming formats**: N/A **Free BYAHO songs**: N/A **Indie songs**: N/A

Music variety: N/A **Speed**: N/A **Webcasts/Videos**: N/A **Radio**: N/A **MP3 software**: N/A

Music/MP3 news: N/A **Chat/Msg. boards**: N/A **How-tos**: N/A **Links**: ✭✭✭✭✭ **Search engine**: None

Search:
This site

Search by:
Artist
Any Word
Buy music: Yes
Ships merchandise: Yes
Price: $101 – $300.

In general, a good way to get **album cover art** for your MP3 player is to go to a site such as **Amazon.com** that has practically every CD for sale. They'll usually show the picture of the CD, which you can then copy onto your hard drive by right-clicking the picture and choosing Save Picture As. Then, you take the picture of the album cover from your hard drive and tag it to an MP3 track so the picture shows on your MP3 player every time you play that particular MP3. But, for something different, try copying and saving some groovy, peachy, and often **psychedelically wavy gravy pictures** found at the San Francisco-based Art Rock Gallery. Instead of looking through CDs, though, get the artwork by going on a tour through more than **101,000 rock and roll posters** and pictures of all the authentic, collectible memorabilia available for sale at Art Rock.com. Some of the memorabilia include T-shirts, concert tickets, backstage passes, tour books, stash tins, **blotter acid sheets,** autographed CDs, gold records, and humble lighters. Buy the stuff if you want to hang it on your wall and stare at it in a drippy-eyed delirium, or if you just need **something to put your weed in.** Being able to put pictures on your MP3 player is just a little nicety that you can do with some MP3 players, such as RealJukebox and MusicMatch Jukebox, and it definitely adds to the *je ne sais quoi* of coolness in the MP3 experience. For another alternative source for artwork tags, check out **www.graffiti.org**, and for an actual CD/album cover site, go to **www.cdcovercentral.com**.

101. MusicStation.com ★★★★★ CATEGORY: Misc. > News > Performance bookings
URL: **www.musicstation.com**

Best reasons to surf this site: A kind of eclectic site that combines being a great source of music news with finding *anything* related to music coming up on TV and BMG and Columbia House music clubs.

Audio formats: N/A **Streaming formats:** N/A **Free BYAHO songs:** N/A **Indie songs:** N/A

Music variety: N/A **Speed:** N/A **Webcasts/Videos:** None **Radio:** None **MP3 software:** None

Music/MP3 news: ★★★★★ **Chat/Msg. boards:** Linked **How-tos:** ★★★★ **Links:** ★★★★★ **Search engine:** ★★★

Search:	
This site	
Search by:	
Artist	
Song	
Genre	
Phrase	
Buy music: Linked	

There are three sections at this three-in-one site, and the first two **really deliver**. First, there's **RockOnTV**. This is your comprehensive guide to any musical event or musician coming up on television during the next month. Whether it be a concert on MTV, a musical guest on **Jenny Jones**, a rocker in a movie made in 1973, Elton John on *The Muppet Show*, or Burl Ives singing "Rudolph the Red Nosed Reindeer," **you'll find it scheduled here**. You won't miss a thing, and you can hook your TV and VCR to the line-in jack on your computer's sound card, so you can record the shows on your Music Match Jukebox or RealJukebox as a WAV or MP3 file. Secondly, MusicStation has a **MusicNewswire** section, which is an *incredible* gateway to music and music industry news. Read the headlines here and then link to the full story. Also in this section, link to music magazines, music reviews, and read the latest press releases. Thirdly, the **CD Club Web Server** section actually connects you to **www.CD-Clubs.com**, where you'll find downloadable catalogs by two very popular mail-order music clubs: **BMG Music Service** and **Columbia House**. CD-Clubs.com is not an official site of BMG or Columbia House, so you can't order the music from here. But you can scroll through *huge* lists of CDs and tapes you *could* be getting if you *could* order from here. Unless you really just want to know every CD and tape that you can't get from here, I recommend that you just go straight to the source, namely, **www.columbiahouse.com** and **www.bmgmusicservice.com**. From this section, you also can link to **www.customdisk.com** and **www.cdnow.com**, at least for now. CDNow may be going out of business. I hope not. CDNow is, or was, an excellent online "has everything" CD store, and it also has/had (!?) that great service for indie bands and fans: the **Cosmic Music Network**. For more "What's On" guides, go to **www.onnow.com**, **www.webevents.microsoft.com**, **www.real.guide.com**, and **www.events.yahoo.com**.

Index

Songfile.com Web site
  ratings for, 247
  reviews for, 248
songs
  files, editing, 140
  searching with Napster, 125
    bit rate, 125
    line speed, 125
    multiple, 126
    search form, 123-125
    waiting queue, 126
Songs.com Web site
  ratings for, 248
  reviews for, 248
SonicNet.com Web site
  ratings for, 211
  reviews for, 211
SonyMusic.com Web site, 43
  ratings for, 221
  reviews for, 221
sorting MP3 Fiend search
  results, 59
sound cards, 24
sound quality, 140
sound source, wiring to PC,
  149-150
sound waves, conversion to
  digital data
  analog current, 13
  distortions of primary
    waveform, 11
  electrical current, 12
  electrical wave, 12
  electrical waveform, 12
  recorded patterns, 12
  resolution, 14
  sample rate, 14
  vibrations, 11
speakers, 24-25
spinrecords.com Web site, 201
StarSeeker.com Web site
  ratings for, 265
  reviews for, 265
StartingPage.com Web site
  rating for, 251
  reviews for, 251
streaming audio, 5
  functionality of, 157
  recording, 156-158
  streaming, 157
subscribing to newsgroups,
  72-73

subscriptions, purchasing, 46
Supershareware.com Web site
  ratings for, 257
  reviews for, 257
swapping software
  CuteMX, 134-135
  Gnutella, 133-134
  Macster, 135
  ScourExchange, 135

T

tags, 147-148
Taxi.com Web site
  ratings for, 249
  reviews for, 249
Team-MP3.com Web site
  ratings for, 212
  reviews for, 212
themes (RealJukebox), 173
TheMusiciansResource.com
  Web site
  ratings for, 253
  reviews for, 253
TheMusicLover.com Web site
  ratings for, 259
  reviews for, 259
TimeWarner.com Web site
  ratings for, 222
  reviews for, 222
Total Recorder
  functionality of, 158
  structure of, 160
TowerRecords.com Web site,
  45
  ratings for, 240
  reviews for, 241
transfer-method for portable
  players, 175
Tunes.com Web site, 42
  ratings for, 212
  reviews for, 213

U-V

UBL.com Web site, 43
  ratings for, 213
  reviews for, 214
universal resource locator
  (URL), 50
Universal Serial Bus (USB),
  182

UniversalRecords.com Web
  site
  ratings for, 222
  reviews for, 223
uploading to FTP sites,
  99-100
upstream data, 125
URL (universal resource
  locator), 50
USB (Universal Serial Bus),
  182

variable bit rates, 143
verification log (MP3 Fiend),
  62
  interpreting, 63-66
  Remove Results, 63
verifying MP3 search results,
  59
VH1.com Web site, 43
  ratings for, 214
  reviews for, 214
visualizations
  defined, 173
  running, 173

W-Z

watermarks. See digital
  watermark
wave files
  functionality of, 9-10
  quality of, 4
Web sites
  Amazon.com, 45
  ArtRock.com, 269
  askmp3.com, 44
  big five record label sites
    BMG.com, 220
    EMI Group, 223
    SonyMusic.com, 221
    TimeWarner.com, 222
    UniversalRecords.com,
      222-223
  Compact Disc Database, 145
  emusic.com, 45
  epitonic.com, 201
  FestivalFinder.com, 269
  FTPMusic.com, 266
  genre specific sites
    AlternateMusicPress.com,
      229
    Country.com, 230

CD-ROM End-User Licensing Agreement

By opening the CD-ROM package, you agree to be bound by the following:

You may not copy or redistribute the entire CD-ROM as a whole. Copying and redistribution of individual software programs on the CD-ROM is governed by terms set by individual copyright holders.

The installer and code from the authors are copyrighted by the publisher and the authors. Individual programs and other items on the CD-ROM are copyrighted or are under GNU license by their various authors or other copyright holders.

This software is sold as-is without warranty of any kind, either expressed or implied, including but not limited to the implied warranties of merchantability and fitness for a particular purpose. Neither the publisher nor its dealers or distributors assumes any liability for any alleged or actual damages arising from the use of this program. (Some states do not allow for the exclusion of implied warranties, so the exclusion may not apply to you.)

Important Note: Some of the Software on this CD-ROM has a "time-out" feature so that it expires within thirty (30) days after you load the Software on your system. The "time-out" feature may install hidden files on your system which, if not deleted, might remain on your computer after the Software has been removed. The purpose of the "time-out" feature is to ensure that the software is not used beyond its intended use.

Additional Note: This CD-ROM uses long and mixed-case filenames requiring the use of a protected-mode CD-ROM Driver.